MAN ENOUGH

MAN ENOUGH
Men of Thirty-five Speak Out

Yvonne Roberts

CHATTO & WINDUS · THE HOGARTH PRESS

LONDON

Published by
Chatto & Windus · The Hogarth Press
40 William IV Street
London WC2N 4DF

ISBN 0 7011 2726 0

'General Review of the Sex Situation' reprinted by
kind permission of Messrs Duckworth & Co.

Printed in Great Britain by
Redwood Burn Ltd
Trowbridge, Wiltshire

Contents

Thanks
I would like to thank all the men I interviewed. They gave very generously of their time and privacy. They offered total co-operation and much trust even when, at times, the experience may have proved less of a massage to the ego than some might have expected.

I would also like to thank the dozens of people all over the country who helped in the search for candidates and showed much interest. My thanks go too to Carmen Callil, Publishing Director of Chatto & Windus and my editor, Mike Petty, for their help and patience.

Jacqueline Korn, my agent, gave wise advice and encouragement, always at the time when it was most needed, which I much appreciated. I would like to thank the Typing Pool and Jude Sharpe who helped with the typing. I would like to thank Barbara Humphries, who transcribed most of the interviews. Her comments, involvement and humour made the work on the book very much easier. I would like to thank my parents John and Nancy, and my good friend Sam.

And I would especially like to thank John, with whom I live. Not only did he share our house without complaint for almost a year with two dozen men unknown to him except for their spoken words, he gave constructive criticism, a lot of support, much love and many laughs.

General Review of the Sex Situation

Woman wants monogramy;
Man delights in novelty.
Love is woman's moon and sun;
Man has other forms of fun.
Woman lives but in her lord;
Count to ten and man is bored.
With this the gist and sum of it,
What earthly good can come of it?

DOROTHY PARKER

Introduction

My work means I often travel alone. Normally, any man who attempts to initiate a conversation, however inoffensive, receives the deep freeze of a monosyllabic reply. This is certainly rude. Experience, however, has taught me that in the most unlikely situations, such as early morning at the buffet bar of the Inter-City to Manchester, a man can go from the inconsequential 'Do you happen to have the time, please?' to the intimate 'Are you married?' in less time than a BR microwave takes to heat his sausage roll.

However, over the last year or so, as I've travelled across Britain to carry out interviews for this book, I've spoken to every man who has approached me. Surrounded as I've been by newspaper clippings and books all more or less on the same subject, the first question has been predictable.

'Excuse me, do you mind if I ask what you're doing?' 'A book about men – or some men.' Initially I thought the response to this might be more ribald than inquisitive; nudge, nudge, wink, wink. I was wrong.

The most common reaction from men of all ages has been a series of questions. Who have you talked to? What have they said? Are men changing? What are you trying to prove? (The answer is 'Nothing' but the implication in the question was made explicit by one man: 'Another book telling us all men are shits, I suppose?')

Often the questions would be followed (before any answers could be supplied) by a man offering a sampler of his own life stitched in dramatic detail. He would then ask if he was considered 'normal' by standards 'nowadays'. He would also frequently describe how men have difficult lives too – how *they* can be the victims of unequal treatment, often at the hands of women.

One man in his forties went into minute detail on a two-hour journey to Stoke-on-Trent. He explained how his wife had never allowed him to become close to the children, never took an interest in his hobbies or friends, always went to bed at ten thirty after *News at Ten* and refused to go out socially.

I asked the man why he thought his wife might behave in such a fashion. He was unsure, he said. He'd always tried to be 'a good husband', brought home a decent salary, didn't booze to excess or philander. They had been married for eighteen years, and it seemed a sad assessment of what one man saw as the extent of his wife's requirements from a relationship; and one wife's apparent inability to perceive her husband's needs.

I asked him if any of his male friends were in a similar situation. He looked surprised. He didn't know, he said, perhaps predictably. 'We don't discuss really personal matters.'

One of the two main reasons for writing the book was encapsulated in his response. Men seem to spend a lot of time talking to each other but very little time actually saying anything which touches on the reality of the lives that they are living.

As a result, as individuals, they frequently seem unaware not only of their own motivations and the roots of their prejudices, but also of the range and variety of attitudes within their own sex. As long as they remain unaware, I believe, they are equally oblivious of the force of their united pressure on women.

My hope for this book is that it gives men some insight, however small, into the lives of other men. It may seem a simple objective, but the more men I listened to in the course of working on the book, the more I realised that they knew little about themselves and even less about their closest male friends.

Traditional men (by which I mean, in shorthand, men who see their role as hunter, breadwinner and head of the household and the woman's function as that of mother, wife and homemaker or sex object) can and do talk endlessly, it seems to me, but usually strictly according to ritual; at work, in the pub, with the wife, out with 'the lads' on subjects such as sex, football, next year's holiday, the mortgage, cars, politics. The aim, at the risk of generalisation, is to say much and reveal little. Except, of course, that you are a Normal Man.

Step outside the formula and talk about emotions, fear, failure, love, joy and you become a loner, a bit 'soft'; less of a man. If one man breaks the chains of convention others might follow, but nobody does, so the myth develops that all men are living a life which few if any at all actually do.

One man I met in the course of writing the book gave an example of this kind of newspeak; the art of communicating while saying nothing (an art not entirely exclusive to men, of course):

'You meet a friend and ask how he is. "Fine," he replies. You ask, "How's business?" "Good," he replies. Two weeks later, you find out he's died of a terminal illness and his business has gone bust. Men exchange information but they don't tell each other much. We're too competitive to confide.'

Inevitably, it seems to me, this kind of non-communication also has a drastic effect on the relationship between men and women. Women are alleged instinctively to 'know' their men. Apart from the fact that men don't always practise the same skill on women – 'I didn't realise she was so upset' – this 'instinct' can also be a dangerous thing. In February 1984 *Options*, a monthly woman's magazine, published the results of a survey which demonstrated graphically how the vision 'Eighties Man' has of himself is not necessarily the vision shared by his partner.

To give a few examples: 80 per cent of women thought their partners had changed 'only slightly', while 95 per cent of the men who replied said they were more caring, better dressed, took sex more seriously than women and worked far harder in bed to satisfy a partner, i.e. they were radically different. 75 per cent of men said they fancied sex less than they used to, while 80 per cent of women thought men were just as keen as ever. 70 per cent of women said their husbands wanted pretty little daughters and macho sons and 90 per cent of men said this wasn't so at all. One woman wrote to say, 'My husband has just looked at what I have filled in [the questionnaire] and says he is horrified at my misconceptions.' Lack of communication becomes a mutual failing. So, my aim was simply to ask men to describe their own lives with as much honesty as possible.

A second aim was to find out for myself how men think and act and feel; what motivates them and what frightens them; what gives them joy and what causes anger. I wanted to find out, in part, so that I could make some assessment, however crude, of the progress or otherwise towards a society based on equality between the sexes.

Such a society does not, to me, mean a male society in which there are more women in men's jobs and a still larger group of females at the base of the pyramid growing steadily more impoverished. It means a society in which work and home life are more balanced in each person's life, if they so desire it. A society in which the mundane tasks do not become the burden of one partner alone. This means not only that women will be able to exercise the choice now denied them by stereotyping and conditioning, but men will too.

I wanted to find out if men, like some women, analyse their pasts to try and explain present behaviour to themselves. Did they have, as women are so often told, a blueprint for their futures from an early age? What had been their disappointments and failures; achievements and personal satisfactions? What place did work and ambition really have in their lives? Who influenced their behaviour most – friends, partners, some idea of what a man 'should be'? Had they ever physically or mentally abused a woman and if so why? In their view, did women (some women) demand independence and then live a life of contradictions?

What did these men think of feminism? Had they tried to change into the mould of the so called 'new man'? Or did they hold fast to ideas that men and women have biologically determined roles in life; the homemaker and the hunter?

I wanted to find out from a group of men what sections of their lives they would *never* surrender in the cause of equality between men and women, what parts of their lives they might wish to change and why. I wanted to find out too what myths and truths and beliefs they held to, if any, to justify their own position and the position of the women in their lives.

I wanted to find out from each interviewee what 'being a man' meant to him. How did his views and actions compare with those of his father and what he in turn might now expect from a son or a daughter? If the man couldn't analyse that change for himself, if it existed, then I hoped it would be exposed in the simple telling of his life story.

I also wanted to find out how a man defined 'masculine' behaviour. Did it differ among men? If there were exceptions to the rule that men are competitive, aggressive, unable to convey emotions, I wanted to find out why – how had that individual escaped or overcome his conditioning?

I hoped to find out if men as individuals had any vision of what they might become should they decide to forfeit the props of chauvinism. Was there much about being 'a man' which they disliked?

Adjustment inevitably brings pain to both sexes. One of the aspects of the male-female relationship I wanted to question men about was the area in which women exercise power and yet refuse to, or cannot, acknowledge that they do – most usually in the house and with the children.

A woman for example demands that a man offer more help in the house; he does so, but for a variety of reasons she criticises his performance until he retreats into inactivity again. I have felt the same sort of conflict myself. My partner and I initiated a scheme a few years ago in which we took turns of a week on and a week off to cook and shop.

I thought I'd welcome the escape from the kitchen. In fact in the week when he was in charge, I couldn't resist interfering. I tried to supply shopping lists, I checked what he bought; I dropped hints on how he should cook such and such and above all I criticised, always disguising it as 'help'.

I recognised eventually that while I didn't want to have all the domestic duties, at the same time I'd been brought up to consider the kitchen my domain, the place where I had power and received praise. Moving towards equality meant forfeiting some of that power, which I found hard to do.

Men face the same problem but much more acutely since they have so much more power to surrender and they are that much more uncertain whether the compensations will be worth it. For example, I recently had a conversation about paternity leave with a senior executive on a daily newspaper. He was appalled at the idea that men should have time away from work on the birth of a child. He was appalled, it emerged, not because of the practical problems – how do we cover for the absent man and who foots the bill? – but because the scheme would reveal the myth of a man's indispensability. If people could make do without him for a month, what might follow? In short, the executive felt he was being asked to concede power in familiar territory for unknown gain in an area he wasn't entirely sure he wished to visit. I wanted to know if other men had considered the impact of such a change in their lives. Had they even begun to think about it?

I had a third reason for writing the book. It is now the vogue to discuss the imminent arrival of the 'New Man'. Indeed, some believe he is already here. The argument seems to be that the kind of social change now under way – high unemployment, the decline in 'macho' manual work, the increasing numbers of women workers, the influence of the 'Me' Decade which prompts men to search for fulfilment in areas other than a career – are threads weaving a chrysalis around the traditional male from which, in due time, he will emerge as a butterfly: the New Man.

The New Man shares domestic duties; gives his family equal or, better still, higher priority over work; the New Man is open with his friends, discusses his emotions, co-operates so his partner can find her own sense of fulfilment too; the New Man is anti-sexist and as a result of all this is also a warm and wonderful human being.

I felt sceptical about the belief that social forces affect human nature so neatly and logically. If man's traditional masculine identity is being under-mined by circumstances then arguably he may well fight all the harder to retain it. He may become *more*, not less, entrenched in his views. I had no facts to back my scepticism but it was another strong motive for wanting to meet and listen to as large a group of men as possible.

The question was, how large a group should that be? I felt it was important to place an individual's opinions within the context of his life, otherwise they would lose much of their value. Given a man's history (albeit as he chooses to tell it) a reader can then come to his or her own conclusions. A man talking at length also has another advantage. If this *is* a time of transition in men's attitudes, it is surely a fragile process. The black-and-white areas exposed so often in polls, surveys and question-naires ('Do you believe women are equal? Do you think equal pay is good, bad, don't care?') in my opinion, either don't pick up on the gentle nature of that change or they exaggerate the strength of its force.

I was interested in the grey areas. The areas for instance where a man may voice one opinion and demonstrate by his actions that he believes in another. Or where he holds two views which appear to be in conflict because he simply hasn't thought through a belief logically (a 'fault' most often ascribed to women). It is the contradictions I believe which sometimes reveal more of the genuine state of a man's mind that his certainties.

It became obvious that if each man spoke to a reasonable length, numbers would inevitably have to be limited. At the same time, I wanted enough men included to meet certain other requirements.

I wanted to have a geographical balance. I also wanted to reflect broad social changes taking place in the 1980s: high unemployment, the switch from manufacturing and heavy manual work to service industries; the technological change within certain traditional industries such as mining.

In addition, I wanted to include the kind of men now affected by the high divorce rate, with seventy per cent of divorces brought by women; men influenced by the 'coming out' of homosexuals; men interested in feminism.

I also wanted to include the kind of man I would not normally have the opportunity to listen to at length – the man who is particularly sexually aggressive; the man who is physically violent towards women; the unrepentant chauvinist.

I wanted to speak to men whose experience does not have any obvious parallel in a woman's world; the fighter pilot in the Falklands with his experience of death and war and 'heroism' as it is defined in a male military society; the homosexual sado-masochist with his experience of pain as a source of pleasure and his intimacy with another male.

In all I interviewed about forty-five men at length. By 'at length' I mean a minimum of four or five hours; more usually the interview spanned a day or was spread over several visits. The final figure of twenty-four was what was considered manageable in terms of a book. The interviews which were omitted were only left out because, in some way, they echoed what others had already said. Obviously in no way do the interviews as a whole pretend to be a social or scientific study.

All the men I interviewed fell into the same age range: thirty-four or thirty-five at the time I contacted them, or on the publication of the book. I wanted again to see what the differences and similarities of outlook might be in one age-span. I am thirty-five, so I knew I would have some shared experiences. It seemed an interesting age for other reasons too. Men in their forties and older may have been able to sidestep the kinds of changes which have taken place for women. Men in their twenties and younger may already have 'naturally' adopted some of the habits of the so called 'new' man, perhaps because that is considered part of masculinity in the 1980s.

I felt that a man in his thirties might have had to give much more conscious thought to these changes in work, at home and/or about himself. If he has adapted any of his ways, he has had to unlearn old habits and relearn new methods. If he has followed in his father's footsteps (presupposing his father to be a traditional man) he may still be under some kind of pressure – however slight – perhaps because of changes in people around him: his partner; his work colleagues; a sister?

In addition, men in their thirties are at the outset of middle age: a time of reassessment for some. They also span three decades of enormous change. In the fifties, women were housewives; if they worked, they earned 'pin' money. By the eighties, women have become much more visible outside the home.

Women have moved into senior positions in industry, local government, trade unions, and now run organisations unique to females such

as the GLC's Women's Committee, with a budget in 1983/84 of £6m.
Also established are Women's Studies, women's refuges, women's history,
women's theatre, the list goes on.

In spite of this the majority of men, however, while they may *know*
that females make up fifty-one per cent of the population, still don't 'see'
them as significant in their economic strategies, blueprints and business
plans. Childcare and equal pay, for instance, still remain 'a woman's
issue' rather than society's challenge. Likewise, women are still not 'heard'
in day-to-day language. Talk about an advertising account executive or
a doctor and the assumption is that she is male.

The structure of society has altered too. Women make up forty per
cent of the workforce; one in seven earns as much as if not more than
their male partners (two-thirds of women, however, remain in the low-pay
sector, battered heavily by unemployment). Only one in twenty families
has the stereotype male breadwinner, mother at home and two dependent
children. One family in six is now headed by a single parent, most
commonly the mother.

In terms of the sexual revolution, the men in *Man Enough* have also
seen change. In the main, they would have spent their early teen years
'wanting it' when it was not readily available. By their twenties, the Pill,
reform in the laws on homosexuality, abortion and divorce, plus the
influence of the hippies and the Women's Movement combined to mean
that, in theory at least, not only were women willing, able and sometimes
more than ready – marriage no longer had to be the bribe.

I consciously discovered as little as possible about each interviewee
before we met, except for the minimum of details – including, obviously,
why he had been chosen (as a single parent, for example). I tried in
this way to bring as few preconceived ideas as possible to the interview.

In order to achieve this distance from the interviewee, I usually asked
a third party to select the actual person. So, when I wanted a middle-
management executive in Derby, for instance, I asked Rolls Royce for a
candidate. They suggested Robbie McGregor, who is, I'm sure, a stunning
advert for the personnel department, but we talked almost entirely about
his private life.

One problem was the matter of truth and interpretation. Individual
men in the 1980s, I was warned, not least by other men, could be devious.
Like Janus, they would show me the face of the 'new' man while concealing
the features of the old.

In 1977, a *Sunday Times* National Opinion Poll of British husbands came to the conclusion: 'Overall husbands emerge as strikingly progressive in their attitudes to women's rights and roles . . . but husbands are far less willing in their actions to share home and family obligations equally . . .' Survey after survey carried out by a variety of women's magazines has since underlined this gap between male attitude and intention.

Cross-examination of every man I met, summoning up witnesses for the defence and prosecution, was neither possible nor desirable. I decided against talking to those who might be close; wives, friends, relatives. I was not constructing *my* profile of a man, I wanted his concept of himself. If possible, I wanted him to speak without feeling on the defensive. At the same time, I wanted to get as close to veracity as I could.

In the end, I decided to place faith in the length of time and the kind of relationship I might develop with each interviewee. If he was posing, I hoped he would find it difficult to sustain the pose effectively. If he was exaggerating, the contradictions would emerge. The contradictions would not reveal 'the truth' he was consciously or otherwise trying to conceal, but they might say something about why a man needs to nurture one or several lies in his life. In the event, men *did* contradict themselves. For instance, a few referred to their 'happy' childhoods and then went on to describe a life which sounded to me like a desert of affection. I have not always pointed out these contradictions, but left them to the reader to pick up.

The reasons men gave for agreeing to be part of the book were almost always one or more of the following: ego; curiosity about themselves and what it might be like to be interviewed; or a chance to make some sense of a process called 'being a man' that they found increasingly confusing. (Some asked me on occasions for my analysis of why they had behaved in such a way at a particular time. I tried *not* to analyse, however superficially, but to ask them to come to their own conclusions.)

Almost all had never been interviewed for any reason – and a majority said they had never talked in detail about themselves in such a way before.

Another consistent pattern was the inability or unwillingness of many of the men to recall the influence of their mothers, even where they had apparently played a large part in their lives. On the whole mothers were remembered in terms of their relationships with the interviewees' fathers, unless contact between mother and son had been based on negative emotions such as anger or what was perceived as over-protectiveness. It is a trait which reminded me of Oscar Wilde's comment: 'All women become like their mothers. That is their tragedy. No man does. That is his.'

In the end, I put down the lack of recall to the fact that mothers were very much a part of the *routine* of everyday life – fathers' interest, by contrast, was either a treat or a threat (if he was about to administer some punishment promised in advance by the mother), because more often than not he was at work, an absent parent for a great deal of the time.

What conclusions, if any, did I come to? Are the men I interviewed different from their fathers? Are there signs of change?

The answer is that for some – perhaps less than the majority – there *has* been a change, but I'm not certain of its significance. I believe each generation of men makes *some* adjustment. Men nowadays may wash up; their fathers didn't. It doesn't logically follow that they therefore also have different views on their own roles and the role of women.

Indeed, I think some observers grow too optimistic about the nature of the change they see today. On the cover of Philip Hodson's *Men: An Investigation into the Emotional Male* is the following statement, on which he elaborates further in the book:

> The Male Chauvinist Empire is crumbling not just in the face of feminist opposition but in the face of economic realities. The traditional stereotype of men as the 'strong dominant providers' is cracking and a major male identity crisis has arrived . . .

An identity crisis may have arrived but it's nonsense to assume from that that the 'Male Chauvinist Empire is crumbling . . .' If this view gains currency then it offers false and dangerous reassurance. Why do so many marriages break up under the pressure of a man being out of work? Surely not because he has changed his traditional habits?

Research now being carried out indicates that an unemployed man will still consider himself the household's head and show no inclination to help with the chores even if his wife or partner works outside the home as well. Yosser Hughes didn't suddenly join the Women's Movement; he didn't even do the housework.

In addition, the father is somebody a boy is encouraged to emulate. In the fifties, a son was not expected to model himself on his mother. Even if the mother held power in the home, it was not the kind of power a boy was conditioned to desire or respect.

At the same time, it seems, some mothers contributed to their own invisibility by accentuating the virtues and status of the absent fathers. Repeatedly men remarked on how their mothers encouraged them to behave 'like a little man' while their sisters were handed the feather duster – an attitude which is as strong today.

Inevitably I had to edit the interviews, but in doing so I have tried to convey the essence of how a man appeared to feel. In some cases, on seeing the transcripts, the men asked that pseudonyms be used. A few did not want to hurt those close to them. More felt too vulnerable, they said, to reveal their identity. Some of those who *have* allowed their names to be published used words such as 'bemused' and 'discomfited' about the image of themselves they felt they conveyed, while not denying the truth of what they have said.

I found that the majority of men in the age group I interviewed were not confused about their role. They may be puzzled about how they communicate 'safely' with women without causing offence by behaviour considered sexist, but they don't seem over-anxious about their identity as 'a man'. On the contrary, some have remained unchanged while others have adjusted well enough to bring rewards which were denied to their fathers.

These men are not 'traditional' men nor 'new' men, they are simply contemporary men. They often *are* more involved as fathers; they can discuss their feelings, at least with one other person; they don't, in the main, uphold a double standard in sexual activity; they expect a woman to enjoy her sex-life; they believe in equal pay (if not in equal opportunity or improved childcare or less conditioning in schools); they may be less competitive, aggressive, and they certainly don't regard themselves as 'macho' – they will even believe the wife should go out for a couple of nights a week so she can develop her own interests.

But what it all amounts to is not a man of the future but a man who has much of the best of both worlds; the traditional male world and the present female world. Contemporary man can now enter what was once considered the exclusive domain of women, such as the care of children, but not to the extent where he equally shares the drawbacks as well as the advantages. At the same time, he sees no need to concede any of his own power or privilege. He still regards the woman's role as secondary. A number of the men I interviewed, for instance, described a greater 'involvement' with their children in terms of the more pleasurable tasks – playing with them, putting them to bed, dropping them off at school. The mundane daily chores, the trips to the dentist, the ferrying to and fro, were still left to the wife. In short, they have adjusted but not, in my opinion, *changed*.

So, is the view entirely pessimistic? I don't think so. Men in the main are obviously in a privileged position. They need a lever of some sort – be it self-interest or the influence of another – to relinquish some if not all of those privileges, at least until they realise that the compensations for doing so are adequate in themselves. And in this women have to play a greater part, I believe.

Women have evaded a simple truth: if they want a man to change, if they want him to share responsibility, to act in a spirit of equality, to be more caring in and out of bed, they should tell him so and keep on telling him until he listens. A man can often be ignorant, innocent, naïve and ill-informed. If he is told the truth, he cannot claim any of these attitudes as a defence; he cannot slip off the hook.

Feminism, I believe, can and *should* have done more to encourage women to tell men what they want, to explain to men how much richer their roles might be in different circumstances. Feminism, I think, has not done nearly enough to provide 'ordinary' women with the arguments to make *their* case. It has not done as much as it might to help men and women in a practical way to live together as equal individuals on a daily basis.

Reasons beyond feminism exist for this failure. At the time the women's movement emerged in Britain, the easiest way for the media to handle it was in terms of ridicule and over-simplification. The symbol of the movement became the lesbian separatist, the man-hater. The image has lingered on, undermining and distracting the women's movement so that at times its main preoccupation has been, apparently, with labels – Separatist? Radical Feminist? Socialist? – and in-fighting.

Such debates are inevitable, and of course take place, but if they are the only voice that is heard in any strength, then the relevance of feminism becomes even more obscure for the ordinary man and woman, already coaxed by the press into accepting a caricature.

The erroneous impression that the only 'true' feminist is one who lives without a man alienates many of the ninety per cent of women who do live with and love men. As a result they don't hear much of what feminism has to say which *is* of relevance to their daily lives. Men's antipathy to feminism comes often in ever stronger measure.

Again and again I was told by the men I interviewed that feminism was about women who want to be men; women who burn bras; women who hate men. Not once was I told it was about a freedom from stereotyping for women *and* men; the right of choice for females *and* males; the end of an abuse of power by the strong over the weak.

Feminism has made *some* gains, for instance operating by stealth like a saboteur in the media. Women's magazines in the eighties, for example, do handle issues such as abortion; the working woman; equal pay. The tone, however, is more often what the woman should demand for herself, less often what she should expect from her man in terms of care, shared responsibility, joint decision-making. How does she couch arguments which, even if they are resisted, will make sense to a man?

Men see almost no distinction at times between a woman asking for her rights and 'nagging'. It is feminism's task to make that distinction so clear that it *has* to be confronted. It is not an easy job, the media will continue to act on the whole with hostility rather than enthusiasm, but at the present time I feel it is a task which is not even being tackled on any serious scale.

Some feminists argue that men should be left to fend for themselves because women need all their energy for their own battles. Left to their own devices, however, how many men will volunteer for such an experience when initially at least they are being asked to make their lives materially less comfortable? Unlike women, what's more, they have no tradition of supporting each other, talking to each other, stepping out of the stereotype.

The more I have listened to men in the course of this book, the more I've felt some of their conditioning is as difficult to live with as that of women. The crucial difference is that the opportunity to cushion the worst aspects of their lives (the crushing boredom of the assembly line, for instance) is readier to hand than it is for women. As is the opportunity to build a totally different life, if they so choose, for themselves and their partners and every woman with whom they come in contact, because they hold the power.

Again and again while writing this book, I was reminded of the schizophrenic reaction of many women towards men. I would spend the day talking and listening to a man who was good and pleasant company. Then, alone on a late-night train with a drunk, or standing at a bus-stop being abused by a man because his overtures had been rejected, I was reminded of what Judith Arcana in her book *Every Mother's Son* calls 'men's enormous sense of entitlement . . . they sort of feel women are on this earth to gratify their needs.'

Nevertheless, I am glad that in the course of writing this book I have met a number of men, not necessarily the majority, and not necessarily men without prejudices, who articulated their potential and their willingness for change. It does not add up to a revolution, by any means, but it *does* underline that to condemn all men is to discourage the few, and to forfeit the only allies women have in the struggle for equality. And perhaps, on reading this book, some men might realise that the struggle for equality is *their* struggle too.

Terry Callow   *Middlesbrough*

On a warm August afternoon, Terry Callow sweats gently inside the Blinkin' Owl at Butlin's while he puts up balloons, Christmas decorations and tinsel. Tonight at Callow's Cavalcade, it is Christmas night. A couple of hundred holidaymakers, the colour of so many beetroots jostling in a jar, will welcome Santa Claus at eleven thirty and sing *Silent Night* and *O Come All Ye Faithful*. They do it every Wednesday night right through the summer season.

The Blinkin' Owl is a massive bar decorated in pseudo-Swiss chalet style. The beams are low and rustic plastic; beer is served in buckets which hold nearly two pints. If the barmaid or man is decorated with a blue plaster you know it conceals a love bite; the seasonal worker's DSO.

This is Terry's Empire. He receives star billing on the daily programme of events, and rightly so. He invented Christmas at the Blinkin' Owl six years ago. He also writes and produces pantomimes starring such favourites as Fairy Liquid, and dresses himself in homemade costumes which turn him into Butlin's Pied Piper; wherever he goes the children follow. His magnetism even exceeds that of the other Redcoats.

At six p.m., Terry sits in the coffee-bar close to the Prince's Ballroom and chats to an elderly holidaymaker. She tells him of her late husband, the emptiness in her life, how she always enjoys herself at Butlin's. Terry listens. His working day began at breakfast and will end at around two a.m. He doesn't have to act as unofficial social worker but he likes to mix.

He is dressed in gold wellington boots, gold cloak, a hat the size of a pumpkin made out of pastel foam-rubber; as a sporran, he has two Christmas balls hanging on gold tinsel, a black leotard and tights plus a set of plastic teeth hanging round his neck to complete the ensemble. 'Give us your autograph, Terry,' says a fan.

At five past ten the doors of the Blinkin' Owl are opened and the long queue outside surges through and makes for the tables at a run. Joke hats are distributed, orders for cockles and whelks and hot dogs placed, rounds are bought two and three at a time to avoid the crush at the bar.

Six nights a week, Terry produces something different. One night it is Old Tyme Music, another Babes in the Wood, another the Miss Whitbread competition and the Worst Singer of the Week competition.

Terry begins tonight by indulging a few fantasies – he knows his audience well enough to understand that their reserves of tolerance and good humour halfway through a sun-varnished holiday are enormous; almost as vast as their thirst for alcohol.

He introduces a regular. A woman holidaymaker in her sixties who has sung every night since Saturday. She could be Dorothy Squires's double. Her hair is white blonde, the Indian caftan is stitched in silver, the lipstick is pale apricot to contrast with the mahogany tan; the jewels on her fingers and rings through her ears flash and sparkle as she wobbles through 'My Way'. The trio of musicians at the back strive to make their musical climax coincide with hers; satisfaction is not achieved. Still, she gets a standing ovation. Terry introduces the final of the Singing Waiters competition.

The men in the quartets have gone for conservative fake moustaches and boaters. The women have opted for more ostentation. Four quite large competitors wear suspenders, stockings and frilly knickers and display them frequently.

Jock Strap and his Danglers are followed by Fag Ash Lil and the Dog Ends, then comes Di and the Bollicals and Slack Alice and the Loose Ones. The audience love it; the humour makes a *Carry On* film seem subtle but nobody cares. 'Poor lad,' Terry says up on stage as a man goes to the seafood stall, 'he hasn't got a winkle but he has got crabs.'

He persuades them to sing, laugh, make fools of themselves, speak to the stranger next door. He keeps going on half a dozen lagers and the adulation. At around midnight, Neil calls in. Neil was a teacher. He likes being a Redcoat. While Terry is homely but extrovert, a small man who fits the word 'cuddly', Neil is more serious, he speaks less often and prefers to reserve his flamboyance for the children. He still looks like a teacher and is not remotely camp. Both are good company. Terry is almost shy when he is not in his public persona. They have been having an affair, as Terry terms it, for seven years. No one at Butlin's knows, although they spend all their free time together. If asked, Terry replies

that they are just good friends. On their day off, they dress smartly, go
out for the day, have a good meal.

They met in Terry's home town of Middlesbrough. Neil had already
decided he was homosexual; Terry is more ambivalent. As a Redcoat he
has had encounters with both sexes. He knew though when they met that
this was something special, he says. Neil's mother had died of cancer just
before. Neil's father had a girlfriend and there was conflict between father
and son. Terry's mum and dad took Neil in and he has remained a part
of the family ever since. Neither parent ever asked questions about the
relationship.

'I knew it wasn't a flash in the pan,' Terry says. 'I knew I wasn't
lovestruck or owt like that, we just got on really well. I believe in love
but not on the scale it's meant to be. I think infatuation is a lot to do
with it, and lust. Real love is a mixture of deepness, thought, mutual
understanding. Everybody needs somebody. Everyone needs someone to
talk to who's close. We might not have much money but we've got our
friendship.

'I don't know why we do get on. We don't go into a deep relationship,
we've been together for seven years and we're more or less like brothers
now. I stick up for him all the time because he's the quieter one. He's
more dependent. We're not that lovey-dovey. The passion side has fizzled
out a bit. But I never was one for jumping in and out of bed. We both
feel the same.

'I see us as an ordinary couple really – not man and wife – none of
that stuff, we don't mix with a lot of camp people or gays, we're just us.

'I don't want to be any different. I've never wanted to be a woman.
I've never acted the woman's part or anything like that. Never needed to
– women have a terrible time anyway.

'I've always said a housewife is an unpaid slave. No wonder women
turn to drink and become recluses. They're left alone all day and when
he comes in, he'll have his meal, sit in front of the telly, fall asleep and
that's it. She'll be there on her own again.

'The icing on the cake's changed a bit. If both work the man gives a
hand. If the man's unemployed, he does a bit in the house. But underneath,
the cake's the same.'

Some of the strength of the relationship between Terry and Neil comes
from Neil's antipathy to the institution of marriage as he has seen it. He
has had several tastes of heterosexual relationships and he hasn't much

liked the flavour – a dislike that has very little to do with sexuality. It's
the possessiveness of women he says he mistrusts. As a Redcoat in the
sixties and seventies he was in a position to make as good a consumer
test as any: 'You were on a pedestal, you had that red jacket on and to
a woman, you were a star. They fell in love with you,' he says very gently.
'They idolised you. It's still the same even with married women and
Gingerbread ladies, women whose husbands are on oil rigs. You always
get chatted up. Then and now, a Redcoat could have a different woman
every night if he wanted that.

'Women behave differently on holiday because I think they feel free.
They've probably been tied to the house for fifty weeks and that fortnight's
holiday is theirs. Nothing's going to stop them enjoying themselves and
they have a few drinks and live out a few fantasies. Not all the women
are like that, but some – if you saw them back home in their own street,
you probably wouldn't believe it was the same woman.

'I've always got on really well with women as friends. They've often
said they can talk to me in a way they don't even open up to their
husbands. I like women, but as friends.'

At nineteen, in his second season at Butlin's, Terry met Lyn. They went
out together and suddenly, one day, she moved into his chalet. She tried
to take over his life, he says. It got to the stage where he was expected to
account for his every move. And equally suddenly, he found himself
engaged.

'She used to try and do my washing and ironing, for instance. But I
like to do my own ironing. I know how my shirts should be done and
where to put the creases in my trousers. I think it's instinct in a woman
to try to be the homemaker.

'I mean, men and women are completely different. Women are brought
into this life to reproduce, just reproduce, reproduce. Like animals really.
The main instinct is to get married and settle down. You do meet those
who have a family and who go to work but they always suffer in the end.
Something always happens because the family's not knitted together.

'The male instinct is to father children and go out and provide. Neil
and I are more flexible but then I don't particularly want my own children
– although I'd like to adopt – and what I've seen of marriage I don't like.
I've never been as bothered by sex as some people seem to be. I'm a happy
person, I like life on an even keel. I can get excited and fiery if I'm in the
right mood, but I don't like that every night. I don't like the feeling I'm

being taken over either – Neil and I live side by side, if you know what I mean – and he's a bit more dependent on me – but I don't mind.

'I look at people in my family who've married and what have they really got? They haven't got owt like I've got. I mean they've families but they've worked in dead-end jobs, they've got mortgages but I don't think they're really happy. They go to work, they go to the club for a drink. It's the same routine. I think that's why they admire me. I'm the one who broke away. I've done what I've wanted to do and I've stuck by it.

'I think deep down my brother Jimmy would've loved to have done it but he didn't have the guts. And I couldn't have done it with a family and kids, not really. I've no regrets at all.'

In September, in the last week of the season, Terry and I meet again. Terry has all manner of plans for the winter. He and Neil will spend Christmas in Middlesbrough, there is the possibility of the Butlin's roadshow, they've saved some money from the season but not much. As a senior Redcoat, Terry earns £80 a week. He pays for his accommodation, a chalet on A line, the manager's line which entitles him to a double bed. Neil is on N line.

'I call my chalet Crossroads,' Terry says, laughing, 'everyone comes to me for advice, I don't know why it is, they always have.

'I mean I haven't got this halo or anything, I can just sit and talk or listen to anybody. You sit with a cup of tea and they pour their hearts out. I've met that many millions of people, now I can judge a person. I can talk to a person and know exactly what's wrong – even Neil comments on it. It's uncanny.

'If I died tomorrow,' Terry says reflectively, 'I'd die happy because I'd know I've done so much. I love people, I love meeting people. I remember when I was a kid, my mum and dad and three of us kids would have a week at Butlin's at Redcar, a taxi there and back and it would cost our dad £20.

'The Redcoats used to go out of their way to make people happy. They knew we were working class, saved for fifty weeks to have a damn good time for that fortnight. Some holidaymakers used to arrive with a carrier bag full of clothes and £200 to spend. They'd leave penniless but happy.

'I've had some fun. All right, I'm not a star. But thousands and thousands of people know me. I've made them happy at Clacton, Minehead, Bognor, Filey. They won't forget me.'

Four months later, we meet in Middlesbrough. Ten years ago, this was a boom area – steel, coal, North Sea Oil, chemicals plus regional grants, wages ten per cent higher than the national average. Now, Middlesbrough and Darlington, like a sad case of dry rot, are riddled with unemployment.

The winter plans had not come to fruition for Terry or Neil. The Roadshow never happened while, as seasonal workers, they had been deemed ineligible for unemployment benefit of £60 a fortnight. Instead, they have been receiving supplementary benefit of £45 a fortnight while they search in vain for work.

Terry comes to meet me at the station, having planned his budget to the penny. He has walked into town, four miles or so from his mother's council house on a new estate. He has enough money to buy two cups of coffee and twenty cigarettes. None of this information is given willingly, Terry would have preferred the illusion to have been maintained.

A diet of chips and cheap food has increased his weight by a stone, so he seems rounder than when we first met. But his optimism has increased in proportion too, in spite of it all.

'I've just come through the worst time in my life,' he says cheerily. 'But I'm sure it's going to be O.K. now. We've been out once on New Year's Eve and that's it. We pay my mum £20 a week for board because she's only on her widow's pension and that leaves £5 a fortnight pocket money.

'We've a big social club in the centre of our estate, they have bingo and a cabaret show every night. Everyone gets dressed up and goes down there and you think, 'what would it be like to do the same . . . I had the money at Butlin's but once we'd had a good holiday it all went. I'll just have to cut down and save harder when the season begins again, there's no way I could go through this again.

'It's small things, really . . . like aftershave. Even if I'm not going anywhere I like it . . . we need batteries for the cassette. But there's no point in sitting down and crying, is there?'

I ask how others might describe him. 'Happy,' he replies quickly. 'A happy person. I wouldn't say I don't get annoyed but I wouldn't kick out at someone just because of what's happened to me. I wouldn't say it's brought Neil and me closer together but we've survived and we're still close.

'But then I never really open myself up to anyone. I've always been able to handle any crisis or whatever myself. I've always got through things without actually asking anyone for help. I cried on the night my dad died. I kept saying, "Why's it got to be me?" He'd never done no harm to nobody, I'd hoped dad would die in his sleep with no pain – and he had cancer for a year. That's the only time I can remember crying.'

Terry is one of six children. He still lives at home with his mother – at least for part of the year. Neither parent, George and Gladys, showed favouritism, he says, and he gets on well with his mother now; Neil gets on even better. When Terry tells the story of Gladys and George Callow, his features soften.

George was nineteen and going out with Annie, Gladys's sister, when he met Gladys. Gladys was sixteen when they married, three years younger than her husband. He was a docker, she was a nurse. He was six foot six, she was four foot nine. Once the children came along, she gave up work and eventually became a cleaner in a bank.

Eighteen years separated the eldest child, George, from the baby, Maureen. Terry was fifth in a line of four boys and two girls. He can remember the girls did most of the housework and his older sister, Pat, was expected to care for the children. The family lived in a two up, two down.

George worked shifts, six a.m. to two p.m.; two p.m. to ten p.m. On the morning shift, he would go and have a couple of pints first, his dinner would be ready and then he'd have a sleep. His wage he kept to himself; Gladys had her bit and extra if she wanted a new dress or 'owt like that'.

Gladys saved. When George retired, the Inland Revenue demanded to know how much Gladys had stored away. 'You never told me you had money saved, Gladys,' George said. 'That doesn't matter, that's my affair,' Gladys replied, 'I'll go down that tax place and tell them it's nothing to do with them what I've got . . .'

Gladys, now sixty-nine, recently had an encounter with two youths in the shopping precinct. They tried to pinch her handbag and she clocked one with a tin of baked beans. The other fled in fright.

Terry's earliest memory, he says, is sitting watching his mother make rag mats for sale out of sack with a peg to stitch through the rags. 'We'd sit in front of a big roaring fire. Dad would come in from work with sweets, a big bag of sweets. My mum and dad used to sing together, close harmony . . . 'Apple Blossom Time'. They did concert shows for pensioners. They got on so well because they married for love, unlike today. But they used to fight.

'My mum could come out with words I'd never even heard of. She could swear. If he came in late after a drink at dinnertime and she was waiting to go to bingo, she'd throw the lot at him . . . liver and onions, the lot. She was half his size and he used to say, "Get her off me," as she had a go.

'If his horse went bad, he'd say to my mum, "That's it. It's because of you. Never shut up yapping at me. You put the jinx on me horses." He used to enjoy a drink and when he came home drunk, my mum could settle him. He couldn't stand being ignored. She'd not speak to him for maybe two days. He'd say, "What have I done? Do you want a cup of tea, Gladys?" "I don't want nothing off you."

'They used to talk through us kids and we'd laugh. "Can you ask your mother so and so . . ." I can't bear that kind of silence now or rows that go on for too long. Women can keep it up for much longer than men and I hate it.

'My dad left home for two days once, but he was back. They cared for each other . . . everyone said my mum wouldn't be able to stand it when he died. But over the last year, she's come round, she's got her family round her.

'I could get my own way with my dad but it was my mum who made all the decisions,' Terry adds. 'Dad was the breadwinner though, 'cos he made the money. My mum had her money from the part-time job. It was a standing joke, anything in the house, my mum would say, "I paid for that . . ." My dad used to say, "You're the only woman I know who's got elastic in her wages . . ."

'Mum paid the bills, she could have anything she wanted from him. He was a very fussy man about eating. He would never eat if a neighbour was in and he would only eat my mum's cooking. He wouldn't even have a cup of tea at his brother's house.

'We'd all go to Redcar for the day and my dad would go to the Races. Once he gave my sister five shillings so four of us could have our dinner – he asked for change, but we'd all had three courses! It were a real laugh.

'He didn't bath us or put us to bed but when we were five or six he'd give us a cuddle, get up to us in the night if we were sick.

'When my father was dying, he called Neil in and said, "This is your home. If you want to go and come as you please, you can. I'm telling you, this is your home." It choked Neil up because no one had ever talked to him like that in his life. I think that's why he thinks so much of our family. We fit together very well. We all do.'

Terry's childhood was splintered by mishap. At three he broke his collarbone; at five, an operation went wrong and left him with a squint in one eye which he still has; at six he fractured a limb in four places; at eight he broke his hip.

'Ma says I was "a fairly quiet kid. You were always quite ordinary like, not into mischief."' She kept the children in or near the house and discouraged them from going out a lot.

Terry says he was and is close to his sister, Pat, who is eight years older, because she used to take him everywhere. 'I remember she had flared skirts. We went to see *Rock Around the Clock* and she was dancing in the aisle. You don't see that now . . .

'Maureen, my younger sister, although she's turned out lovely now, was always crying. She was proper spoilt. She'd sit in a corner and cry and when my dad got home, she'd say, "Dad, our mum's hit me." And my dad would say, "Oh come here." If she was sick she'd tell him she was getting into their bed . . . we boys never bothered, like.'

George was Catholic, Gladys Church of England. Terry went to a Catholic College but refused at fifteen to continue to go to Confession in spite of priestly pressure. Sex, he says, was never mentioned at home. At the age of twelve, he still believed girls got pregnant by kissing. His mother had all her children at home but at seven and eight and nine, Terry says they believed the midwife brought the baby in her black bag. 'We'd save milkbottle tops for weeks and give them to the midwife in return for a baby. Even when I was seventeen, mam wouldn't say "she's having a baby" or mention the word "miscarriage". If ever anything to do with sex or kissing came on the telly, my dad wouldn't watch if we were there. Once *The Killing of Sister George* was on and they both went to bed but my mum watched it recently with us and thoroughly enjoyed it. She's more open now . . .

'I'm the only one not married of the six but she's never put pressure on me. She's got enough grandchildren to keep her happy. She doesn't want explanations, she just accepts. She's very strong.

'I think it's in the way of things,' Terry offers, 'boys are closer to mothers, fathers are closer to daughters. I was close to my mum because she was always there. I mean I was never one for going and putting my arms round her and cuddling her. I was never a mummy's boy, I was a swot. But I think our mum and dad admired us all, they pushed us, even if we didn't go the way they wanted us to go.'

At school, Terry did well academically. He had a group of friends with whom he still remains in contact. They went on to be teachers, which is what George wanted Terry to be.

'I've always known what I wanted for myself. I wanted to be different. Friends are on £12,000 a year now but they say they envy me the variety. They admire me. I'd already produced *Cinderella* at school and at fifteen I used to sing. I didn't have a good voice but I began to develop a personality.' At nineteen he applied for a job at Butlin's. No one in the family thought he'd be successful. 'See I've proved you all wrong,' he said when the letter arrived. He began at Clacton on £8 a week and hated it.

'I had all the terrible jobs, seeing people into meals, I'd play all the worst parts like Dracula. I never saw the bar or the ballroom and I was a northerner amongst Redcoats who were southerners . . . but I stuck with the holidaymakers and gradually by the next season it got better. My mum and dad used to come and see me and I think they felt quite chuffed. I was – and am – famous in my own way, you know.' The tone is wistful rather than self-important.

We talk about appearance and vanity. Terry says he used to worry terribly about being plump. At Butlin's, he explains, his waist is usually thirty-four; at home it has crept up to thirty-eight, but he'll lose it once the season starts. 'I used to think, Oh I hate being plump, now I think, Oh well.

'Looks have never bothered me. I know I've never been a nice-looking person, I'm just a plain ordinary kind of a person. I don't care what people think, it's what's in here that counts. I mean when I was a kid, I used to get called cock-eyed. I used to get hurt but I don't even think about it now.'

Terry has spent some of the winter months writing new pantos for the summer season. His ambition, he says is to produce shows, make an album. 'I'm not competitive, I don't want success. I've made a thousand people happy so I've got what I want but I'd like to branch out now. My shows have worked, people have gone. That's bloody marvellous,' he says without a fleck of the boastful about him. 'Now my goal is to make people happy producing shows.'

If Neil became more successful it wouldn't bother him he says. 'I am what I am. I've got something nobody else has got . . .'

At one point in the previous season, Terry says Neil had become jealous of his relationship with Alan, a young barman, and Anne, a middle-aged woman who was employed as a supervisor. 'I explained that I wouldn't dream of going with anyone else, I don't want to and I explained to Anne too and she was very nice about it. I think jealousy is a waste of time.'

One other of Terry's ambitions could only be fulfilled if he won the pools. He'd buy a big house 'and fill it full of kids and give them a proper home. We'd have a rota for all the housekeeping. Girls one day, boys the next, both treated the same. I had to do the washing up, why shouldn't the boys? I had a marvellous upbringing but I'd be more involved if I had children. I'd talk to them more about life, answer questions. I'd cuddle them a lot. When kids are shunned, that's terrible . . .'

The kind of life he lives now, he says, is far removed from the perpetual motion of Butlin's. He and Neil get up around nine thirty, they do a bit of housework for his mum and cook the dinner for the three of them; corned beef hash or egg and chips. In the afternoon, they watch television or listen to Gladys reminisce or go for a walk. After tea of eggs on toast, Terry reads the paper upstairs and Neil and Gladys watch more telly. They both love soap operas.

'I hate *Dallas*. I call it *Dysentery*. But Neil and my mum love it. She's a television addict. The two of them get on very, very well indeed.'

In the afternoon, Terry's older brother often comes over. He is separated, he had a golden handshake from the docks as well as compensation when he fell and broke both his wrists: £50,000 in all. 'He bought his own home, everything is immaculate. He comes to see mum every day which is good. He doesn't work now, the interest on his building society account is probably enough to keep him all right. He has everything but he brings mum his washing. I had a terrific row with him about it yesterday. I said, "Don't you think she's got enough to do?" I says, "I can understand you bringing your shirts up for Ma to do because no one can iron a shirt like your mother . . . but towels and sheets!" He's got a washing machine and a tumble dryer.

'She started washing at ten a.m. and she still had the tumble dryer going at a quarter to nine at night. She won't let anyone else do it. She says, "While I have breath in my body I'll do my own work."

'She's getting older now, so she'll tell you a story and the next day she'll repeat it all over again. You can't say nothing, it's as if she's in her own little world. When my dad died I told her I'd stay, I wouldn't go back to Butlin's. She said, "You go back, that's what your dad would've wanted." She still says that.'

The last time we spoke, it was March and Terry and Neil were due to leave the next day and return to Butlin's for a new season; out of anonymity back to the limelight. On a previous occasion, Terry had said, 'I don't know how long it will last with Neil. We could decide tomorrow that we've had enough, he may decide or I may decide. I might decide to get married one day. I mean, we are happy but should something happen . . .'

In March, Terry still had all his dreams and plans for the future. 'We'd like to go to Australia to see Neil's sister, we'd like to go to Disneyland and Washington. I'd like to go to Rome. There's places I'd love to go to and maybe we might get there some day. We've got to do what we can now. At least we've got a job, we've very lucky. I think next winter, Butlin's might even find us some winter work . . .'

Derek Carter   *London*

A woman lies by a swimming pool dressed only in a pair of mirrored sunglasses. She is thin and greased and her lips pout easily. A man walks into shot in a suit and another pair of mirrored glasses. His back to the camera, he simulates cunnilingus. The camera concentrates on the images of 'ecstasy' on the woman's face.

A little later on in the half-hour video, the same woman appears naked with a female partner and for several minutes they apply suntan lotion and explore each other's bodies. A third sequence has a different woman, again more upmarket and carefully groomed than the participants usually are in soft porn, who persuades a garden hose to do all manner of things to her body. The cost of the video is £22.50. It is part of a series, a video 'adult magazine', and it sells extremely well in this country and in the USA.

The house, in one of the wealthier parts of London, is Georgian. A Porsche Turbo is parked outside beside a customised Volkswagen. Inside, Peter and James, the two silver-haired tabby Persian kittens with whiskers on their faces like old men, play in a series of rooms furnished only with decorator's equipment.

Derek Carter and his wife, Sue, moved into the house a few months ago. Eventually it will be plush and original but not flashy, with a good deal of money going into such detail as the tiles on the kitchen floor. Derek is slightly smaller than average, unassuming; he looks as if he plays sport regularly, and he says he is about to leave for a local gym where he will work out on the Nautilus equipment.

Derek has built up his soft-porn video business over the past five years, and his turnover is now £2m a year. Porn is one of the fastest-growing sectors of the service industry. It can also be one of the nastiest. Derek stipulates no erections, no penetration, no humiliation, no violence, no under-age sex, no coercion. A ban dictated largely for reasons of marketing, and one which still leaves plenty of scope.

Sue is twenty-five. They met a year ago and were married shortly after. She was then selling advertising space in a magazine. She now works with

Derek on the administration side. She loves the business, he says, she is far more interested in it than him, far less inhibited. Sue is slim, friendly, energetic, without make-up, dressed in jeans and a jumper. She resembles the probably rather popular head girl in a mixed progressive boarding-school. Both Sue and Derek speak in the accents of the middle class.

Derek Carter's apprenticeship for the porn video business spans two years of a four-year degree in Business Studies; pyramid selling, an advertising agency, second-hand bookselling, film editing; and finally a job as a successful photographer for a monthly soft-porn magazine.

If people ask him what he does for a living, I ask him, what does he say? 'I've never worked that one out, actually,' he replies. 'I've never had a pat answer. I'm usually tongue-tied for a few seconds. It is controversial to say you're a pornographer. Funnily enough,' he adds without intended irony, 'it's a bit of a conversation-stopper.

'Very few reply with nudge, nudge, wink wink sort of thing . . . They usually say, "Mmmm . . . would you like another drink?" They go very pensive and say, "I knew a man once who . . ." I'm not at all the sort of person who's deliberately shocking by any means, but certainly when I was a photographer I got quite a lot of money out of doing something I basically knew nothing about and that gave me a sort of smug feeling. It wasn't sacrilegious but it *was* kind of anti-establishment and iconoclastic. Sort of Up yours. I liked the idea of being totally accountable to myself for my own time, not employed by anybody.

'Several close friends took a rather stupid moralistic stance at the time . . . so I don't see very many of the friends I used to have. I have a new fairly small circle now. I'm not particularly gregarious so it never worried me that much.

'People used to say to me, "You'd probably like to go into advertising . . . you'd probably like to be a fashion photographer . . ." As if soft porn was only a means to an end. As if there's some innate good quality in flogging frocks to ladies or some real social benefit in taking pictures of cans of lager or cheddar cheese. That to them was more important and clever and worthwhile.

'My attitude is maybe a little simplified but it's fairly straightforward. I think there are very few things people actually do in their working lives that are either "good" or "bad" — except perhaps for people such as nurses and doctors. The majority of us are just earning a living. I don't feel any guilt about what I do. It's just a job.'

How does he react to the charge that porn causes harm? 'I believe there will always be the oddball whose interest in the bizarre might well be fanned by looking at a magazine, although I imagine they'd be on to something much stronger than we are selling,' he replies.

'I'm prepared to accept that someone, somewhere, could be adversely affected. At the same time, I know a lot of people derive a lot of solace or help from it. And a lot of other people just think it's fun.'

Derek Carter devises all the 'plots' of his videos, he writes the scripts, directs the filming and then edits the product. How does he know what the audience wants?

'Instinctively I know. It's something *I* would like. I know without any trouble.' It is a job a woman, or at least some women, could do, he says. He began in photography working as an assistant for his then girlfriend, Pam. They had met when Derek was in his early twenties and she was about the same age and married. They had an affair and eventually lived together for eight years 'off and on'. Pam's ex-husband was editor of the monthly magazine they both worked for and he is now Derek's business partner; the strain in the relationship has been forgotten.

'Pam could do it very well. She understood exactly how things should be presented and what people wanted to see. There are umpteen ways to work and Pam always worked on the most basic, fundamental, professional level. She was extraordinarily sympathetic. It had absolutely nothing to do with sex whatsoever.

'She taught me something very valuable. I felt there was some mystery to it all. "You've got to be a professional photographer before you can know about such things . . ." Pam made me realise anybody can do anything and it started a whole new philosophy for me.'

I ask how he reacted at first in the photographic sessions. Presumably, if it didn't arouse him, it was not going to sell?

'I can remember being very embarrassed initially. It was the idea of all this naked flesh around. The first we did together we had a location near my parents' house, for which my parents never forgave me,' he smiles.

'We photographed the model in the river. It was a novelty, the idea of a girl taking all her clothes off. Later it became a switch-off. Partly because Pam was always there which ensured it was never anything more than was going on and partly because you soon learn anyone who gets involved in what they're doing emotionally is going to come up with a bad product at the end of the day. You can't really do two things at the same time. You're only going to get half of both of them.

'You know, hump her another time by all means, but put it out of your mind on the day. Everything we did was always done with cold professionalism, which was always appreciated.'

Pam, he says, came from a working-class background and married at sixteen. They met when Derek was a copywriter and she was the secretary at an advertising agency. 'I was about twenty-two then and fairly obnoxious, I think. A prat, I would guess. I was very shy. My dad had bought me a Fiat 124 Sports Coupé which was a medium flash motor and I shared a flat in Hampstead with three guys. I met Pam and we had a really peculiar relationship.

'She was also incredibly shy, very vivacious, funny and amusing. Although she came from a working-class background she spoke extremely well. Her husband is probably now one of my closest friends although at one stage there was a man with a shotgun on his way to visit me, that kind of thing . . .

'The affair drifted on for ten years. It wasn't right for me and it was what I was doing through my own weakness. That and the drifting characterised all my early years. I never for instance thought whether my relationship with my parents was good, bad or indifferent. I never thought about what I should be doing. For a long time I was the kind of person things happened to rather than the sort of person that made things happen and for that reason I was not a strong personality in many ways.

'Pam understood that exactly. We had an incredibly self-conscious, self-aware affair. Sort of laughing at each other's ineptness. It was very funny, like something out of Jacques Tati.

'In the end I found it a strain working together and living together. I needed to feel a sense of independence on a very selfish level, especially as Pam was extremely puritanical. That's not probably the word to describe it but she was very, very inhibited . . . She wasn't interested in people at all. She was introverted and unflamboyant although she could be flamboyant on occasions. As a general rule she'd much rather sit at home so I was leading a very isolated life.'

I say it's ironic because some people must imagine that the life of a pornographer is bound to be saturated in sex. It must be assumed that Derek Carter is a proficient lover, leads a salacious life, generally resembles some men's fantasy of how they would like themselves to be.

He says all those assumptions *are* made but on the whole he has always separated his work and private life. The kind of woman he likes tends not to be the kind he sees in his work, except for a brief fling. He sees his work as a profession, with a few extra perks perhaps. He is in fact still inhibited about sex and wouldn't rate himself very highly as a lover. 'I mean how do you really know?' He was at one stage obsessed with sex but that was simply because he wasn't getting any. He does not believe in monogamy however. A belief Sue abides by willingly.

'Sue is a very, very uncomplicated person,' he explains. 'She gives off the most fantastic positive vibrations. She is extremely energetic, unpossessive, which is unusual in my experience. As long as she receives the requisite amount of affection from me, as much as she can get, then it's of supreme indifference to her what I get up to.

'I'm certainly not monogamous, not as a set rule. I'm more demanding. I'm much more possessive than she is and she respects that so she is monogamous. She wouldn't want me to have an affair but she wouldn't mind if I had a fling. It's not important to *have* a fling, it *is* incredibly important to feel that you can if you wanted.

'It's a weakness but it's a nice feeling for all the reasons men and women can identify with . . .'

He goes on to make an observation about the porn industry. 'There is no bullshit. I think probably because people are more purged. I mean it's just so straightforward and that's the beauty of it. Nobody has pretensions. Nobody I know and work with spends time trying to get themselves a bigger desk or a bigger expense account . . . you know the little social strictures which exist in the straight world, if you like.'

I point out that he, unlike some pornographers I have met, does not appear to indulge himself in conspicuous consumption; no heavy gold rings, necklaces, wads of notes, no exhibitionist displays of power over women. He seems to be more at the Gucci end of the market.

'I would say yes, that what I'm describing is only my own environment,' he agrees. 'There are two or three photographers who are like me and who aren't saving up for Rolls Royces and wearing gold bracelets. I see it more as a business proposition than a way of life.

'I know some men in the business are just very weak characters, in it for different motives – but money is still the prime one.'

Upmarket or downmarket, it is nevertheless a business to do with the selling of flesh, the exploitation of women, the use of their bodies as objects. Derek Carter knows the arguments by heart and he has his answers ready. First, the women.

He says that from a photographer's point of view there's a certain amount of play-acting. 'You do all the simple silly things, you tell them they look pretty or "You look fantastic!" That kind of thing . . .' Doesn't it make him cynical about women that they can be so gullible?

'Some, yes. But to be honest I never really extrapolate that information and extend it to all women.' You mean, I ask, that they're not women as such, but products? 'Yes. I don't just see them as the female gender. But a lot of them *are* stupid and incredibly gullible. It's something I've certainly never exploited. They've always survived extremely well working for me, less well working for other people.

'Most notably the ones who came from the country. They began by working for me and have been very well protected and very well looked after and then they moved on to do fashion and beauty and within weeks they're doing drugs, living with black men and generally getting screwed up.

'They're more likely to be exploited working in straight commercial environments than they are with me. With me, there's no bullshit. Nobody is lied to.'

I ask what sort of women he used in magazine photography as models. 'Again, contrary to what one might expect, they were nearly always working-class girls who had usually or very often a very moralistic approach to what they were doing. Often they were married. It usually represented a holiday that they wouldn't otherwise have got. Some of them were quite Roman Catholic in their approach to life.

'They were married and they slept with one man. There was the working-class ethic . . . earn a bit, have a holiday in Benidorm, maybe a kid next year. Dead straightforward. Whereas the middle-class girls fucked anyone senseless but the idea of them taking their clothes off before a camera was totally outrageous. "I'd never dream of doing anything like that . . ." But in fact totally amoral in every other respect. They wouldn't give a damn who they fucked but they wouldn't dream of exhibiting themselves in the magazines.

'The business does attract men who are highly motivated towards women,' he adds. 'They get into the habit of exploiting them because there's a constant stream of very pretty, very gullible and very stupid girls just passing by their noses. So it's inevitable that they should get into the habit of exploiting them . . .'

I ask why someone like himself, in his thirties, doesn't just tire of it all. Surely the novelty must wear off? 'It's not a matter of "once you've seen one body you've seen them all." That's a total fallacy. It's an appetite, it's not a curiosity that's satisfied. It's something that you have to do very regularly, like eating.'

Doesn't it then escalate, I ask? You may begin with soft porn but end up requiring a diet of video nasties?

'Well, you always wind up with what's permitted and videos that are commercial are always the ones that get the distribution. What I do is always engineered to be within the bounds of what this society sees as socially acceptable. But I don't think it *does* escalate. I've been totally submerged in it for a long period of time. I don't think there's anything abnormal about my attitude to sex.' Have you, I ask, got less interested?

'Possibly,' he replies. 'Well, less curious about it . . . In our videos we don't have any sex with violence,' he continues. 'That is out – rightly or wrongly – probably very rightly in my opinion. That would be considered obscene and likely to deprave and corrupt. I know I don't deprave and corrupt, I may even do some good.'

I say that there doesn't seem to be much correlation between men, the women they actually know and the unreality of what they see on the screen.

'I can't really claim to be an authority on why people watch,' he replies, 'but they will use it as a jumping-off point for a fantasy. I mean it's a pretty girl with no clothes on and men never tire of looking at that. A lot watch them with their wives or girlfriends. It's something which surprises me more and more. I meet more and more women who are into it, who actually enjoy it. I know a lot more uninhibited women now than I used to . . .

'There is an absence of pornography for women. There is to some extent a myth that women don't get turned on visually, although I think it's certainly true they get turned on to a lesser extent or less frequently than men.

'I think it's to do with a basic physiological level. I have an erection but for a woman it's a more elaborate arousal ritual. It's a lot more complicated than a male one. A male is fairly easy to stimulate and arouse, whereas I think women are more complex.

'They have tried to tap the female porn market but it winds up with the magazine dropping the cookery pages and being sold to gays . . .' I suggest the failure may be because what is presented is a *male* idea of what female taste in pornography ought to be?

'Yes,' he replies, 'I'm sure it probably is. I don't profess to have any idea what women would like to look at.' How does he avoid repetition in his 'plots'? 'With difficulty,' he says and smiles. 'It's a mistake to think, Oh, we must keep changing it. What the punter wants to see is pretty girls with no clothes on playing with themselves, each other and anything else that is available. There are no statements made. The approach has to be absolutely minimal.'

Inhibition is supposed to be part of a woman's makeup, so how does he persuade his actresses to lose those inhibitions on screen? 'You try not to get them too raw. You try and get them when they've done it a couple of times and you lead them into it in the easiest possible way. You do it by having a very sympathetic film crew. We try to create as pleasant an atmosphere as possible. It's a totally working context. That really makes them relaxed because they know then they're not parading themselves emotionally. Nobody gets off on what they're doing and that's what makes them relaxed.'

Does he think women perform in front of the camera in ways they would perform in the privacy of their home? 'Oh yes. They're more likely to do it in front of the camera because they're being paid to do it. They do exactly what they're told. If they start to enjoy it that's an added bonus. The enjoyment for me is in the editing – I mean insofar as you have to make it work.

'What you get on film is always a little bit rough. They're certainly not having orgasms all over the place, it's more mechanical than that . . .'

He does get turned on himself during filming at times, he says, but on the whole the worry of the whole exercise can kill desire. He recently went to the States and wrote a script, built a set, cast fifty women in the film, hired the crew and directed the film in five days; a functional matter rather than sexual.

'I did quite enjoy that. What I'm saying is that you do get turned on by it but at the same time you're watching every detail, looking at the clock. I admire some people, they're as cool as cucumbers but I'm rushing around a bag of nervous energy. So in reality, usually by halfway through the day, you're fairly bored with all the antics.'

He doesn't get propositioned very much by women in search of jobs nor is there much of the casting couch involved. 'I keep things quite neatly segregated,' he says. 'A lot of girls want to do porn because they enjoy it. A lot do it because they're the centre of attention or they want a holiday or they think it's Showbiz.'

Derek Carter's father runs a successful engineering company. He sent his son to Harrow and Millfield. Derek also has a sister who is four years older. As much of his childhood was spent away from home in school, he feels slightly distanced from his parents, he says, 'they're sort of the Old Codgers.' He smiles, tongue in cheek. 'We had a lot of affection but I know that my parents feel guilty that they didn't bring us up the right way.

'The recurrent thing has always been, "Where did we go wrong?" They know what I do now and their reaction is "Where did we go wrong?"'

Derek Carter describes his father: 'He is a very forceful character, highly self-disciplined, self-motivated, well organised. He is a perfectionist in a slow, ponderous way. The problem will be solved at the end of the day, which is totally different from me.

'I tend to be slap-happy about things, slapdash, whereas he is meticulously efficient. He didn't do much with us because he was very busy. He was always grafting away.

'My mother is very Scottish, a great believer, well they're both great believers in the work ethic. She's not religious in the traditional sense but she's very puritanical. The house is always freezing cold and they derive satisfaction from saving energy. They could afford to heat the town but they don't. They're doing up the bathroom now so it's very El Ritzy and the other day my sister said, "What the hell's the point in having this extravagant bathroom when you know you've only got three minutes of hot water in the house?"

'It's a very regimented house and my mother is never happy unless she knows exactly what the agenda is for the day. That always used to be discussed at breakfast, exactly what would be achieved that day - and if things weren't achieved, my mother was not a very happy woman. So there was very little frivolity. Although she's very sweet, she has this incredibly strong urge to be achieving things all the time. Doing things of value.

'She was a housewife, now she grafts extremely hard for a number of charities. She's a leading light in conservation, population control, the World Wildlife Fund . . . she does it all in a very unsocial sense, no coffee mornings and so on. She's not interested in people, she just gets on with the job in hand.

'They're not interested in other people's lifestyles, how other people live or eat or what cars they buy. But they are very happily married. Although I see them very seldom now, I can't believe how like them I'm becoming. In the last two or three years I've become frighteningly similar . . .' The main similarity, he adds, is in leading a much more simple life than he once did. 'I'm less and less interested in material things . . . I don't want to make two million, then four million, then eight million . . . I realise now those things don't matter.'

The approval of his father used to be very important, he offers. 'It was important to me that my father knew that I was successful. Of course that sort of backfired because he doesn't approve of it. He's more Victorian in his attitude than my mother. We get on fine but certain things we do not talk about such as my work, absolutely not.'

Derek Carter found Harrow neither a happy nor an unhappy experience. 'Kids aged thirteen to seventeen have an awful lot of energy to work out. They either worked it out on the playing fields kicking shit out of each other or they established very much of a King Rat pecking order.

'Everyone was kicking the psychological shit out of the person below them. If you were down the bottom, your aim was to survive. If you were getting towards the top your aim was to be popular. I was in the middle. There were all sorts of psychological tricks and points to be made. For instance, if people visited you in your room you were a cooler dude than the boys who went visiting.

'At that age I don't think you make value judgments, you just accept. So I wasn't particularly happy or unhappy. What you had instilled in you at an early age is that it is very important to be successful. You knew that it was all a game and you had to keep scoring points to stay in the league.

'The ability to manipulate is very hard to lose. It's hard to relate to people in a natural relaxed manner afterwards. I found it very difficult with people for a long time. Cool was the name of the game and you never ever allowed your guard to slip if you had any sense. If you did you were jumped on and crushed.

'Everyone had a best buddy but it was on a very basic level. You never poured your heart out or any of that rubbish. You'd discuss the things you thought were cool because, remember, it was the sixties. You'd discuss how to behave and you'd take the piss out of the other guys. You formed a nucleus because there was strength in numbers and if you could surround yourself with a cluster of cool dudes then you were secure.

'Again my father's approval was very important. He went to Harrow and he wanted me to do well. I wanted to do well for him but I could never motivate myself to work hard. I was always extremely lazy. I always found it extremely difficult to achieve what he expected.

'At the very end of the day it might have been one way I had of getting his attention. Maybe that was true but I don't think so. I could never relate what I was doing at school to what I was going to do in the future. I mean I've always known that I could do pretty much whatever I set my mind to do and being at school bore no relation to achieving that goal whatsoever.'

Did he, I ask, have a conviction that he would be rich and famous? 'Yes, that was typical Harrow arrogance. If nothing else they did instil a belief that the world was there for your gratification. I never imagined that I wouldn't be successful.

'Harrow made you incredibly uptight and self-conscious, just so self-aware that you disappeared up your own arsehole. You felt everything you did wasn't quite as good or quite as cool as it should be. Everything was style and no content.

'I've always slagged the school off and said I'd never send any kids of mine there but I'm also eternally grateful in some respects that I *was* sent there. If they had sent me to the local day-school, I'd still be working as a solicitor's clerk or something equally dreary. Harrow gave me a will to succeed. I met a lot of other people who had a similar sort of idea: that life would smile on them from here on out.'

Derek was sent to Millfield to get some A-levels. While there, he made friends with Matthew, the son of a very rich bookmaker, rich enough for the two of them to spend school lunchtimes in upmarket restaurants and holidays in London doing what young men would, presumably, all like to do if they had the resources.

Derek fell in love and so did not get very good A-level results. Eventually, his father found him a job in the advertising agency which handled his company's account. It was there Derek met Pam, shared a flat with three men and eventually moved in with the landlady who lived on the ground floor. He was in his twenties, she was in her forties. He ended the relationship as he ended quite a few in those days, he says, with very little consideration for the other person's feelings. It was cowardice rather than malice.

'I was totally irresponsible, it stems from school. I have a recurrent dream about being at school for another year. I'm there to pass exams and on the night I'm dreaming, it's maybe the fifth or sixth year that I'm back again to take these exams. There are new boys and girls and I'm still not made prefect or monitor because I'm too irresponsible.

'I was totally irresponsible, I wasn't a good leader or motivator of people or anything. The Hampstead lady was one of those things that just happened. It wasn't a positive move, there was just a low resistance to it. It just happened.

'I think I must have been extremely selfish and unswitched-on when I was younger. I just drifted through relationships, using people and getting whatever I wanted. You know being reasonably charming and not being an out-and-out cad.

'A lot of women did want commitment but at that stage, I was never prepared to give it.' He lost his virginity at eighteen, and has never considered himself anything other than adequate in bed. I ask if women's desire for commitment nevertheless gave him a sense of power.

'Yes, in a small way. It made me feel better. I'd been striving for years and years to feel that I was getting it.

'I was still a man's man. I still talked about getting laid with friends and all that. It's all so unlike what I am now, I've lost touch with it. I mean I am so different from how I used to be . . .' He pauses for a long time. 'That's what I would like to think. One gets very arrogant about thinking that one has changed . . . especially if you think it's for the better. A number of things have made me feel as if I've changed but I probably haven't very much.

'When I left the Hampstead lady,' he continues, 'I know it was very painful for her and I felt a cad over that. I never ever confronted issues in those days. I never said, "Look, I don't love you and it's not going to work out." I'd smile, kiss, kiss, "Well, you know, *che sera sera* . . . that's the way it's got to be." I always tried the line of least resistance, I never really took a grip on anything, I'm afraid.'

Eventually, Derek Carter became a film editor and met Sally again. Sally had been at Millfield with him, left, married, and when he heard of her later, she had just separated from her husband. 'She was incredibly insecure. She was very extrovert, very lively, both her parents had died when she was young. She was very clever in the way that frantic girls can sometimes be.

'You know, the ones doing English A-level who write very quickly and can concentrate very hard and pour it all down. She was very good. She was always a nutty girl – "Oh, I'll get married tomorrow, I'm not doing anything else." I felt guilty about it for ages afterwards because I rang her husband and, this is an example of how devious I was, I told him I was getting married and wanted to invite Sally to the wedding.

'Her husband was so upset because they'd just split up and he gave me her number. He said, "Oh it's been a nightmare," and all I wanted to do was lay his wife. I wasn't looking for a long relationship, everything was short-term in those days. It might be something as silly as "Sally's a model, well maybe I'll hump her a few times and she'll introduce me to a few more nice models . . ." You know, incredibly naïve, Will o' the wisp, get pulled by the nose in whatever direction.'

Sally, he says, became besotted by him. He found her gauche, slightly irritating. Then she became ill, and while she was in hospital he took a decision. 'I decided that this was going to be it. She lay there so feebly I decided all the guard that I'd had from Harrow I'd drop. I decided I'd do the right thing. She was a nice girl, she loved me very much, I'd look after her. It wasn't based on love, it was based on the fact that I felt I could afford to drop my guard because I thought there is no way this creature could ever slap me in the face.

'She was very clingy and slightly clumsy in everything she did. She wasn't really what I thought was "right". I was totally orientated towards games playing. Coldly analytical on exactly what step should be taken next. I never ever dropped my guard.

'I think the name of the game was to further project one's image of oneself, or how one should be. It was just a code of behaviour. It certainly got women to adore you. There was no long-term plan. You know, you'd be out when a woman rang up, that sort of stupid super-score sort of thing.'

What happened, he says, is that as soon as he declared his love, Sally grew cooler and he became utterly obsessed. It was an obsession which lasted three years. He felt inadequate because while he was a humble editor, 'like working at the gas-meter factory', she was leading an exotic life as a successful model.

'I felt I'd failed so badly. It annoyed me so much that I'd wanted her and eventually, in my own terms, I hadn't been good enough. I hadn't been successful enough, I hadn't been witty enough, rich enough or any of the things that at that time seemed extremely important.

'It was a real sense of inadequacy. I knew she was a flake. She could behave in the most extraordinary fashion. You could be having dinner and she'd walk out to wave goodbye to somebody and you wouldn't see her for an hour because she'd be in the back of a cab with whoever it was.

'I couldn't handle it. I always related it to me. It was always a reflection on me. Everyone told me, "You must be mad."

'I got obsessed with the idea too that if I could become successful, everything else would fit into place. I would automatically be witty and very interesting and very rich and I would have her then and get my own back.

'It took a long time to develop to the point where I actually hit her but it's definitely true, once you get the habit it's difficult to stop. It was very hard to break that first taboo and do it. I think she hit me a few times first . . . You do feel regret but then the next time . . .

'She'd be driving back from somewhere and suggest to the taxi driver, "Why don't we go off to Greece for a week?" And they'd go. She got married eventually to a barman when they were both in the nick on a drunken driving charge. She proposed to him. That marriage lasted about a week.

'She was an emotional mess but it took an awful long time to rid myself of the obsession. In a peculiar way I enjoyed it. I've never been able to rationalise it. But it gave me a real urge to be successful, to crack it.

'I saw her again a year ago and it was such a shock to the system, because frankly she was none of the things I remember her for. Having thought about her every day for three years, it just went Phut! like that. It completely disappeared. Thank God! If I *had* felt something for Sally a year ago, it would have meant I hadn't got anywhere, done anything, I was just the same weak wanker I was then.'

He returned to the arms of Pam but it was not until he met Sue that his life got in balance again. She has, he says, helped to restore some of his faith in the uncomplicated, spontaneous, non-manipulative side of love and life.

'I look at Sue's family and I realise things about my own family. Sue for instance is incredibly physically affectionate with both her parents. She constantly throws her arms around them, she will discuss any topic you like in the most simple and basic way. She will express her emotions without any barriers at all.

'They just tip out absolutely unhindered. There is no self-awareness at all in the way she deals with her parents or her two sisters. That is completely different from the way in which I deal with my parents. I don't think it's a male thing because my sister is the same as I am. I think it's to do with family rather than sex.

'I had to decide to leave Pam and that was very traumatic. It was difficult and unpleasant. It was the first time in my life, I suppose, I'd actually made a crucial decision, as a result of that I feel much more positive . . .'

Sue proposed to him. He was 'rather frightened' about the idea initially but he's never regretted it since. 'Sue is very positive. She knows exactly what she wants and she's extremely happy with her lot. She is much less inhibited than I am. She's curious about everything and will try anything. She is very open about it all.'

He also felt timid about the idea of children, but now 'the wheels have been set in motion', he feels happier.

'If I had a son it's difficult to know how I'd bring him up. If he was like me, he'd go out and make all the mistakes that I made. I'm actually quite an inhibited person, so I'd find it difficult to be a very natural father. I will endeavour to because I know that's what I have to do.

'I would have him at a day school. I'll have time for him because I've lost a lot of my silly motivation for success for the sake of it.' If he had a daughter, he would let her be whatever she chose to be – although preferably not in the business. 'It's only a means to an end.'

The Women's Movement, he says, hasn't paid him or his business much attention. 'I think feminism has had its first flush of success. The issues that it's raised have been duly noted. Feminism has gone as far as it can go, humanism certainly hasn't. I think it's pointless to make a distinction between the sexes. It's a decisive mechanism rather than a unifying mechanism, we need a better quality of life for both sexes.'

In the past, he says, he always knew materialism wasn't an adequate god to worship but he couldn't see much else to take its place. Recently he has begun to get interested in the more spiritual side of life, partly under Sue's influence. He eats health food and has given up heavy drinking.

'She is far more in tune than I am. She's slightly clairvoyant. Her energy is quite pure.' On a more practical level, how do they divide the household chores, as they both work full time?

'It's never really been an area of dispute,' he says. 'I think if I had to do it, I'd hire somebody else. It's not really a problem. Sue doesn't feel self-conscious about being housewifely. She doesn't feel like a "house-wife" if she does the cooking a lot . . . But then I don't make her cook a lot so . . . I think neither of us is the dominant partner, I think we're evenly matched. If she wasn't as strong and as forceful a person as she is, I'd be the dominant one. She is independent, the kind of woman I'm attracted to. What I like about her very much is that she is always what she appears to be and she always says what she means.

'I think she's sexually uninhibited because of her childhood. She had lots and lots of affection and she's never been frightened to give it in return. With me, she never played games. She told me she loved me – probably long before she did,' he adds with a laugh, perhaps revealing more about his own skill at game-playing.

He intends to move out of soft porn gradually, he says. It is a means of making money, not a way of life. He would one day like to make a 'Guru' feature film or perhaps launch a range of cosmetics along the lines of Beauty Without Cruelty.

'Until recently,' he offers, 'because all the goals I had been conditioned to aim for are very "man"-orientated, I've always been glad I'm a man. Everything I held as being important and dear like not getting married, getting laid as much as you can, being in control were "male" things. Having said that, now I'm less goal-orientated, I wouldn't mind being a woman.

'Women have a sort of clichéd Mother Earth quality. They are more spiritually with the ticktock of the universe than men, I think that's a conditioning thing. I think men are so souped-up and hyped-up they lose all touch with the rhythm of things. I do envy women quite a bit.'

Winston Clarke *Birmingham*

Winston can dance; *really* dance. The kind of dancing that doesn't require a partner. Winston also has style, *natural* style so, at eighteen, Winston is made. All he has to do is 'be' Winston and he earns himself admiration, status, free drinks, entry to the clubs, friends, women. But he doesn't really have time for friends or women. Not close friends or deep relationships, anyway. All he wants to do is *dance* and be seen; night after night, dance and be seen.

All of which keeps Winston *very* occupied. So occupied that he doesn't have time for work. In the day, he drifts around Birmingham centre, passing the time, allowing others the glory of being seen with Winston, the man who is hot shit in every disco. At night, he's out dancing; no drinking, just dancing, oblivious of the women who vie for his attention, uncaring if jealousy is demonstrated. He has courtiers who will take care of that. Winston is untouchable.

Naturally enough, this is not Eric Clarke's idea of a bright professional career for his son. Dancin', nightclubbin', where did he go wrong? Naturally enough, being the good Jamaican, God-fearing, husband-respecting woman she is, Sarah Clarke supports her husband. So, at eighteen, Winston moves out and moves in with the family of a friend living on the other side of Birmingham. He is given free board and lodgings, he needs no cash in the clubs, his very presence pays his way, his clothes are sold to him half price from local boutiques. Who needs money if he has Fame?

Besides, Winston believes that the dole is *so* unstylish, he couldn't lower his standards to touch it. Mr Clarke senior can't fathom it out – he came to Britain, the motherland, almost thirty years ago from Montego Bay because here he believed he could build his family a future. He came to Birmingham, the heart of England, because wasn't it called 'the city of a thousand trades', the 'workshop of England'? He used his skill as a carpenter and he *did* prosper. First he sent for his wife and one daughter, then for two more sons and finally all eight children. He has a home in a pleasant house in Aston. Mr Clarke had achieved it all because he is a craftsman, a manufacturer, a maker of goods; a man of standing in a world now gone by.

Some sons have followed in his footsteps, one has become an electrical contractor, another a plasterer; but what about Winston? The black sheep, an 'entertainer', a member of the service sector now drowning Birmingham's traditional past in wave after wave of conference centres, hotels, restaurants.

Winston doesn't care. He has his suede shoes, his parka, his scooter, he is a black mod and he dances on to the Beatles, the Rolling Stones, Tamla Motown, Wilson Pickett, the Supremes. He doesn't yet worry about the practical details of how he will *remain* famous once the dancing palls. That comes in his early twenties. And by then, he is a married man with a baby son to support.

Winston Clarke no longer dances today. He has become his father's son again. He hopes he is on his way to being a prosperous man. He is a builder, a small businessman, a hard grafter. Winston owns a three-bedroom terrace with a stone fireplace, open plan and a nice Chesterfield sofa. He drives a white 1980 Alpine. He dresses carefully, still with style, from his soft navy-blue flat peaked hat to his trimmed moustache and deep blue suit.

He likes to drink in the best places; the bars of Birmingham's four-star hotels where a monogrammed coaster under the glass adds twenty-five per cent to the price of the contents – in Winston's case the contents are usually vodka (*good* vodka) and lemonade. He likes the company of women. Lovers provide the fertilizer for his vanity. Where once he let his feet dance a manifesto on his behalf, now his tongue is in charge. He flirts. He deals in lavish compliments, long pauses before he answers the most trivial of questions, the implication being that he is treating every word with his undivided attention. He practises the old-fashioned courtesies – chair drawn back, car door opened, he walks on the outside, closest to the road. 'Has anyone ever told you you have beautiful eyes?' he says.

He enjoys making love to women. He likes a woman to occupy a traditional role in life not because he believes that this is her 'natural' birthright but because he fears that if she abandons such duties they will fall upon him. He sees little value in the rewards that a revolution in male and female attitudes might bring him. He discusses the iniquities of the pressures on him and his fellow men but for all their disadvantages he rates them more highly than the pain he believes he might have to endure to adapt to a different order.

Winston knows himself well, he says, he is in touch with his own feelings, he would not wish to be a woman under any circumstances. And yet he proves to be a strong advocate for women, warning of the dangers of what he describes as the 'false freedom' which women are now trying to achieve. He wishes them well in the struggle because if they win, he says, it will make his life all the richer without any undue discomfort. He intends no sarcasm.

The Clarkes are a middle-class black family. In Jamaica, Sarah was a prominent woman in the parish; in Britain, she tended to remain more at home – except for functions of the church. In the last ten years, since almost all the children have left home, the Clarkes' relationship has grown stormier, Winston reckons.

His father has land in Jamaica and wants to return home, Sarah is happy here. Eric enjoys a night in the pub, Sarah disapproves. In the lives of the eight children, particularly Winston's older brother and the sisters, the parents were strict. Winston, being the middle child and male, had it easier. He says he was his mother's favourite, his father worked hard so he saw him less often.

Winston's mother and sisters did the housework. Affection was there but neither spoken nor demonstrated that often. At Secondary Modern school, Winston was captain of school football and came up against very little racism. He came up against his father's belt rather more frequently.

At eighteen, Winston ceased to be a virgin. He slept with a girl at a party and was too drunk to remember much of the detail. He may convey the impression of cool connoisseur-ship of sex, he certainly implies that in his chat, but in truth, he says, he has always been inhibited; unwilling to discuss details of conquests with the other lads. So they called him Virginlegs.

At nineteen, Winston began going out with Billie. She was the same age and worked in a boutique. Eighteen months later they got married. She wanted it, he decided that if it didn't work out, he could always get a divorce. She was white and both sets of parents opposed the marriage for a variety of reasons, not least that it was too short notice, they should wait and have a proper *white* wedding.

The two married in a registry office and a year later Gregory was born.

For another year after that, Winston says, he tried to be a good husband. He didn't exactly do much in the house or help with the child but he didn't go out as much as he used to, he didn't transgress, he didn't pursue other women. Then, he just got fed up. He began to think of missed opportunities and his desire for Fame.

He began seeing other women, he went for auditions as a dancer, he worked as a male model. And still his reputation was solid enough to give him some kudos wherever he went. He became a salesman. He sold double glazing, electrical components, insurance. Eventually, in 1972, he left the family and lived in London for a year, wheeling and dealing. He and Billie separated many times again and finally divorced a year ago.

They still see one another all the time, she hasn't anyone else and if she did, Winston says, he'd just have to learn to live with it. Greg, now thirteen, lives with him. Suddenly, a couple of years ago, Winston realised that if he didn't try harder he would be in danger of losing his son's friendship.

'I used to think, Oh he's only young, there's plenty of years left, I'll pay him some attention later. But it doesn't work like that. In the meantime, the kid's growing up. Now, we talk a lot. I try to help him as much as I can but he pretty much leads his own life.'

Billie reacted aggressively when she found out about his affairs, he says. He himself has slapped women a few times but only in retaliation and only once on any occasion. He talks about the use of force when it is conjoined with sex.

'A lot of women now let a man go so far. Touch her top half, touch her private parts, when it comes to intercourse, she says no. If it was me, I'd just forget it. I've been in that situation but in actual fact I think some women like to be forced. Sometimes the man is too anxious, he rushes it and the woman isn't ready yet so she puts up a struggle. A lot of the time women call it rape. A lot of the time where the man says the woman is willing I think that's partly true. But I don't think there's ever any need for violence, some men are just that way inclined.

'The thing is that men today have it easy. They can pick up a woman today and go to bed tomorrow. The man doesn't have to make any promises, although the older woman, those who are divorced and separated, probably want a longer relationship. Girls between the ages of eighteen and twenty-eight are different. "What do you want to do?" they say straight out. "Screw me or what?"

'I don't like that kind of woman. It doesn't interest me, it's dead and gone. I'd rather find out first what we have in common. I'd rather have a woman between the ages of thirty and say forty-two.

'I couldn't go to bed and just satisfy myself, the woman has to be satisfied too. It's OK if it's just a passing ship but even then you're trying to be good because your ego is involved.

'I think women are liberated to an extent – but liberated to what? When it comes down to it a man still needs a woman, a woman still needs a man,' he says.

'If a woman comes along for a job with me as a plasterer or an electrician, I'll hire her if she can earn herself money and the company money, great. I see separatists as a form of racists. What I'd say to that kind of woman is, "Right, go and buy yourself a little place in the country, form your own community, then see." It doesn't make me feel threatened because I don't believe it's something that would spread very much. When it comes down to it, we need each other.'

Winston has some sympathy for women today. It is so much harder for them, he says, to find a good man. In the past, the man had to commit himself to marriage to get his quota of sex. Now there is a free market, why should a man strike any kind of a bargain?

At the same time, he says, much of what was once considered the male responsibility in life is now being shared by the female; the female has double the worry and half of the rewards. Women's roles may change radically in fifty or a hundred years, he says, but only if society changes radically too.

'Nothing's altered, not much anyway. A woman can sleep with a man, she can go anywhere she likes but she's not better off. In a sense she's worse off.

'It's OK for women to talk about being liberated in a professional capacity – but even that's a tiny minority. And it doesn't apply much at all in a domestic capacity. At the end of the day, women still do the chores. Can you pass a law saying they must be liberated from the chores?

'If the man and woman in an individual couple want a change then that's OK. But the women in my experience are less interested in their own liberation and more interested in how much harder they can push their husbands to earn more, be more successful. In my experience, in arguments, women are always complaining. "If I'd married John instead

of you, I'd never be in this position," or "I've given you the best years of
my life and what do I get?"

'Women today have been drawn far more into society, they're far more
aware of what's going on,' he offers. 'The man alone used to worry about
money, the bills, the mortgage. Now, the woman is also conscious of these
worries. She says, "I've heard they're laying off men from your place, will
you be one of them?" She worries about his job security; she knows about
the bills, so she's taken on even more of the burden than before.

Men have a hard time too, Winston says – unless they happen to be
good-looking, rich and drive a sports car. 'Rejection is a big thing for a
man. The majority of men aren't good-looking. They can't make themselves attractive with make-up like a woman can.

'They go to nightclubs and the glamorous women won't look at
them. It's very, very competitive. The beautiful girls always go with the
best-looking men. Men are always comparing themselves with each other.
They are very impressionable. They want material possessions, I'm not
interested in that . . .'

What he *does* want is success because that will bring him money and,
though he doesn't say it, perhaps some of the recognition which has faded
since those early days when he was Winston, the dancer.

'A Ferrari or a Roller, they're necessary accessories for a man,' he says,
contradicting himself on the matter of materialism. 'Then you've got it
made, you're a somebody. People who've known me a long time,' he
adds, 'have always said I'd be successful.'

Winston now has a girlfriend of thirty-four. She is white, unemployed,
'glamorous'. He has been out with black and white women but he prefers
white women because they demand less, they are 'freer', he says. Winston's
girlfriend stays with him three or four nights a week but he likes his own
freedom too. The freedom to search for love, he says. If, that is, he knew
what love was.

'Love is a bond between two people,' he starts out confidently. 'It's an
attachment. Love is a thing which you feel towards a person which is
warm . . . What is love? It's difficult . . . perhaps there are so many forms
of love. You can love the person physically but domestically that person
might be hopeless. Some people could put up with the domestic side but
I expect a certain type of standard where everything is clean and things
are in order . . . Still if the other person wouldn't do it and I really loved
her I suppose I'd do it myself . . .'

What he wants is what everyone wants, he says, 'security'. 'One woman. Most men want to be dependent.'

Winston doesn't have close friends, only acquaintances, he prefers it that way. If he goes out in the evenings, he does the rounds and will always meet up with someone. He wouldn't call himself lonely but he likes somebody to come home to in the evening.

He can have a 'man-to-man' with a male but prefers to confide in a woman, 'they are more understanding'. Image, the impression he creates, is vital to Winston but he can lay that aside and speak the truth if he wants to. He could tell a woman he felt a failure, for instance; 'It would all depend on how I said it and how well I know the person.' On the whole, he trusts only his own counsel.

Winston says men today are far more open anyway about their feelings – irrespective of the women's movement – 'It's one of the potholes and downfalls, men are interested in themselves far more no matter what is happening to women.'

He would call himself a romantic but not an emotional man. Of course, he cried when his grandmother died but tears are only shed on occasions such as that. At seventeen, his feelings were bruised when a girl he went out with for nine months went off to read Economics at university and he never saw her again. It's not really a tale of our times because no woman has put her career before him since – or even made him suffer.

'I think I've hurt other people. I don't deny that. Like a lot of men, I've created a situation in which a man wouldn't have felt hurt but a woman does. It's being able to understand that.'

He tries to understand women's feelings but at the same time he knows he also tries to hide his own. 'It's inbred in us. We've all got to be John Wayne.' His son Greg isn't so stereotyped, he says. 'He can handle himself but he's not a loud child. I wouldn't say that he's polite but he's sensitive. I give him – not a lot – but a certain amount of affection. I think he's inherited some of my views on women. He helps in the house but only just. Like me as a child, he helps a bit, cleans the windows . . .'

If he felt Greg was becoming too much like a 'sissy', Winston says he would spend more time with him 'doing masculine things'. 'But he's OK. He likes sports, he's mechanically minded, he likes clothes, he's got a girlfriend.

'In the end,' Winston offers, 'a woman does look up to a man. A man can stand the strain. At the end of the day, the woman still looks for guidance and strength from a man, either mental or physical strength.' All of which does not mean that if he had a daughter, he would discourage her if she wanted to be an engineer. 'If she had the brains and she was happy, I'd say go ahead.' If she came home and announced she was a lesbian, however, Winston is less certain of his feelings. 'That would be a difficult thing really. I wouldn't like it. I'd try and stop it happening at an early age. I wouldn't throw her out, I don't know how I'd react. All that's only just happening, isn't it?'

At times, Winston says, he thinks his days as a black sheep were more pleasurable. Now, occasionally, when the pressure of work is intense, the bank is screaming, and the bills come in, he asks himself, What's it all for? You've only one life. But in the end, he says, you *have* to work for it. 'I wouldn't say I'm contented. No, not contented. Financially, no. Socially, no.

'I'd be contented if I had dough and I didn't have to think about it. That's when you know you're contented. After all, it's like being taken care of – that must be content, to have someone take care of you.' Possibly, only a woman could give him the answer. 'You've got beautiful eyes, you know,' Winston says.

Trevor Cherry *Bradford*

Valley Parade is the ground of Bradford City Football Club. As the team's fortunes have risen and fallen so has the name been adapted: Death Valley; Happy Valley. In 1911, the first year of the FA Cup Final, Bradford City won the Cup on home ground with a crowd of more than 39,000 – most of them workers in the wool mills.

Now the cobbled streets remain but the rest of the scenery has shifted somewhat. Many of the mills have closed, nearby is the Tawwakkulia Mosque; the Bangladesh People's Association operates in a terraced house and half a dozen Bengali sweetshops sell candy like saffron and bright orange jewels. What Bradford City needs to pull in the crowds is a good Pakistani lad with a gift for football, a manager once announced.

The player hasn't yet appeared, but on the wasteland in front of the club a dozen or so Asian boys kick a ball around, simulating all the excesses of pain and joy seen on *Match of the Day*.

A couple of years ago, the Fourth Division 'Bantams' were in danger. The club had built up debts of over £300,000, the gate had fallen to as low as 3,000. Fans lived off a few brief moments such as the time the team reached the quarter-finals of the FA Cup in 1976, only to be beaten by First Division Norwich City.

The club has now been retailored. The council has bought the ground, the board of directors has had an overhaul, a local appeal raised over £40,000, economies have been made. In December 1982, Trevor Cherry, then playing for Leeds United, was appointed player-manager.

The manager's office is about the size of a sitting-room in a palatial caravan. Two windows give a view of the pitch. A desk is covered in papers and has room for two telephones. A television faces the desk. In one corner is a cocktail cabinet made of Melamine. Stacked against it are boxes of Marathon and Twix, prizes for 'the lads' when they play five-a-side.

Trevor Cherry is in his thirty-fifth year – twenty-one of them have been spent playing football. He is in the Trevor Brooking mould; decent

51

short haircut, no shirt open to the navel, no gold jewellery, casual clothes of the sort Val Doonican wouldn't turn down.

In his twenties, Trevor Cherry was described as 'Andy Pandy with muscles', a man with an unassuming air who became ferociously aggressive on the field. In one year he managed eight bookings in eight months. 'Cherry only *looks* as if he packs as much grit as a Cordon Bleu egg custard,' wrote one sports reporter in an appropriately cautionary tone. Even now, he seems mild, pleasant, ageless. He sits drinking tea with his assistant player-manager, Terry Yorath.

One of the teenage apprentices knocks on the door. 'Do you want a sandwich from the shop, gaffer?' he asks. Terry Yorath remarks that footballers tend to sacrifice everything for the sport, including their wives, and only wake up when it's too late.

He says he thinks the game holds some very traditional male ideas. He knows players on only £100 a week who *still* won't allow their wives to work. At the same time, he offers, some of the girls believe that once they marry a professional football player, that's it. They think they're in the money – but the game doesn't provide riches for all; not in the Fourth Division, it doesn't.

In the first few months Trevor Cherry took over, also playing centre back, the Bantams lost fourteen games out of fifteen. Now he has just had a run of fourteen matches without defeat. For his efforts, he earns £25,000 a year plus a Rover car – a drop in salary from what he earned as a Leeds United player but he wanted to move into a managerial role.

Football seems a sport of contradictions. The player epitomises traditional 'maleness', often marrying young and behaving as a chauvinist at home; yet, as part of the team, he comes under the rule of the classic matriarch – the manager. He is told what to do and how to do it and those who rebel, such as George Best, usually end up as the vanquished rather than the victor; disciplined or banned altogether from the nursery.

It is also a sport which often expects a man to put his 'work' before his family and friends – the reward being, in part, enormous adulation, predominantly from men. The female world lacks an equivalent. On the field, the footballer is also – within rigid limits – allowed to display more feelings than some men demonstrate in a lifetime, but does that necessarily lead to greater intimacy in the relationships within the team? Are the cuddles and kisses more of a ritual, or are they a genuine form of communication? I wanted to see how one man fitted into this world.

In 1971, at the age of twenty-three, Trevor Cherry, also known as 'Pip' and 'Grasshopper', was captain of Huddersfield Town, a team only just in the First Division. 'My target,' he told reporters confidently, 'is an England place and I expect to get one.' Five years later, he got his place, of course, and went on to play for England twenty-seven times.

In 1972, he asked for a transfer from Huddersfield Town. The team had been relegated, he explained, and he had to be realistic. 'I can't see Second Division football doing my game any good and I'm at an age when I should be making progress, not going back . . . I'm sorry for the lads . . . I'm sorry for the club . . . but there comes a time when you must decide what is best for yourself and your family.'

Leeds paid £100,000 for him and he stayed with the club for ten years, becoming captain for two years and playing under half a dozen managers including Don Revie, Brian Clough and Jock Stein. At one stage he was hailed as a natural successor to Nobby Stiles and Alan Mullery: 'Trevor Cherry is the new England hitman . . .' He himself said he had always been a bit anonymous in the eyes of the public because he was surrounded by internationals.

The modesty persists today – ask why he is self-effacing in a profession of egos and he replies in two words: 'My dad.'

'My father loved football, he'd do anything for me to play and my mother had the steadying influence. My father was very critical. The times he told me I'd played well, "but why don't you . . ." He always had to have a follow-on. I think that was a tremendous help. He never told me I was a good player.'

Trevor Cherry was born and brought up in Huddersfield. His father was a fitter, then an estimator, with ICI. His mother worked as a private secretary. His father died in 1981, his mother a year later. Their deaths, he says, devastated him and his own family, his wife Sue and the three children, Ian (fourteen), Darren (eleven) and five-year-old Danielle.

'My mum and dad were just an average family. We didn't have many material things, we lived in a council house, we didn't fly off to Spain every year but we had the basics, I was very close to both my parents. It was a very happy time, a perfect childhood.

'The biggest disappointment of my life was that they didn't see me at Bradford. My dad would have considered that a success; going to be a manager from a player. My parents loved my children too. They were always at the house wanting to babysit when we were off doing things.

They were part of the family and they were taken so quickly, I don't think you ever get over it.

'My father was just coming up for early retirement, at sixty-two. He loved gardening, he loved fishing and golf, he loved sport. He had everything planned with my mother to really live his retirement and it never worked out.

'I think it's affected me a little bit. I've always been conservative, I believe in saving things, I've planned my future very carefully. I've never wanted to be a footballer who had a lot of money and ended up with nothing, but their deaths made me think more about living for today.

'My mother was the careful one. My dad wasn't really bothered about money. She ran everything. She ran the house, my dad would help out, to be fair, but he was a very basic man, if you like. He liked tea on the table when he came in from work but he'd help.

'If my dad could go footballing and do what he wanted to do, he liked a pint, that was his lot really. It suited him fine for my mother to sort everything out.

'In the evenings when I was a young boy, six and seven years old, he'd spend four nights a week with me playing football. We lived near a mill yard and we'd go up and he would literally spend hours with me just on our own. He always believed a good player was one who could head a ball and we'd do that night after night.

'I got to the stage when I wanted to be out with the boys when I was thirteen or fourteen. I can remember, for instance, saying, "Mum I want to go with the lads now, they go to the game on the bus . . ." My dad used to take three or four of us in the car. It was very hard. I wouldn't say we had an upset but it was hard for my dad to understand that I wanted to grow up a little bit. My mother understood but he'd always turn up to watch us play. I never wanted to stop him coming because he saw me progress. I played for the Huddersfield Representative team and the Huddersfield YMCA which my father played for before me.

'Looking back, I think my mother had a sensible attitude to football. My mother always wanted me to have a good education and my father wanted me to be a footballer.' He tells the story of when he was due to play for the under-eleven school team. He had been off school with a cold and the headmaster sent a note: 'I don't mind if he doesn't come to school but I certainly want him to play in the Final.'

Trevor Cherry laughs. 'My mum went absolutely spare. "I want you to get education." But later she always enjoyed watching me play.' He was offered a place as an apprentice with Huddersfield. His mother said she didn't want him to be an ex-footballer at nineteen with no future, so he became an apprentice electrician – joining the club later.

'I always wanted to be a footballer – it's every boy's dream and the dream of a lot of men too. But I always had in my mind that I wasn't good enough. I could always talk to my mother about feelings. My dad didn't understand things like that, I don't think I could have sat down and talked about sex with him, I could with my mother a lot more.

'My father was a super man, a very pleasant man, he would never say a bad word but he did enjoy the basic things in life. To be honest with you, I'm a different nature from my father. I'm perhaps a lot more forceful, I perhaps want a lot more than my father I dare say ever did. I think that comes from my mother. My dad was very easy-going and perhaps I'm not. But I learnt a lot of good things from him.'

Trevor Cherry says his mother pushed his sister on too. His sister, he believes, is more intelligent, she found school work easy. She had a series of secretarial jobs and is now happily married with a daughter, three dogs and a husband who has a heating business.

'Nowadays players laugh at you when you sit down and talk about sacrifices,' he offers. 'I think the sacrifices *have* to be enormous if you're ever going to be a good player. My father was the best one for discipline. He used to say to me, "If you don't go to bed before nine o'clock you shouldn't bother to play tomorrow because you've not had your rest." My father set the standards which I've always followed.'

It is an attitude of mind he applies as manager. 'A manager,' he says, 'can do anything to a player and I certainly do as a manager. I've got to decide what time a player comes in to train and what time he goes home, what he does and where he does it. I can make players' lives unbearable really, but that's the last thing I want.

'I would say I've got a perfect relationship with the team. They know exactly what I expect. I can have a good laugh, I'm one of the lads when I play and train but they know I've got certain standards and disciplines. They respect them, they know I'll tread on them like a ton of bricks if I had to because they've already seen me once this season with one of the boys so they know I'm capable of it.

'I can penalise wages for a fortnight but I've never thought fining is an ideal way. Or I can have the lads training seven days a week.'

He doesn't order his players not to drink, he leaves it to their judgment, the test being their performance on the day of the match. I say it's a kind of subordination not usually associated with men, more commonly expected from women, so why do they put up with it? 'That's the game,' he says simply.

Trevor Cherry rates George Best as one of the best players in football, and what he believes Best needed was somebody who would 'get a grip on him and say, "Look, I'm going to run your life for you because you're not capable at this early age . . ."' (George Best has explained that it was precisely the over-protectiveness of the system which made him rebel.)

It's easy when you're young and 'an ordinary lad' suddenly in the money and limelight to start drinking and becoming involved with the women who are always around. Trevor Cherry says he avoided the pitfalls because of his belief that how he behaved was linked so strongly to how he performed in a match. 'Too many people say, "I'm a good player." The only way you prove it is by going out on your next game and playing well.' He also married when he was 'coming up twenty-one' – a good policy for any serious-minded player, he suggests. 'I must be honest with you, to be a footballer it helps a lot.'

Sue is six months older than Trevor Cherry. They met at seventeen when she was a shorthand typist and he was an electrician's apprentice. 'I've been very fortunate. She didn't marry me for my money or whatever money I've got now. She's seen my career from the start and helped me through it. We married because it seemed the right thing to do at the time.'

Sue is more extrovert than he is, he says, she enjoys a drink and a social life: 'At the beginning she didn't accept things that I couldn't do or wouldn't do because I had to stay in form. She's got used to it now and we've moulded our lives around it. I mean we're no angels, we go out quite a bit but I think anyone who kids themselves they can lead a normal life and play football is a fool.

'Sue is my best woman friend. I can talk things over with her and she knows if I'm wanting something more from life, she understands. I think she understands me quite well.

'She knows my moods. She can tell better than anybody if I'm on an upper or a downer. I think she manipulates me. I think all women learn to do that. I think perhaps I do the same to her but not so much.'

I ask if he feels proud of his wife. 'Yes, I think she's adjusted very well.

I think it's nice to have a wife where you can be in any sort of company without having to have your arm round her and say, "Are you all right?" We've met a different level of people. We can socialise with anybody now.

'I think she would like to believe I'd walk away from football. I don't think she wanted me to come into management. She would have preferred a total break. What I said to her is, "If I don't make a success with a fair chance at Bradford, I won't keep going to clubs lower down. I either want to do better for myself or get out." As long as I think I'm achieving something and getting some satisfaction that's fine.

'I run all the financial side, Sue runs all the household. I'm not fussy about standards, I just like it to be clean. She buys things for the house, I just don't seem to have time for that. She looks after the children – with three that's a full-time job – I have the involvement but she's there every day to do it.'

I ask if the marriage has been smooth all the way through. 'No, I think we've changed. I was talking about it to my wife earlier. I think your wife resents you going away a lot when you're younger, just purely from the fact of being a wife. She didn't resent me travelling to places like America, Brazil, the Continent, all the places I've visited – she just resented me being away from home.'

Did he ever feel that in the time he *was* away, he missed out on family life? 'Yes, but I think the thing is from a purely footballing point of view, I wouldn't have missed going with England for anything.' You had to put football first? 'When you say that, I found I could spend more time with my children than most businessmen. I could drop them off at school before I went training and pick them up again at four o'clock instead of being a father who got home just in time to give them a goodnight kiss.

'I want to spend time with my children probably because my father did everything for me. If I wanted to go fishing my dad would take me.'

Now he says he is at the club from nine to five, five days a week, he plays on Saturdays and two or three evenings he goes scouting, attending matches. He keeps Sundays for the family. He offers an illustration of one of the penalties of football. On the birth of his first son, he took Sue into the hospital on Friday and went off to Cardiff to play on the following day for Huddersfield.

On Friday evening, Trevor's mother phoned to say Sue had had a

seven-pound boy. Half an hour later, she phoned again and spoke to
Trevor's manager. The baby had swallowed some mucus, he had been
christened and he was in danger. The manager took the decision not to
tell Trevor until after the match. 'He argued after that there was nothing
I could have done if I'd gone back home. But if your wife's there and my
son had died, Sue would have resented two people for the rest of her life.
Fortunately, he was fine when I got home.'

Had Sue asked him to stay with her during the birth and not go to
Cardiff? 'Oh no,' he replies. 'She wanted me there when Ian was poorly
but not before. She understood about the game.' What would he do if a
player asked for a fortnight off because his wife was having a baby?

'Two weeks off? Well he couldn't do that. There's no problem with it
being born. I'd accept that. I do everything for my players. I give them
days off if they want to take their wife to the doctor and things like that
. . . but a fortnight would be difficult.'

Trevor Cherry says he also missed his sister's wedding because of
football. He went to Germany for a match instead and the manager
'played hell' with him afterwards. 'I never told him it was my sister's
wedding and he said it was one of the things I should go to. Looking
back, he was right, but I was so involved in football, I felt missing a game
meant losing your place. Probably I lacked confidence in myself as a
person.'

In the seventies, Trevor Cherry was not included in the Leeds team to
play in a European Cup Final although others felt he had played well
enough to merit inclusion. He discovered he had been dropped when the
manager read out the names of the team.

'Privately I was very bitter because it was the biggest game of my life.
I probably coped with it well because I spoke with Sue about it. It was
probably the worst week of our lives, it was also the week Sue's mother
died of cancer.

'Sue didn't really need a football problem when she had a week of
problems far bigger than football will ever be. The other players felt for
me. Players always feel it's unjust if you're dropped. Even if you're playing
badly, you never accept it. I now get on very well with the manager then,
Jimmy Armfield, time heals, but the way he left me out was a terrible
way of doing things.

'I didn't feel depressed. I think that's a sign of weakness. I think you've
got to think your way round things. I don't get depressed as a person. I

probably have a lot of inner feelings which I don't talk to anybody about. I don't believe in having weaknesses. I'm not a male chauvinist or anything, I just think I can cope with anything so long as people leave me alone and give me time.

'I don't think I'm a worrier,' he offers. 'Sue would probably say differently. She can always tell if I've got things on my mind because I go quiet. I think she'd like me to discuss things a lot more with her on the football side.

'When I get the sack, I expect it, if great managers get the sack there's no reason why I shouldn't, I've already worked out that I won't mind, if I've had a fair chance.'

I ask if he feels any guilt that he has put football first on some occasions. 'I don't feel guilty about things I've done,' he says, 'because I do try and do everything right. I feel perhaps a little guilty towards Sue. I could have done a lot more with my social life, I could have lived a lot more. We're starting to do that now. But then I wonder, would I have kept the standards I've now got?'

Sue Cherry attends aerobic classes and has a life of her own, her husband says. He thinks she feels 'pretty fulfilled'. Would he mind if she now decided she wanted to go back to work? 'No, I wouldn't mind at all. If she thought she could do it. I know if it was a business, she wouldn't blow a lot of money and keep on blowing it. She knows how I feel about money.

'I think it's my job to be the breadwinner. It's probably an old-fashioned view but I know if things went wrong, Sue would be willing to go back to work again. But she doesn't feel she wants a job at the moment. Danielle is now at school and Sue's enjoying her spare time.'

He is, he says, a careful man with money. He carries only one credit card, which he's used three times. He has a Yorkshireman's way of paying cash for everything he has, he points out with a smile. 'I've made a lot of money in football and I've used it wisely. I could say to you now I could probably retire from football but I'm not one to sit at home all day. At this stage, I want more from life.' Like his father, Trevor Cherry loves cars. His ambition is to own a Mercedes, but only when he is financially secure enough to ensure that he can continue to run it in perpetuity. 'If I was sacked today, I'd still have all the things I've got now. I'm probably too security-minded but I think football guides you that way. I've seen too many players end up with nothing. Even a good player can get carried away with the life. I think we're fortunate to be paid for playing a game when ninety-five per cent of people would pay themselves to play.'

At Huddersfield and Leeds, he says, the atmosphere was competitive but he never came across jealousy, nor did he make any permanent friendships except for 'one or two'. However demonstrative on the field, off the field, 'it's ships in the night, you're acquaintances, you're on good relations but you don't keep in touch outside of football.'

He doesn't have a male best friend as such but he and Sue and three other couples meet regularly – the men are outside the game, one is a dentist, another one owns a steel business, a third has an electrical company. 'The wives get on very very well. We're all very close. I've told them, "The day I get the boot I expect you to come out the same night for a meal." I know they'd be there without thinking.'

In conversation, Trevor Cherry seems relaxed, so where does he draw his aggression from on the pitch? 'I've been brought up on that,' he replies. 'That's my nature of play. Probably wanting to do too well, especially in my first season at Leeds. I was playing in a different position, I found it difficult.

'I mean I've never been an angel as far as kicking. I can honestly say I've never injured a player seriously, it would be the last thing I wanted to do. But I've always been strong in a tackle. I've always been taught from an early age to look after myself.'

Does he, I ask, think there are qualities men have that women lack which enable them to play better football? And I remind him that Sweden now has a women's football league.

'Yes, I've got to be honest,' he says. 'I'm all for it. If you can produce a women's team good enough to play against us, fine. But I think physically it's going to be difficult to produce a woman who looks like a woman but who can perform.

'It needs aggression. I think there are exceptions among women that you can throw at me who *are* aggressive and keep their femininity but not on the whole.'

Violence in football, he says, is part of a wider problem 'a terrible social problem with discipline', part of the same spectrum which includes the rape of women. He thinks that attributing the blame to the demise of the family since women began to work in large numbers is 'rubbish'.

'A lot of people might say, "How can you say women getting raped has anything to do with football?" But I think you can associate it.' It's all about violence. Rape needs a stronger penalty as a deterrent. 'Now, to me, people should get killed for it . . . people get two years. I sympathise totally with women, I think they get an absolutely diabolical deal.' He thinks a stronger deterrent should also be used to deal with football violence – two years' imprisonment or an on-the-spot fine.

Only twice in his life can Trevor Cherry recall crying, once when his father died, and once in his first season with Leeds when he played in the Cup Final and his team lost. 'In my early days, I wouldn't go out if we lost, I'd stay in and watch *Match of the Day*. Football was everything to me in my younger days. Sue used to get very frustrated. Now, no matter the score, I can play with the kids or go out with friends if that's been arranged. My private life is now totally separate from football.'

What does he think are his faults? 'I have plenty of them. I probably want things done too quickly. I expect everybody to do things as I do them and make decisions quick, nice and clean. I don't like dilly-dalliers. I want a lot of things out of life to come too quickly to me. I don't relax and just let them come.'

He is now within two pounds of the weight he was when he signed on for Leeds United twelve years ago. He always tells people he doesn't have a weight problem but he says he is actually careful about what he eats, he still trains hard. What price has he had to pay for so much self-control? Does he think he is demonstrative enough at home? Does he cuddle his wife, for example?

'No,' he says honestly, 'that's probably one of my failings. I'm not a warm person, no. I don't have a lot of sympathy for illness and things like that. I don't want my sons to be like that. I don't think it's a good thing. I don't know why I'm like I am really. I don't think you set out to be, I'm not a hard man or anything like that. And I'm close to my family but I just can't do fiddly little things if you like. I like things plain and clear and straightforward.'

He has ambitions for his children but not in football, 'unless they were really good because it's always difficult to follow your father'. He looks at his boys now and he is both envious and pleased. He had a bike and a football at their age, they have computers, colour tellies, 'everything, or to me they seem to have everything'.

He tells his sons to treat girls as they would treat their sister. He has the same standards for Danielle, 'although obviously', he adds smiling, 'with fathers and daughters, it's different. I suppose you think at the time,

Well I don't want her to go out with a boy because . . . But that is part of a girl becoming a woman. All we can do as parents is set the guidelines.

'I'm probably soft with Danielle because she's a girl. My wife wanted a third. I can't understand people who say, "I want a girl instead of a boy" or the other way round. It's nice to have both.

'Danielle plays with footballs and the boys will play with her toys to play with her. I don't want to make her a tomboy and I certainly don't want to make her into a doll-like thing. But there's no way with our family life, everyone mixes in.'

Danielle is free to be what she wants to be in life, he says. His mother always worked, she had a good education and he doesn't believe that women's only role is as a homemaker – how much men should contribute in help when the woman is both worker and mother and wife he is slightly less clear about. 'Well, I think the man should give a hand if he can . . .' He smiles, perhaps at his own evasiveness.

Does he have a different relationship with the boys and Danielle, I ask? 'Yes because they're older now,' he answers. 'She's a lovely little girl and I like reading bedtime stories but my relationship with my boys is that I just take them with me. I take them out for meals, we treat them as grownups really. I take them to football matches, I try and let them do the things I do.

'There are times,' he adds, 'when you think, crikey, I've been unfair to the kids. I've been out every night this week at football matches, dinners, I've not seen them. So I'll probably take them out for Sunday lunch, "Let's even it up a little bit" . . . You find you commit yourself to things and they seem to pile up into a really busy week and time goes by.'

The only point which he holds to rigidly with the children, he says, is a ban on smoking. It has caused arguments with Sue, who says it's impossible to stop them if they decide to smoke. 'I'd stop everything they had if I thought they were smoking. I don't hit them. I hate hitting my children. I think they have enough discipline in the tone of my voice but I wouldn't give my children a penny if I thought they'd go out and smoke.'

He is not content with his life now, he says, because it is not in his nature to be content, but he has a good home life and he hopes he has a fair chance at Bradford. If it fails, he may open a garage, do something outside football altogether. He can respond to constructive criticism well, he offers, but he has never loved the publicity attached to the game.

I ask if he is vain. 'No,' he replies instantly, 'I'm not. It embarrasses me if I'm recognised. I like it on the pitch but not away from the game.

'I think I've been a good steady player but I was never what you'd call outstanding. I've played in good teams but I've never been over-confident. I look at other players and I think, I wish I could do that. That's probably why I've got as far as I've got. I've never been as confident about my ability as other people.'

As a footballer, he is now living on borrowed time, he points out. 'If you're playing well, they say, "He's doing all right for his age." When you have a bad game, they say, "He's slowing down, he's over the top."' He smiles wrily. 'I'll need a little bit of help from others to tell me when it's time to stop. I might know in my own mind but I'm not sure; the enthusiasm for the game carries you away. But I've got my friends who still come to the game and at some time they might say, "Listen, you're perhaps getting to the time when you should think about calling it a day." And I'll probably listen.'

Bill Cobbs   *West London*

'Well, Mr Henry sir, you're in for £20.29 – what do you want, cash, Barclays, Yankee Express? Barclaycard, very wise, squire. Have you got a Gold One? No, well that'll do nicely sir. And a couple of quid for Eddie, thank you sir. God bless you and may your God go with you and be careful. Thanks very much, bruv, cheers.'

The customer leaves. The phone rings and Bill Cobbs picks it up.

'Westgate Tyres, good evening sir, what can I do you for? No sir, we don't do Semperit tyres. Semperit is mostly made by Pirelli, a lot made in Northern Ireland. A good tyre; a very good tyre, squire. Where do you live? Hendon, what near that bloody police college? You're near Shepherd's Bush, have a look in the Yellow Pages, you want White City Tyres. Cheers mate. God bless you.'

He puts down the phone and grins. 'You never know, it might be one of the governors seeing if I'm helpful to the customers.'

In June 1977, Bill Cobbs put on his Chester Barry suit, white shirt, red spotted tie and slip-on shoes, climbed into his lorry and met the governor of the soon-to-be-opened Westgate Tyres. The governor was parked outside the premises in his Jag. He took all Bill's particulars but he *never asked* for a birth date. Bill knew he was all right then, he knew he'd got the job. No birthdate, no checking with police records, no evidence of any form.

A couple of days later Bill Cobbs was handed the keys, £100 for petty cash and became the manager and sole employee of Westgate Tyres on £2,500 a year plus commission. Now he has young Eddie, sixteen, to help, £15,000 worth of tyres in stock and a nice little business on the side. Bill has always fiddled. He and Eddie can change a tyre in minutes. Eddie stays silent, Bill provides the chat. And decides the price.

Take a tyre for a Jaguar XJ6. The recommended retail price is £84.75. The wholesale price is thirty-seven and a half quid. Bill says if you arrive dressed smart in a A-registration Jag, he smells money. £84.75 times four to you, mate. If it is a friend or someone with whom he has been fucking about, you'll get them at cost. Stands to reason, don't it?

Bill loves his job. He does it well. At the back of the warehouse where the tyres are stacked is his small office. Friends gather in there for a coffee and a chat. Or rather, a listen. Bill does the talking. He is around five foot eight, dressed in orange overalls. Underneath are the remains of his Mod past; a buttondown shirt, smart jumper, Levis. He bears a smudgy resemblance to Steve McQueen but he doesn't rate his own looks much.

The office is the size of a coffin and almost as sparsely furnished. It has a desk, one chair, an electric kettle, piles of reference books for tyre prices, a pay telephone, a few photos of boxers pinned to the wall – Dave Boy Green, Frank Bruno – and the obligatory calendar for some piece of mechanical equipment which, in the month of January, is being advertised with the help of a large pair of breasts. Occasionally, the office will store a case of scotch or a pile of meat or some other little bit of business Bill has conducted. He's always been a thief, he says.

Often, if times are slack, Bill will stand in the well of the warehouse and survey the High Street. He waves to the girls in the bakery opposite, sends Eddie over to the Asian supermarket for a jar of coffee ('the pale stuff, none of that dark muck') and passes comment. 'To fuck her would be nice,' he says, 'to make love even better.' And 'Hasn't she got an 'andsome pair of tits. All right, darlin?' And 'What's a nice bird like you doin' in a banger like this? Now what can I do for you, darlin? Hasn't she got a lovely pair of legs, Eddie?'

Sexism in Bill's book is one more way of showing a lady, girl, bird, tart, she's appreciated for what she's got.

Bill earns £125 a week and makes at least another £80 a week tax-free. He works hard for it, he deserves more just for the patter. He could persuade the owner of a shire horse to invest in a set of Firestones. 'The chat?' he says. 'That's just to gain their fucking confidence. They say, "Oh I remember that bloke, we'll go back for the fucking tyres." It's all front, it's a show, this is a fucking stage. You're here to perform, make them feel welcome, a bit special, make 'em laugh, remember their names, don't take the piss too much. No one likes the piss taken out of them. All that old balls about "God bless you and your God go with you," I nicked that from Dave Allen.'

Bill on thieving

Bill has had six jobs since he left school at fourteen. His first job was as a BR guard. He got the sack after a week because they found out his age.

Next he worked in the warehouse of an upmarket grocery, wines and spirits company. He listened to the drivers who brought in deliveries, sized one up and bang, wham, they were in business. At one point, Bill was nicking up to £100 a week. Then, he says, he got greedy. He nicked a pallet of Martini Red, twenty-four boxes with a dozen bottles in each.

A big policeman came down and called Bill 'Billie', then he shook him so hard, Bill cried. Bill not only confessed, he grassed on three others. When he appeared in court, Bill's dad was choked, his mum said, 'Well, what's done is done.' Bill was sent to a remand hostel, at sixteen, his first time away from home. He cried at night for his mum. He went back to court and had to pay a compensation order of £800 at the rate of thirty shillings a week. 'It took nine years to get that money out of me.'

After, Bill did a bit of labouring, he fiddled a Heavy Goods Vehicle licence and became a driver, he worked on the Thames Barrier and he became a sign erector on the M1. Whoever hired him must have had a dry sense of humour – or just enjoyed a risk.

'They didn't think fucking much of me and my jokes. London Airport that way. St Albans the other, know what I mean? Anyway I had enough of that. It was so cold as the snot was coming from your nose, it was turning into fucking ice. I thought fuck that.'

Eventually he ended up in a sack factory. He stayed six years and got done for receiving several thousand hessian sacks. He'd actually pinched them in the first place but he got done for receiving and was given a six-month jail sentence. Then he got nicked for nicking in jail. When you were eating Christmas turkey, he was eating bread and water.

Bill was working in the prison kitchen helping the chefs. He saw one prisoner come out with a ham sandwich. 'Where did you get that?' 'In the fridge.' Bill walked out of the kitchen with one slice of ham and a screw called Mr Williams was there. 'A great guy, Welsh guy. "What are you eating, boy?" he goes. "Ham sir." He grabs hold of me by the scruff of the neck, smashes me against the fucking fridge, knee in the bollocks. He goes: "I've got seven hundred fucking blokes in here. You're stealing food from their mouths. You are fucking nicked."'

Bill got ten days' solitary confinement and three days bread and water. He hates prison with a rage. He hates it almost as much as he hates dirt or uncleanliness of any kind. 'You don't know, you don't know, you're shit in there. You tip out the piss pot and smell the urine and shit of seven hundred fucking geezers . . .

'Some people don't realise these things, they break your arms, break your legs, get someone to fuck you. It happens. I had a screw come round who'd taken a fancy to me one night. He gave me a fag and he sat down on me bunk. I took a puff then gave it back to him. I'd twigged. "What's the matter," he says, "don't you want to be friendly?" So I says, "No, no," like that. I felt fucking frightened. What if someone else had come with him and held me down?'

If you tell Bill that's the kind of fear some women have about men, he answers with a long silence.

Nicking, he reckons, must just be his nature. Until three years ago, he was the only one in the family. Now his dad's a bit bent too. Mind, Bill's reformed. In his own way, of course. 'I haven't got the bottle for it now. Once you've had a taste of prison life, you don't want to know. If you're going to be bent, it's got to be in a very, very, soft way. If you get nicked it's only a fine or probation. See what I do here now, I could get sacked for – flogging second-hand tyres. It's not that it's illegal, it's just against company policy. That's me; just softly bent,' he grins. The thing about Bill is that you trust him even as you doubt.

Bill on his best friend; that was . . .

Bill and Frank Armstrong went around together for seven years. 'We were together so much people thought we were poofs. He was a soppy bastard, soppy, but he had a lovely personality plus he had the driving licence. I was on a ban so we always used his car. He had no mother, she died when he was very young and he had a very old dad so my mum took pity on him. He used to eat round our house a tremendous amount.

'We'd go out in the car, cruise along the road, usual stuff, take turns to chat up the birds. "Go on, it's your turn," "Where are you going sweetheart?" All that old bollocks. We'd be in the pub, put on the Searchers, the Hollies, the Beach Boys, play the machine, have a light and bitter. Get drunk together.'

Then Bill met a girl. 'Instead of me outrightly saying, "Look I can't go out with you, I'm going out with her tonight," I done a dirty. I was supposed to meet him in Lewisham and I didn't turn up. He got the whistle and I never see him again for a year. I didn't tell him because I didn't want to hurt his feelings. I think he understood. Sometimes you've got to be wicked to be kind.'

Bill on his children

'I'm close to my kids, they're my life. They both know how to wind me round their little finger. I bollock them – "Oi, shut up, I'm watching that. Be a good girl." But ten minutes later, I'll grab hold of Lucy, I love to get hold of her bum because it's such a tiny bum . . . she's so little with big blue eyes . . .

'My kids are diamonds in the sky. I knock two penn'orth of fuck out of Darren – not Lucy. I don't hit him but I hurt him. I grab hold of him, you can tell by the way I'm holding him that I'm hurting him . . .

'I gave him a load of old records to play and I leave a box of new records down there and it's my own fault, he's only a kid and he plays them. "What have I told you, leave them alone." And he bares his teeth at me, "Grrr," he goes. Him frightened of me – is he fuck!

'What do I reckon Lucy will be? I reckon she'll be Prince Edward's fucking wife. She'll be what she wants to be, the wife will encourage her, she's into all that. But I expect she'll marry, settle down. I don't want her messing around like my slag of a sister. No one fucking respects that.

'Lucy and the boy sit in the bath with me. I stand up washing my legs under my crutch and all that and she'll go "Ain't you got a big winkle, dad?" So I goes, "Leave it alone, you mustn't do that, that's naughty." And she goes, "Mine's big, en it dad?" She doesn't like to be left out. She's got a mind of her own.

'The kids are special but not all day every day, I need a break of it's "Dad this" and "Dad that."'

Bill on Princess Anne

'You don't know what I'd fucking do to her, do you? I'd made her fucking ache. I'd fuck her so hard all night it would hurt. To me she is an 'orrible woman. You can't physically go up and hit her but you could drink her up at a party, get her to bed and do things that Mark and no one else has ever fucking done to her. I detest her.'

I ask Bill if that would give him pleasure. 'Oh yes.' Would he use sex as a weapon against any other woman? Has he ever done so?

'No, I'm a pussycat really.'

Bill on his dad

Bill's dad used to work in a rubber factory, packing Marigold gloves, French letters, scrap to be shipped abroad. He had four children, two boys, two girls, the eldest being Bill. He favoured the girls, according to Bill. His dad is six feet tall: 'He's a gambler, a womaniser, a miserable bastard when his horse runs out. Fucking flash? There's nothing like my dad; green illuminated socks, black patent shoes, red shirt. He's a hard-looking bastard. He's got ginger hair, green eyes, a broken nose like mine. He's sixty my dad, still very upright but all his fucking teeth are missing. He won't have false teeth. He loves to talk about sex.

'He always took an interest in my older sister, he's got no time for blokes. He'd rather be in the company of women. Sexually, I like to be in the company of women, other than that, I don't want to know them as such. Don't get me wrong . . .

'I prefer men because I'd rather brag like we do and talk about lorries, talk about money, music . . . My mum was a rotten housekeeper. My dad would hand over so much a week, she was in charge of the bills, but she always ran out.

'She worked nights, cleaning in a hospital eight till eight. She worked fucking hard, my old mum. That's what used to fucking grieve me. She'd say to my dad, "Got any money dad, so I can get to work?" He'd say, "I've got no fucking money," and I'd think, what a cunt.'

At thirteen, Bill took up boxing. In his first fight, the other kids had boxing boots, silver shorts, green velvet tops. He had a pair of white PE shorts, a white vest, plimsolls and 'a pair of fourteen-inch fucking gloves they supply for wankers. I lost before I fucking got in the ring.

'I got home that night and I figured, I won't let anyone know I've fucking lost, I wasn't marked . . . So I goes, "I've been boxing, dad." He's watching fucking Ward Bond, *Wagon Train*, the old cunt. "Oh yeah." "Don't you want to know how I got on?" "How did you get on?" I says, "I lost." "You're no fucking good then, are you?" I thought, you cunt. That was it.

'That was the only fight I fucking lost. He never, never took any interest. He would never fucking come and watch. Never, never, never, never, never . . . I couldn't give a fuck, I'd say, *not a fuck*. But it used to hurt me.

'I run a disco. My dad came to see me for the first time a couple of months back. I think he was quite impressed. I think he was fucking proud.'

Bill on his mum

Bill's mum is tiny and swears more than Bill. She worked nights. When she got in from work in the morning, she'd sleep until five p.m. and go to work again three hours later. 'My mum's mouth is fucking rotten. Many years ago, she'd hang over the balcony of the flats and go, "Billie." I'd hide. "I can fucking see you down there." Everyone would look round. "Get up them fucking stairs, you Hungarian bastard." That's a mother for you.

'On a Saturday, I'm going shopping with her and she'll go up to the man with the fucking fruit and veg and she'll say, "Give us two pounds of tomatoes. I want them as hard as the man I sleep with . . ."

'I'll tell you what my mum's like. She's like Hilda Ogden but she's lovable. She goes round like a tramp but the house is fucking spotless. She used to give me a good hiding with her fucking fists until I learnt to stick up for myself. I told her to fuck off and leave me alone.

'My mum and dad fought something rotten. She used to say, "Your old man was the first and he'll be the fucking last. I'll tell you all about him one day, son. The old bastard."'

She's had four children, Bill says, so she's had to be four different kinds of mother; one for each child. 'She'd talk to me, like mum's stuff. I used to go into the bedroom on the way to school and ask her for money for cigarettes. She'd say she hadn't got any, "Take a couple of fags from my bag instead."

'If I asked for money to go to the pictures with the other kids, they'd get eleven and six, fifteen and six, I'd get half a crown; a fucking dollar. I felt really sick.'

Bill did more of the chores than his sisters, he says. One sister, Mary, learnt that if you did it badly enough, you didn't get asked again. At ten or eleven, Bill's job was to collect the family allowance, go down Westbourne Grove buy mince, carrots, fags for his mum, come back, get the dinner ready.

'I'd think, right, mum's in bed so you can't do that bedroom, so I do out me and my sister's bedroom – there was only two of us then. Make the bed and do all the bedroom, living room. In them days we didn't have a Hoover, we had a carpet sweeper. What we had was lino and you had like a 74-square carpet. Your job was to wash and polish all the way round, with the hard old Gumption shine, all the skirtings, fucking lovely . . .

'If I didn't do it, mum'd say I was a lazy dirty bastard. She wouldn't hit me but – don't get me wrong, who wants to live in shit and dirt? I don't. I could never do washing and she never asked me to do washing. I couldn't do ironing but I could fucking clean. I can clean windows, clean floors, clean taps, clean an oven.

'My mates didn't take the mickey, they didn't mind what I used to do. We had different parents, their parents would be out pissing it up Friday, Saturday, Sunday night. They'd be sitting outside a fucking pub – I wasn't, I was indoors with me mum and dad with a load of sweets or a cheese and onion sandwich, something like that.

Bill on his sister, Mary
Bill has two sisters. He says he idolises his younger sister, Kathy. She is twenty-three and, while she isn't virginal, 'I know for a fact not one bloke could get her into bed . . . she's cute, she watches the drink, she says all the right things and takes no notice of this Come on darling, I won't do nothing to you business . . .'

Mary is thirty-one and Bill says she is a slag. His definition of a slag is a woman who 'takes anything that comes into the room so long as it can make its cock big and it can come. Then she can fuck it.' Mary is separated with two children and is a part-time barmaid. Mary's score on men, by Bill's own admission, couldn't match his score on women – but Bill says women should follow a different code. He can't say why, only that a 'girl is different'. She should be 'respectable'.

'How would you like to sit at the table and find out that your sister's pregnant, and you go to her, "Who fucking made you pregnant? What's his fucking name?" "I don't know," she says, "about four hundred geezers get up the Arts Club." And I've looked at her, I've looked at my dad, I goes, "You are a shit cunt," this is at a Sunday dinner table. So my old man's picked up the fucking carving knife, not to stick in me, he's pointed it at me. He says, "Never, never talk like that at my fucking dinner table and never call that to your sister." I said, "It's a slut, it's a shitter,"I says, "four hundred fucking blokes and she don't know what one fucked her."

Bill on other women
Bill says: 'I'm to the stage in my life now, if someone walked through that fucking door, providing that I can fucking see there's no fucking scabs under her legs and she ain't got a growth in her fucking teeth – if

she's randy enough, I'll fuck her. If I can smell or see any fucking dirt there – herpes, I wouldn't even let her give me a fucking blowjob.'

In practice, he seems a shade choosier. He often gets propositioned; he says women offer sex instead of a credit card for their bill. One woman he fancied wanted a discount of £25. 'I decided no, not even for Ursula Andress.' Then there was the woman in her fifties from the Family Planning Clinic.

'She had big tits and very skinny legs but she attracted me. She said she worked for the Family Planning and I thought, fucking hell. It turned me on, I suppose, because she knew all about pricks and cunts and bollocks, didn't she?

'She came in here in a big, dirty great big American Cadillac, her son's. Now she says she hasn't had sex for fourteen years so I thought, this must be . . . , you know, wanting some stick. So anyway, after we finished doing the car, she left a couple of quid, I said to her, "If ever you're passing, Mrs Brown, do come in and have a cup of coffee."

'I couldn't fucking get rid of her – coming up here day after fucking day, fetching glass cups, coffee cups and coffee. She's sitting there and I go for her – on my life – I goes, "Mrs Brown," I goes, "I'd love to knob you." So she goes, "Knob me?" I goes, "Fuck you." "Ain't I too old?" she goes. I said, "How old are you?" She goes, "Fifty-two." I says, "No. I'd make love to you." She went all quiet, she went away, a few days later she comes in. Now she's sitting on me fucking lap and I was getting bad, I was getting right horned up. We made a meet one night and I backed out. She come down and bollocked me the following day . . .

'I backed out because I tried to picture her with her clothes off and . . . I like to imagine things I do and I'd taken all her clothes off and it looked like a fucking map of Ireland and I went, "Oh no, I couldn't, I couldn't."'

Bill says he was innocent until the age of thirteen when he had intercourse with a girl of eighteen, 'a simple bird who spoke with an impediment.

'I'm telling you now, honest to your face, that I was fucking green. I had no sex talks at school. I knew the words fuck and cunt and all that in a joke but I didn't know that you had to put that inside a woman, to do that to have a baby. I didn't fucking know that. I found it out one night, the hard way, when I got the horn and I come over all fucking wet and there was some old slag who showed me what to fucking do. I'm telling you straight, that was a dirty old cunt that was, she stunk, she was dirty. It felt very funny – it hurt me . . . I was quite excited. I went and told all me mates. I said, "I've had a bunk-up." They said, "Who did you fuck?" I said, "Susan James." They went, "Oh, fuck me. You'll get the pox." That was it.'

Bill can't understand his friends' taste in pornography. At least not that which involves lesbians, 'lezzies'. Any form of homosexuality he dislikes intensely. He knows some women like pornography from personal experience, he says.

'I've had a woman grab hold of me, watching a fucking blue film. I have, straight. All sitting there on the fucking settee and a hand's come over and started going over the top of my fucking cock. I already had the horn and she fucking knew it – then BANG everyone was fucking.

'Now my wife'll look at a blue film, she don't mind watching them just touch sexually at the top but when she starts seeing that wet cock going in and out of that cunt. Then she sees that cock-sucking, which she cannot stand, it makes her feel sick. Then she sees all that come come over, she goes, 'That is rotten.''

Bill also says he dislikes posers, like Clarke, the man from over the road, who comes in bragging.

'He's been fucking a tart – when I say a tart, don't get me wrong. Names are never mentioned. I could go out with you for a drink tonight, take you into a place and I bet you out of ten fucking birds in there, I've fucked eight of them. But I wouldn't tell you. Ones who are right dirty cunts, ten to one I wouldn't even fucking tell you, I'm so fucking ashamed. But Clarkey's been fucking a tart over there in the café. Now you imagine a person who's been cooking fucking food all day, its hands are greasy, she's been going to the toilet, she been having a piss . . . You've got all that smell from that food, all that smell from her hands, pulling her drawers down, sitting down there. She's going like this, she's wiping her fucking self. Then you get Clarkey going in there at five o'clock at fucking night, take her out the back and . . . You know lovemaking is lovemaking but he says, "Come on, give us a blow job." She gets down and gives him a blow job. So she says to him, "Now, you give me a fucking blow job." So, she's not even washed her fucking self, dirty cunt. He's down there, he's giving her a blow job out. And he's telling me, he goes, "You want to fuck that. That will go through the fucking book." I'm going, "Oh yeah." I'd rather sit there and wank meself. Don't get me wrong.

That will fuck anything. Look at his missus. Oh that is revolting, that is a fucking dog, that is a dog. She'll sit there, she'll sit there and she'll go up to you and she'll go, "I fancy you, Bill." Now I know she's winding me up so I go to her, "Yeah. What about your old man, though?" "Oh fuck him, he won't know." "But I know your old man. Not only that, you're winding me up you bastard," I goes, "your sex life with Alan's good?" "Yeah, you want to see his cock, Bill." So I goes, "What do you mean?" She goes, "Like that." I said, "Fuck off. Fucking break your back with that." "Anything, me." "What do you mean, anything?" "Fucking bananas, anything." I says, "Does he stick a banana up you?" She said, "Oh yeah." The Clarkes are like that, they're them kind of people; posers.

'He brought some photographs in here and he's standing there and he's got his cock out and they took a Polaroid picture of him. And there he is with his cock out. I said, "Look at all them people behind you." He says, "Fuck 'em." And he did have some hampton there, you know what I mean? So then he gives you a picture of this fucking old shit cunt he's living with, she's about thirty-five, forty and right horrible – she's sitting there, she's got no bra on and she's pushing her stomach in and there's these little tits. He says, "What do you think of the girl then, Bill?" And I'm looking and – you know, what can you fucking say? I'll be honest with you, if that was my wife. I swear I'd do something chronic. But my wife is too quality for that.'

Bill on his wife Jill
Bill met his wife when he was seventeen and she was fifteen. They married five years later. Bill says he doesn't love Jill but he has chosen her to be the woman of his life. Until the children came along, Jill was a legal secretary. The children are Lucy, two and a half, and Darren, five. Bill sleeps three nights a week at his younger sister's house because the journey from his own home to work takes ninety minutes. Bill says he will screw women in the office but rarely in the evenings. 'I've got steak at home; mincemeat here.' He'd be 'as sick as a dog' if his wife behaved in the same way. He'd give her a going-over.

'I can honestly say my wedding day was the best day of my life. I felt very proud when I turned around and see her walking down the aisle all in white. Not one bit of black on her that day.'

Bill first met Jill walking down the street. She agreed to meet him and his friend later with her friend. Bill and his mate turned up at the right time. The girls took fright and fled at their method of transport; a black hearse with 'Bonnie and Clyde Incorporated' painted on the side. On the second attempt, the boys took the girls to an Italian restaurant in Croydon. Bill ate his meal with his coat on; he was afraid to take it off in case he revealed the lining laced together with safety pins.

'I remember the first time I met her,' he says, growing almost misty-eyed at the memory.

'She had a lovely petticoat on. She come walking along and she had what you called champagne tights on, them light coloured tights, a little pair of high-heel shoes, a little coat what the Queen wears, even today, that kind of style, and a little scarf around her neck tucked into her coat and a little black bag. I said to my mate, "Look at that, I'll chat that."

'. . . I'd been with young girls who don't swear, don't smoke and they speak pretty nice, they was all right but there hadn't been a bird that I said to myself, "I'd like to spend the rest of my life with her." Then after seeing this bird for a couple of times, I thought, fuck me, she ain't bad she ain't, she's sensible. And she was sensible. Her clothes were sensible, her speech was sensible, she was well educated in that she used it. Cor, fuck me, she was well educated in that sense . . .

'But if you saw my wife, you'd say, "How you fucking married her, I don't know." She is *ugly*.

'We're completely different. Our speech is different, she don't swear, she don't smoke, she don't drink. Her speech – she speaks proper. She speaks proper English. Come on, fuck me, she worked with solicitors for fucking years. She's the brain box.

'Her dad is a lorry driver, he's a thief, he's a fiddler though, he's one of us. Nice man, hard bastard, with his kids. I mean, hard bastard in the sense, don't you ever fucking hurt them or slag them off. He loves his kids. Me mother-in-law, she's a beautiful woman – fat old prat, but she ain't bad, she'd do anything for you.'

Bill says he was ready to settle down because he'd had enough of the single life.

'I'd been around. I had money, I'd been to prison, I had cars, I had clothes, I had women – I had women, I was only a boy – women, you know fourteen, fifteen, sixteen, eighteen-year-old girls, fucking finished with them. Going into the other fucking class now. The ones that want you to call mumsy and . . . I'd had enough.

'I'm not saying it to be flash – at least six years of my life was, you imagine the Beatles now, Paul McCartney, if he was to retire tomorrow – I was living that kind of life. Going out – doing what I wanted.

'Oh, I was tired. Do you know what you can go through with all that? You get fed up. It's the same routine. Pick the bird up, go in the pub, take her out for a drink – "Port and lemon?" – "Port and lemon" – all that old bollocks. "Want to come to the pictures? Come out for a ride. Want to go to Margate at the weekend?" – Bang, bang, bang – scored, don't fucking show up the next night. Right, where shall we go to pick up another fucking one? Do you know what I mean?'

Sex, Bill says, is dependent upon hygiene. 'If I have a shower or a bath every night, brush my teeth, I can have a bunk-up any night I want with my wife. If I don't do them fucking things, I don't get a bunk-up. I'm classed as a dirty smelly bastard – although she don't swear.

'I can honestly say if I have a hundred bunk-ups a year – which is only a figure – she might ask for two bunk-ups out of a hundred. She won't make the start.

'I won't fuck of a morning. Your body smells and you're not there. I don't think you are.

'I mean there's plenty of fucking nights when I get the fucking hump, when I can't have a bunk-up, she'll say, "No, I'm too fucking tired." I'll go, "But it's my fucking right to have a bunk-up." I get all fucking silly. I turn round to her and I say, "See you, you prat, tomorrow night I'm out, I'm gonna pay for a bunk-up, I am out. I'm gonna fuck and I'm staying out all fucking night, you can have the fucking lot of this." I get uptight, "I've lived to regret the fucking day I married you" and all that old bollocks. She says, "Go on then," then she shuts up, and that's what does me. Instead of giving me some of the mouth she shuts up. She just lays down, moving her bum – she does it more, you know, moves it fucking more, does it more – very wicked fucking people women are. She fucking knows it, she knows I'm all noise and chat.

'I've hit her in temper, yeah, and I'm telling you now, I am fucking ashamed of that, I am ashamed of it. And I've never hit her often.

'She knows the truth, at the age I am now, I'd rather wank, I'm telling you now. I'll have the fucking hump with my fucking missus, "I don't need your cunt." I'll come downstairs and I'll fucking wank sitting watching that telly. She's in bed. It don't bother me, and I've got friends who'd do the same as me. I don't understand these fucking people who do it. I don't understand those who rape or who do fucky forcing things to children. No no, not for a bunk-up. Oh, as a kid you meet a girl and you put your hand up. In them days it was called a bit of fucking finger wasn't it? I mean if you get a bit of finger or a bit of fucking tit and you didn't have a bunk-up, cor fuck me, to get that far you was there. But you would get the bird who would pull your hand down and you'd push away, you'd rip her fucking knickers. That's as far as it fucking went, if she said no, that was it, that was it. I can honestly say to you, if I can't get a bunk-up with this and this and this; that is it, I'd rather sit here and fucking wank.'

Home life holds limited attractions for Bill. One afternoon movie on the television and a bottle of Pimm's to drink then the novelty of being home on a Monday wears off.

'I had a week at home last week. It drove me fucking mad. There's nothing that would make me swap places. Them fucking kids!

'It's hard work at home. That is hard work. When you've got children – getting them up, getting them washed and dressed, getting yourself ready, get them off to school, get them off to nursery, come back and do a bit of housework and whatever else has got to be done. Go back up to the nursery – pick them up, fetch them back home, give them something to fucking eat, do something else – bit of ironing or a bit of fucking washing, back up the school at half past three to pick the boy up, back home. Do a dinner, miserable bollocks the old man comes in – give him his dinner, don't chat too hard in case you fucking upset him. After that, start washing up, sit down for five minutes – ironing board out again. That's six days a fucking week that job. I help on a Sunday – I cook the dinner or wash up or help her wash up and I'll do a bit of housework – only in the living room and the lounge, that's all I do, and the kitchen maybe. I never touch the fucking stairs and I never touch the bedrooms and I never touch the bathroom.

'We've talked about swapping jobs. She says she'd earn more money than me which she would do. But I'm fucking frightened of being at home. I've got my freedom here at work. I love my kids, they're my life. But Sunday's my day with them and even then I'm inclined to shout about a bit. But they're diamond.

'My wife tell me off. I'll call something, say, an 'ankie. And she'll say, "It's no such thing. It's a handkerchief." She'll pump Lucy full of stuff about a career and all that too.

'All our times are happy to be honest with you,' Bill adds. 'I row with her a lot now, I rowed with her last night when I fucking got in. She's got cystitis, you know what that is. She's in terrible fucking pain. As soon as I got in she says, "Can you just wait for your dinner while I run round to the doctor's?" When she came back, she grilled me a nice chop. I know it's better grilled but I've told her again and again not to. So I ballocked her, I said, "I want it done in the pissing oven." Later, I told her to go and have a salt bath.'

Bill says he believes kissing and cuddling is for bed, not for the daytime, and he says "I love you" a couple of times a year but Jill knows.

'I've got one woman in my life – my wife. Now unless I go home and catch her in bed with fucking half a dozen men, one fucking her up the arsehole and one fucking her up the cunt, nothing would turn me off of her. I picked her, and I'm not being old-fashioned, because I'm a bastard to her, and she's a bastard to me as well . . . My love for her is my love, that is her. I'd never leave her for another fucking woman. Now people have said to me, "Oh no, no, no, no, no, if you come across the woman you love you'll fucking leave her." I come across women that I knew before my wife who were fucking beautiful women – beautiful – beautiful dressers, good lookers, smell nice, teeth nice, good fuckers, but they're not my wife. She's different from the rest: a gem.'

Jack Dorset *Leeds*

The housing co-operative is in the Sheepscar area of Leeds. It is run-down, but some of the Asian families have introduced the colours of an artist's palette into the grey and grit; terraced houses and shops are painted lime green, yellow, bright blue.

The co-operative has taken over a line of houses; thirty adults and twenty-five children. Some live communally, others live in single or two-bedroom units; a few live as traditional nuclear families. At the rear of the houses are three large gardens, more like allotments, where vegetables and flowers grow, tended by Jack amongst others. The co-operative meets regularly to discuss issues, decide on applicants who want to join the scheme, talk out problems.

Jack lives in a four-bedroom house with Cathy and John – three separate individuals, but they eat together in the evening and take turns to cook. Each week for two or three days alternately, Jack's three-year-old son, Matthew stays with his father. Jack works four days a week as a science teacher in a local comprehensive.

He has only been in the job for a few months and he has a strong desire to leave. He has been a member of the alternative society; now he wants to work for change on the inside. He has twenty-five in a class and he prefers smaller groups; the policy of the school is more academic while he prefers the practical side of teaching. His ambition is to own and run an organic market garden. Jack is tall and slim and speaks quietly and hesitantly, constantly correcting and recorrecting himself. This may be because on several fronts recently his life has undergone great change; the beliefs he once felt certain about he is now questioning.

The sitting-room is large and comfortably shabby. The back windows give a panoramic view of open land; the city is only in the distance. In one corner of the room are a stack of Matthew's toys including a doll's house, xylophone and a cookery range. Decoration is provided in the form of potted plants, rugs, a treadle sewing-machine which doubles as a small table. Jack makes a pot of tea and Cathy comes down briefly from upstairs to claim a cup. Matthew's room has just been painted shell-pink, a conscious attempt on his father's part to break away from stereotypes. 'But in the end,' Jack says, 'Matthew will be what he wants to be and I'll accept it. Even if that means he wants a career in the army . . .' he adds, smiling wryly.

Jack was born in Leicester and read biochemistry at London University, then did a year's teacher-training course. In 1971 he moved to India. He worked for two years in an International School 'teaching rich kids and diplomats' children', then he moved on to a project working with Indians. He was by then able to speak Hindi and remained with the project for three years.

'I had a vague sort of social conscience when I left England but really I wanted to travel and help a bit, I suppose. I lived and worked with Indian and European volunteers the whole time and it made me much sharper in my analysis of myself and the way society works. My idea when I went to India, for instance, was, Oh India's dirty. Then the Indians I knew would say, "Why do you wear shoes in the house? Why do you use toilet paper when it's smearing shit and why do you sit in dirty water in the bath?" It really reorientated me.

'The idea behind the project was that you physically helped to bring about change. You actually built schools and water-supply systems and so on. It was a lot of manual work and it had quite an influence on me. I feel now what you do is more important than what you say. You know: "Do it, and don't talk so much about it."

'So when I became aware of feminism, it was less a matter of what I felt or how I should talk about it but more the practical side – fifty per cent of childcare and domestic work, stand a bit back from the idea that only I and not the woman had a career. I suppose that's stuck with me. The hardest part is that you have to retreat.

'If you keep trying to put feminism into practice, you find yourself in a corner with no space. You narrow yourself down to nothingness. You step back all the time from women so they can have their rights and you end up in that corner.

'For instance, letting strident women in the co-op have their way. I'm saying, "Look, I agree I might have a sexist past but I'm sorry, I'm still going to try and judge this issue on the facts; not whether I should take a pro-lesbian or a pro-feminist or a pro-separatist standpoint . . ." I feel you keep conceding and you're not sure what you're left with . . .' He says none of this with affirmation, always as if it's a newly-formed thought, so fragile it might disintegrate under surveillance.

Jack Dorset says communal living has always appealed to him. He feels nuclear families are 'stifling', 'not really the right way'. At teacher-training college, he shared with two men; in India he lived communally, and then, when he lived in Switzerland for two years, he moved into a communal house where Helen was living.

'Helen didn't just want us to be a couple. She felt we should be a couple with others around us so it was not so intense and you could have your own space. In the end, she had the problems with the two others we lived with – I enjoyed it. It made relationships much richer somehow.'

In the present house, Jack and John have only just moved in so a system has yet to be worked out. 'Relationships seem so short these days,' Jack says. 'When I came here, I said to Cathy I would like to think we're going to try and see it out at least for a fixed time – now it could be one year. And not pack it in if it gets difficult, but she didn't quite favour that . . .'

Prior to the co-operative, Jack worked with remedial children in a scheme which folded because of lack of money, and lived communally with two lesbian women plus Terry who cared for two children. The relationship, in spite of the fears of Jack's father that it might be misunderstood, was platonic.

'I saw Terry as being my alternative family. Him and his kids and me and Robin. Terry wanted to move into this co-op but he got rejected by some stupid woman who had a grouse and she persuaded the others to vote against him. I was really upset, I felt my family had been cut away from me. I feel a bit more O K now.

'I used to think stability and permanent relationships are important. But now I think my relationship to Matthew is stronger, we don't see Terry or the kids much and it doesn't matter any more that Terry isn't here.

'I'm confused about relationships. I'm not in one at the moment and I'm not sure any more how essential they are on a permanent basis. I don't know what commitment is any more. I mean I'm committed to this house – more to the bricks and mortar than the people in it, in a funny sort of way . . .

'People say by the time you're thirty-five you should have all that communal living out of your system. I haven't. I read Aldous Huxley's

Island and his sort of mutual adoption society. I'm sort of moving in the direction of collective childcare, I've seen it work quite well.'

He and Helen visited America three years ago and saw a community where children were looked after communally and the parents had what they called 'Prime Time' in the evening when they put their children to bed and had a 'parent-child relationship'. 'Helen said, "How could you like that sort of place, Jack, it shows how far apart we are . . ." I suppose that was the sign . . .'

Helen is Swiss and two years younger than Jack. They met in India and then lived in Switzerland for two years. She was a nurse, Jack an organic market gardener. They returned to India and married so that Helen could have her visa extended. In the early years of the relationship, Jack says, he formed certain impressions about Helen. He believed her to be a feminist, in favour of shared childcare between man and woman; a person who had a commitment to communal living over life as a nuclear family.

At twenty-nine, four years ago, Helen had a strong urge to have a child. She felt time was running out and her father had recently died. 'I remember she came back from visiting the grave and her mother had said something like out of death must come rebirth, that sort of thing. I had wanted to wait a year or two but I did have a commitment to children.

'I remember that particular night, she said it quite strongly, she put quite a considerable amount of pressure on.

'Still, the minute he was conceived, I felt fine. But while the marriage didn't change anything, Matthew's birth did. We stopped sort of relating to each other. Now, looking back, I can see we hardly had any time.

'We both worked three days a week and took turns with the baby, we barely had time together.'

Jack and Helen returned to England to live. Helen had wanted to make the move but she found she was unable to get work as a nurse and she was, in any case, confined by the fact that she was breastfeeding Matthew. In retrospect, it was a time of confusion for her, Jack says.

'In England, Helen had to decide was she my wife, Matthew's mother, a nurse, someone in her own right . . . why was she in England at all? I helped with the cleaning and caring for the baby but I think that made her feel she had no domain of her own left at all.

'It undermined her because I had a part of the house and I had my own domain as well in work or gardening or whatever.

'We did discuss it and came to an agreement: "OK, you do two rooms and I'll do two rooms." But then she would always insist I hadn't done my rooms properly. I don't know if it was the Swiss mentality or her mother's influence. I used to say, "Look, if you want me to do these rooms, you have to accept the way I do them."

'I used to take Matthew with me when I went gardening but Helen said that that meant I wasn't caring for him properly, I should pay him total attention.

'Now when I look back, quite a lot of what I thought Helen wanted in life was forced on her by me.'

Helen left two years ago. She now lives in a nuclear family with Kevin, a teacher, twenty-three miles away from Leeds. She has just had a second child. Jack says he felt nothing but positive feelings about the new baby and he is glad that Matthew has Kevin, a third adult in his life – but he is bewildered by Helen's reactions over access to Matthew since they separated. At first, she agreed Matthew's time should be split in half. Now, Jack says, she wants Matthew to see less of him so he can become more a part of the new family which she has established. She also fought against Jack's attempt to have joint custody – and won.

'In court I played it very low-key,' Jack says. 'I didn't say she is a bad mother or that Matthew was better being totally with me. I said he needs both of us. If I had been given custody on condition that I give up my job I would have done just that. The magistrate automatically gave custody to Helen. He even overruled the welfare officer who had re-commended we split the week between us.

'Now I have to negotiate holidays and I worry because Helen is cutting down on the time I have. Once Matthew starts school . . .'

I ask if his experience has made him sceptical about a woman's ability to change from traditional views, given that Helen had once been in favour of shared care?

'Perhaps it was more my fault,' he says instantly, 'I may have projected on to Helen the sort of person I wanted her to be. Perhaps she never was into equal childcare . . . although she said so . . . Like anyone, she had contradictions. For instance, at times she liked me working part-time so that I could be at home more. At other times, she complained that we didn't have enough money to live on . . . I think she wanted more of a breadwinner, though we managed financially.'

Jack has been part of a men's group for two years. Leeds is particularly active, perhaps as part of the reaction to the murders of Peter Sutcliffe, the so-called Yorkshire Ripper. I approached men's group and asked for a volunteer who would agree to be interviewed. One man said yes and then his girlfriend objected. He, in turn, recommended Jack. Until we met, all I knew about Jack was his age and his interest in feminism.

Men's groups began in this country in the 1970s. Most seem to have a life of a year or so and then they splinter. In addition to groups and occasional conferences (where the issue which often overwhelms proceedings is whether or not women should be excluded), several newsletters and magazines are also published sporadically, such as the *Anti-Sexist Men's Newsletter*. A masochistic desire to accept any punishment meted out by women is one fairly frequently recurring theme; a desire to become involved in childcare is another.

The dilemma facing some men – at least as mirrored in the editorials of such magazines – is how you assist women without stealing their initiative and taking over as the traditional male is said to do. How do you seek help from women without 'draining their energy and distracting them from the real fight'? How do you behave towards women when you are their enemy and yet you wish to be their ally? How much do you have to grovel, if at all, in reparation for the sins of all men?

Relationships between men are apparently easier. In groups, men learn to talk of their emotions, in theory at least, they shed competitiveness, learn to trust, discuss their own sexism, talk over the relationships they have had with fathers and other men in their lives, try to understand male violence.

A debate which has affected many men's groups has recently taken its toll on Jack's group. In jargon it is a conflict between therapy and the political. In plain English, the question appears to be: should a man concentrate on his own development, 'Personal Growth', the Californians would call it, or should he step outside the group and the boundaries of his personality and take action – campaigning on issues such as equal pay, pornography, rape?

The idea that both activities may be possible does not seem to be popular. Jack says he feels caught somewhere in the middle. At present, the 'men's movement', if one exists, seems even more riven than the women's movement. During the deterioration of his marriage however, Jack found advantages in his men's group. He had somewhere to talk about his feelings and somewhere where he could let the tears flow. But the response of some of the men was alien to how he felt.

'They said, if a woman wants to take a child, we should allow her to do so. They argue men have yielded too little in a patriarchal society and that that would be a small sacrifice to make. They felt that to insist on being 'a father' was a hangover from the Victorian man possessing his wife and children. I didn't – and don't – feel it's a matter of being more or less feminist. I feel I'm a parent and I have a right to some of Matthew's time . . . I think the child *needs* a relationship with both parents.'

Jack says part of his interest in Matthew may have roots in his relationship with his own father. He is now retired but was an export sales manager and travelled fairly continuously.

'I felt he was the father in the home. I'd drop into his factory sometimes but his presence wasn't really felt in the family. The family sort of split between my mother and me; my sister and father. My mother and sister hated each other. My youngest brother came when I was twelve and my mother really resented that as she'd nearly got rid of the children.

'Once or twice she said to me she would divorce my father. She couldn't tolerate this man less intelligent than herself – her inferior, in a way. Now she'll say, "Oh it's important that we stood together for the kids." She can't face working through some of the things she says.

'I think it was the security of the home. She's sixty-five now. In our marriage, she blames Helen, she feels she should've stayed for Matthew's sake.'

Immediately after the separation, his parents urged Jack, he says, to allow Helen to look after Matthew so that Jack could be free to establish himself with 'a nice car and a house'. 'They come up every six weeks or so and I think they're still trying to work it all out.

'I remember when I left university, my father shook my hand. There wasn't much physical contact. I hug Matthew all the time. I try to think about the nurturing aspect. I think a lot of the language comes from women, they sit and talk with children whereas men do things. I saw this pamphlet from the Health Education Council called 'Parents, Your Child Needs You', it was multi-racial and I thought that was good but it was very stereotyped.

'The father took the kid to the park, the mother cleaned its teeth, put it to bed, cleaned the house . . . I sent a letter to complain and they wrote back saying, "Yes, it was very difficult . . ."'

'I take Matthew to the urban farm and library, I clean around the house, we cook and bake bread together. He sees me as a household person and not just a special trips person.

'I am sort of aiming to bring Matthew up in a non-sexist way . . . the woman next door, for instance, is a carpenter and Matthew sees her a lot doing woodwork. I can point fingers at what his images of women should be but my major concern is the man/child sphere and how I can do the best in that area.

'I'd like to talk to Helen's husband, Kevin, about Matthew but I think Helen would think I was trying to undercut her authority. It's funny in spite of what I've said, she's also a very strong person, that's partly what attracted me. In the men's group, they asked me to express my anger towards Kevin but I didn't really feel any . . . perhaps it's deeply hidden . . .'

In the meetings of the men's group there have been discussions, co-counselling, massage sessions, non-competitive games, trust games . . . 'You stand in the middle of the circle and close your eyes and let yourself fall . . . you have to trust others to catch you . . .

'In discussions, we pull each other up on vocabulary, I use "girl" and I get pulled up on that.

'In the context of the men's group, we hug each other a lot. I still think I've got a lot of inhibitions about that. I couldn't do it with a friend in the street. It's not something I feel very good about. I still back off even with Terry or John. I think, Am I supposed to do this? Perhaps I could work it through if I had twenty or thirty years . . .' He smiles broadly.

'In the group we talk over problems such as what you do when you fancy someone. If you see them in the street and you fancy them are you objectifying them? How do you show you fancy them without being sexist?' He laughs. 'We've never really discussed that one in detail . . .

'I didn't lose my virginity until I was twenty-one, whereas some of the men were screwing at fifteen. I remember at college there was all sorts of bravado, but when it really came down to comparing notes in the third year, only one fellow had actually screwed . . .

'After Helen, I had a relationship of four or five months with someone in the co-operative and she was very much into penetration. She said there aren't many women in the co-operative who are into it . . . With Helen penetration wasn't always the force that was important. I remember just before we broke up we hadn't had sex for a time and we did sleep together. I felt I hadn't pressured her at all. But after she said, "I just did it to make you happy," I felt really let down because I thought it was a mutual thing.

'Men don't have to see penetration and ejaculation as the only form of gratification,' Jack says, 'I've experienced sex many times without it and felt equally fulfilled and gratified. It's the exception to the norm, but I have felt, that was great, without penetration.'

Jack says he does have one-night stands with friends and women he meets but he is wary of a longer-term relationship; his main focus is Matthew.

I ask him how he feels about separatists. 'Well, they have their own living space . . .' Isn't that sexism in reverse, I ask? 'I'm not sure. I'm not frightened of giving a comment. I haven't thought through where I stand. I don't think separatism is really the way forward . . .

'I think as men we should try and do our best but we shouldn't feel guilty. When Terry and I shared with two lesbians, four of their friends came from Greenham. Terry was responsible for writing an anti-sexist newsletter and he was away when they read it.

'They wrote him a letter in turn, "Four angry dykes" they put. "We have read some of your stuff and it's very suspect. Men are all shits and the best thing men can do is throw themselves in a lion pit." The letter was left on the table. They were cowards in a way, they didn't even say anything to me. They should have tried to engage me in discussion but in a letter it's easier to write "you shit."

'Terry had done a benefit for Greenham only the week before and there he was being stuck in a lion pit. I want to hear women if they're angry, I even agree with a lot of it but I don't think calling men "shits" is any way forward. Often your closest allies, the people you most love, give you the shit. I think that's true in the feminist line.

'I think women *should* do things on their own,' Jack adds. 'I support Greenham for instance but I like to have contact with mixed groups too. Bill, a member of our group, didn't like the women we had one mixed evening with – as a women's group he felt that they were middle-class, they didn't have a radical analysis. I thought they were OK . . .

'I feel resentful that I can't have children,' Jack says, 'I asked if I could adopt one and they said no, nuclear families only, sort of thing. I don't know what the chances of fostering are. I feel quite envious of the physical experience of childbirth . . . that feeling that "It's actually come out of me, it is a part of me . . ." It's five minutes for the semen but nine months for a woman.

'What I do know is the men's group has helped me to develop. I'm uncertain of a lot of things now, wary of relationships. I don't know how to judge people any more, I'm worried about the future for Matthew and me but I don't feel bitter. I think change *is* taking place. People *are* living in lots of different ways, not just the nuclear family. I hope the way I live will become more accepted. Of course, you've got Margaret Thatcher and her Victorian ideas pushing the other way, and the Government cuts, but still. I think society *does* sort of roll onwards and the feminist push is the biggest push in the right direction there is at the moment. Men are changing but women have to change too. I mean I wonder whether Helen wasn't really always a traditional family-type person, she seems happier now in some ways. Women are saying we want gains in all these departments but then neither are we going to let go of what we've already got. I think they have to let go of something . . .' He says it with great hesitation.

George Hyatt   *Devon*

Six English Belvoir bitches, black, tan and white, stand transfixed in the door of their outhouse, silhouetted in the light of a late afternoon. It looks like a canine Victorian family portrait. Another thirty-four bitches howl with pleasure as George Hyatt pulls ears and whacks noses. Tails are as thick as whips; paws seem as large as paving-stones. The bitches radiate strength. Some are gummy, teeth worked loose by a diet of raw meat. Some look battered; old cuts and catastrophes leaving scars.

Next door, forty dog hounds, some of them stallions used for breeding, are yelping in disapproval that George Hyatt is not paying them due attention. Next season, George Hyatt, Master of the South Devon Hunt, will have bred all eighty hounds himself. Their pedigree dates back to 1802 and he is, he says, ferociously jealous of their fidelity.

'It's sport the hounds want and that's why they are devoted to me. I show them sport. They'll follow me through the middle of London. I could take my hounds through Piccadilly in the rush-hour and I wouldn't lose one. I could never see me walking out on them. Somehow they make me feel good. If they could talk, I wouldn't need friends. I'm their boss and I'm very jealous of that.

'I don't let other people touch them. I've only just let one of the whippers-in take the hounds out. Still, they know I'm the Master. If he walks left and I walk right, they follow me. I'd like a wife now but she could only become involved with the hounds on a staff basis. She'd have to come behind the hounds.

'I'd be scared that she might take over. I've worked these hounds and no one's going to take them off me.' He delivers his message mildly but meaningfully.

The hounds run sixty miles, three times a week. Their lifespan ranges from four to six years – depending on whether they are good stallions and bitches and therefore suitable for breeding. Twenty dogs are put down each year – an activity George Hyatt does himself out of affection and respect, he says.

'You can't keep them unless they're good . . . And you get the ones who do naughty things. They won't hunt properly, they skirt or they whizz round the other side of something to meet the fox coming out and that's not the way we do it. It's unethical. A dog over four seasons will get a bit independent. It's most extraordinary, there's a pack discipline. If one gets lost and it turns up half an hour late, the others will go for it as if to say, "Don't you dare do that again."

'The stallion we've got now is brilliant at his work. He's got tremendous fox sense. He'll never go over a wall without going down the wall each side first. He'll find foxes like nothing on earth. For instance, we'd been hunting a fox for about an hour and the whole pack suddenly turned and marked a fox under a rock but this old stallion didn't want to know. When we dug the fox out I felt a bit sorry for him because he'd realised it was a fresh fox – not the original one we'd hunted. Foxes smell differently and he knew.

'I cry when I put an old hand down. I cried for a week when I had to put Stratford down. I won't let anybody else do it though.

'I'm more likely to cry over a lovely bitch. We lost one last year. She was just about to whelp and she went off and got killed on the road. That really upset me for a day. I rang up my best friend and cried down the phone to him. What was so great was that he sent me another one – he's a professional huntsman in Ireland you see.

'I do get used to killing. We kill a lot. We use two hundred bullets a year with foxes, stock on farms and we've got a knacker's license as well. I've been brought up with death. I killed horses as a jockey. I am used to it and yet I'm also very sentimental, I'm not afraid to cry. I never have been . . .'

A little later, he and Mark, one of the whippers-in who live on the premises and help with the eighty hounds, eight horses and the organisation of the hunt, take the dog hounds for a walk. We go far enough so that Pulsford, the village of three houses which is George's and the hunt's home, hides in a pintuck in the hills. To the west is Dartmoor, to the east is the sea. The nearest large town is Torquay.

George shouts Tally-ho and the hounds, as one, pelt down a field like a terracotta and black-and-white patchwork quilt on the move. He knows most of the hounds by name. If he forgets, each hound has the first two letters tattooed on the inside of one ear . . . Poacher, Pontiff, Dunlop, Durham . . . 'Have you seen anything like it?' George Hyatt asks as the hounds race back to him as if powered by undiluted zest. 'Have you honestly seen anything like it?'

George Hyatt has been Master of the South Devon Hunt for two years. The hunt meets three times a week, ten months of the year. In the two months it does not hunt, in June and July, the puppies are trained on two-hour daily bike rides. The hunt covers an area of 150 square miles, including a quarter of Dartmoor. The land belongs to six hundred farmers, a fifth of whom hunt; only three farmers refuse the hunt access to their land. Members also include dentists, barristers, solicitors, housewives.

Their Master has the kind of face one associates with the country and good health. His conversation is built on respect – which he likes given and received. He believes in tradition. He never uses a Christian name until he is given leave to do so. He addresses 'his' farmers as 'sir' and expects to be addressed in the same manner by the whippers-in who are his employees. On the days when the hunt meets, he says he should be referred to as 'Master'.

'You might think it very old-fashioned,' he says, 'but I think certain conventions *should* be maintained. I get on with people but sometimes they can't understand what happens to me when I get on a horse. If after the hunt, people rush back to the pub, drink pints and have a gossip, that's a terrible insult to me. At the same time, I hate it if somebody has a go when hunting and I tell them off and they answer me back. Inwardly I fold up like a pack of cards. I show anger but I'm terribly hurt underneath. I'm too proud to say I'm sorry because of my position. I also get terribly frustrated if I don't shoot sport; terribly.

'Yesterday, for instance, we had an awful day. The fox ran circles around us, one fox handed over to another so it was like a game of tag. At a certain point, a fox was standing on a stone wall looking down while the pack went sailing past. A bad day's sport doesn't make me happy.'

Britain has 198 hunts, and members pay subscriptions which range from £25 to several hundred pounds a year. All have Masters, many also employ a professional huntsman who oversees the day to day running of the hunt. George Hyatt is a joint Master. His Co-Master, 'a marvellous man', provides a good proportion of the finance. George acts as the mechanic, as it were, ensuring that the machine operates efficiently.

His income comes from the raw meat donated by local farmers, some of which is fed to the hounds and some sold on the market. The two whippers-in receive twenty-five per cent, George the remainder. His salary amounts to about £3,000 a year plus accommodation. 'I can't afford to have friends,' he says half in joke. 'If I go into a pub and buy a round it wipes me out for the rest of the week.'

The accommodation is a cottage almost untouched since the time when Utility was chic. The sitting-room has a low ceiling, a large desk, some comfortable chairs, a television and video which George, a former steeple-chase jockey, uses to record the afternoon races. the only other programme which interests him he says is *The Sweeney*. The *Sun* is the newspaper he reads most regularly but he takes *Horse & Hound*. On the walls are prints of racehorses; foxes' brushes decorate the pelmets. The colour scheme, developed more by default than design, is a chestnut brown, the temperature is chilly, the atmosphere fairly damp.

The dining-room is large and dominated by a massive table. On one wall a small carpet is hung. It is woven in luminous psychedelic colours with a satin sheen. It depicts a group of five dogs playing pool. The wolfhound holds a half pint; the bulldog has an eyeshade and a cue. The carpet was a gift from George's younger brother Tom, at a time when he worked as an agricultural adviser to King Faisal in Saudi Arabia. George says the caricatures tickle his sense of humour.

The kitchen is also spartan. A pot of stew is on the stove; creamy milk has been left by a farmer; the Aga slowly cooks baked potatoes for supper. Cooking and housekeeping is done by Debbie. 'Debs' is in her twenties and lives in the flat upstairs. The two whippers-in share the bungalow next door. Debs is also the girl groom and does both jobs for £50 a week. 'I mean, would you do all that for £50?' says George, slightly incredulous. He regards Debs as his closest friend.

'I *am* close to her. I have cried in front of Debs. I mean I might as well be married to her but it isn't sexual at all. She's got a boyfriend, she could be married to a nice partner but she likes the life here. If I come back from an evening out, I usually go and sit and talk to her before I go to bed.

'It's not boss and staff. She's very disrespectful of me, which is the only thing against her,' he adds, tongue in cheek. 'She calls me "sir" in public but then she'll always go a step further. Like last week on the hunt, she called out, "Sir, excuse me." I thought something was wrong so I said, "Yes Debs, what is it?" "Sir, excuse me, but when are you going to start showing us some sport today?" Cheeky thing. I was laughing, it was so funny. If anyone else had done it . . . She's got that kind of devilment about her.

'We had a terrible row once about her father being on National Assistance [sic]. I had a go at her about it and she got into the car ready to leave. It was a real bust-up. We literally fought each other but then we eventually made up. You probably can't understand the relationship,' he adds, more as a question.

The work is continuous, seven days a week. Last year, George took only a few days off, and Christmas day. Today, a Wednesday, begins as usual at seven. He mucks out two horses while the whippers-in clean the hounds' outhouse. He then has to drive to retrieve Sapling, a bitch puppy. Until the hounds are old enough to train, they are kept by farmers, 'the keepers'. Sapling had gone missing and been found. A second farmer asks George to pick up the pair he has because they have become a nuisance. By the time the truck returns to Pulsford, George has a cow with magnesium deficiency in addition to the two hounds on board.

Out again, he collects some booze for a dance on the following night; some corn for the horses and me from the station a dozen or so miles away. In the afternoon, he makes arrangements with the farmers whose land he intends to cross on tomorrow's hunt, he clips two horses and sees to the hounds. In the evening, he eats supper alone because it is Debs's day off. Wednesday, he says without a hint of irony, is an easy day.

Hard work, poor pay, but the compensations, George Hyatt says, are magnificent. 'People tell me I'm very dedicated but I'm not. It's just a way of life for me, do you understand? I'm very lucky because I'm almost arrogantly in love with my job.

'I've been hunting hounds here for six seasons, I must have killed perhaps three hundred foxes. I've heard hounds hunting a lot. I can promise you now the excitement, standing there on a good or bad day. If I double the horn, tally ho, tally ho, they know that means fox and they'll come like bullets. It's the noise the hounds make that gets me . . . It sounds gorgeous in a big valley.

'You see the hounds leaping up in the air to get the scent and the one who picks up the scent, speaks. You know his voice . . . The hounds howl with happiness when they hear the horn. I sometimes giggle like a kid with anticipation.'

George Hyatt was born in Stanton in the North Cotswolds. He is the fifth generation to hunt. 'The first time I remember hunting they killed a fox. I jumped off my pony and went to see. I remember the smell, the steam coming off the hounds. I can still smell it now. I can remember going back home, my father taking my pony on the leading rein and I recall looking down on the hounds and thinking, one day I'll have my own hounds . . .

'I had an older sister but I was a great success with the family because I was a boy. My godfather is a farmer and gave me a hunting whip for my christening. I was petrified when I was first taught to ride but I got used to it . . .'

The news that he was going to become a Master did not please George's father even though he is one of a small band of only 450 in the country, all members of the Masters of Fox Hounds Association. 'He went bananas,' George says, 'I shouldn't be a Master, I'm not the material. The material is gentleman, money. I'm a farmer's son, I should be a farmer.' He says it with humour.

As a Master without a private income, he explains, he is caught between two classes. A professional huntsman would have a better salary, some security such as a cottage in which to live during retirement. Still, he has no intention of giving up – perhaps he will move on to a grander hunt in time, but he will not give up.

In the stables, George Hyatt introduces the horses. One killed a man, he says. The horse flattens its ears. He threw his rider on to a cattle grid which broke the man's back. 'He is as soft as anything though, all front. We ride these horses hard like motorcycles. We have a thing about life and death being mechanical.' Then he adds, suddenly softening, 'But we're infinitely caring in our own way.'

In another outhouse, his hunting equipment is laid out. Four red coats made by Webbs of Exeter at a cost of £250 each; nine pairs of riding boots, a large amount of tack and his hunting horns. When he gets a new horn he drives up and down the motorway practising. 'It sends lorry-drivers crazy.' If he practises closer to home, it sends the hounds equally daft. Hollering too is an acquired art. If he hollers 'Lu lu' for instance, the hounds know to look upwards for the fox.

'I can remember going out as a child with the professional huntsman at home. I was sent to do what the men do, to see the fox at the end of the day. I stood underneath a tree, as Daddy told me so that the fox wouldn't see me and I watched it come out. I watched the fox go by and I tried to shout but I had no voice. The Master was in such a temper.

"Learn to holler, boy," he said. I had about ten baths that week, so I could practise in the bath.'

At lunchtime, we visit a local pub. The landlord is fairly new and has agreed to the hunt meeting there on the following day. He will provide punch and sausage rolls. 'That's terribly good of you, sir,' George says and it suddenly becomes very easy to visualise him in prep school. He is conscious that his job includes being a diplomat, he says. He has to keep the local farmers happy although by nature he is not gregarious. As a child he had a stutter. 'If someone asked me my marks in class I used to hate to say seven out of ten. I could never get the seven out. Now, the stutter comes back if I'm nervous. If I give an after-dinner speech, which I have to do, I say, "I stutter and I shan't mind at all if you look at each other when I do . . ." I've grown less self-conscious.

'I'm a man of moods, I suppose. I don't like parties much, I don't like pubs – unless they're quiet. I like to be with a crowd having fun, letting its hair down, but not for long. Perhaps it's because I don't like people?' The question-mark which often lingers over his speech appears again.

In the time we spend together, George Hyatt becomes more and more of an enigma.

I find him very easy to like but difficult to fathom. The contradictions in him challenge curiosity.

He tells you that at times he is awesomely lonely yet, to an outsider, he also appears utterly content. He says he does not like people but he has all the cultivated charm of those who consider themselves naturally gregarious. His conversation often reveals that he is both sensitive and sentimental. 'I'm a good cryer,' he says early on in the day, 'I cry very easily . . .' And he does come close to tears without embarrassment when discussing subjects which he considers close to his heart. Yet in tandem with this sensitivity is a certain toughness which he says contact with death and the cycle of life in the country makes inevitable. He appears almost bashful and naïve on occasions but goes on later to discuss women – the women he knows tend to be much younger or married, and seem to occupy a very small compartment in his life – with a certain confidence and an almost total absence of machismo.

At one point, we talk about contentment. He says he is happy overall but his moods do dip and dive. 'I mean I shall probably feel a bit low after you've gone tonight. Tomorrow I'll probably be OK again. A lot of how I am goes back to my childhood,' he volunteers.

George Hyatt has a younger brother and an older sister. All three had a difficult time in childhood with their father, a time George Hyatt prefers not to talk about because the relationship has now improved. It has improved without any discussion of the past between parent and child.

The relationship is at the root of why he wants to succeed so much, George says. 'I will not be beaten. I will *not* be beaten. My family's taken four hundred years to move a mile and a half in the Cotswolds. My mother's very proud of the Hyatt name, the family. There's been pressure on my brother and myself to get married otherwise it'll be the end of the Hyatts.'

At seven, George was sent as a weekly boarder to prep school. Each week, he would cry until the Wednesday. On that day, a letter would arrive from his mother. 'I was in tears, "Can I come home?" I missed my pony, a wonderful grey pony. I felt terribly homesick, perhaps because my mother showed us a lot of love.

'I used to try very hard at school and get into an awful state about homework. I was a very dedicated rugger player when I was at school. That's why I was a dunce because I spent all my time playing. It also meant that while the kids were a bit cruel about my stutter, they respected me. I was quite popular.

'I played in all three school rugger teams. I was always the idiot who picked up the ball from the scrum. At that time I didn't seem to have physical fear. I'm a very bad man to fight. If I was in a battle, I'd be the first over the trenches. It's not bravery – I'm a bit of a coward actually. I used to feel real fear before a race as a jockey. I don't have breakfast before a hunt but that's probably due more to excitement now. But as a child I had this terrible pent-up anger. It's as if I stored it all up and it would come out at once.

'At school when I did get into a fight, I'd fight so they could never stop me. Perhaps three would have to hold me back. Now,' he adds self-deprecatingly, with a smile, 'I'm more likely to dissolve into tears, get rid of it that way . . .'

I ask him if he perhaps has a high opinion of himself as a sportsman and a low opinion of himself as a person. 'I would agree,' he says without hesitation. 'I try hard at sports. All sport to me, if you try hard enough, comes right. I've taken all the openings I can in life. I'm a trier, a doer, a worker. All my life I've worked hard – forget the reward. The idea is that

I've felt I've done my best. I do get irritated when others get somewhere without trying so hard, but on the other hand I get along with people fairly well. Racing taught me that.'

At home, the Hyatts had a housekeeper and a nanny. He remembers his mother as always being busy. 'She's good looking. I wouldn't fall in love with a woman like her. I mean people tell you you always fancy someone like your mother. I don't. I love her intensely but I wouldn't want to marry someone like her. She can be quite dominant.

'She's very emotional. She kisses her girlfriends goodbye. I say, "You don't have to kiss me, mother . . ." I can't stand that. I think I sometimes set out to annoy her on principle,' he adds, smiling. 'I eat my meals in the way she told me not to. I put my elbows on the table. She can't stop me . . . it's a great joke now.

'I don't make enough of either of my parents really. Father comes down to stay here but he's off home again as soon as we have the slightest argument. The first time I won at racing he took us all out to dinner, which was tremendous. If I was racing, he couldn't watch, mother was different. I used to have quite bad falls and she'd run straight past me. She'd stop long enough to say, "Are you all right?" and then move on to look out for the horse to check how it was.'

In his late teens, George Hyatt's father helped to finance him as a steeplechase jockey. 'I remember telling Dad, all I want to do is get round the course. Then all I wanted was a winner. I got one winner, then two, then I won Cheltenham. Then I got two winners in a day, then three winners in a day. It went on and on then I'd done so much damage in falls, it started to really hurt and I cut out of it.

'I'd existed on 850 calories a day. I would kill if I saw you eating a Mars bar. I used to eat glacé cherries and cakes at four in the morning and then panic and have to try and cheat the scales by taking one stirrup off . . .

'After the racing, all I wanted was a pack of hounds. I do get obsessional about some things.'

In his twenties George Hyatt had three significant love affairs. One continued for three years secretly because it was between himself and a stable girl. He still feels that it wouldn't be acceptable to marry beneath his station. He doesn't think he'll marry now until he is fifty or so – and then the main motivation will probably be companionship rather than love. 'I have dozens of girlfriends. I fall in love terribly quickly then all hell is let loose for a week. But I turn it off straight away at work.'

Locally, he tends to take out farmers' daughters in their teens. He doesn't worry about cradle-snatching, he says, and he'd prefer to marry a virgin. 'It's a tremendous boost for a man's ego.' He can see a number of attractions in having a wife. 'I'd worship her, I really would. I wouldn't expect her to be the perfect housekeeper or anything. I'd just ask her to be faithful and not run off and to give me lots of affection.' In reality, he thinks his life is too hard for a woman to share – although he is considered a prime candidate as a husband because of 'Redcoatitis' – the glamour which a Master is considered to have – erroneously, George insists; not entirely with conviction.

In the past, he has had liaisons with married women. They are experienced, they do not seek anything more than a sexual encounter. He does not regard himself as much of a lover, he says with absolute honesty. Nobody ever told him anything. He learnt by watching nature – not the best guide in terms of the more subtle aspects of the art, he admits. He has also learnt by trial and error. 'I'm not a good lover because I don't show my feelings enough. I don't like being that vulnerable.'

He feels sorry for any girl he takes out in the area. The immediate assumption is always that she is going to be Mrs Hyatt.

'The girls down here are lovely girls. They want to be farmer's wives. They don't really know what men are for . . . that sort of thing. Farmers marry farmers, jockeys marry jockeys. Girls will marry who will have them and whoever's got enough money to keep them . . .'

If he did marry and his wife wanted an independent career, he wouldn't mind in principle but he couldn't see how it would work on a practical level. The horses and hounds would need attention as well as him. He draws his lessons from nature, he says, the male is always the hunter, the stronger partner. He expects to be the breadwinner because of instinct, not as a 'right'. He suddenly grows sentimental. 'Sometimes if I'm on my own in the evening, I really *do* miss having someone I'm close to . . . but not many people I know are happily married. And I don't particularly want children. Having said that, though, I haven't gone and had myself sterilised or anything so perhaps I don't mean it . . . ? Someone you're very close to *would* be marvellous.'

In the afternoon, accompanied by George's three terriers, Otter, Stoat and Pâté, we visit an outhouse where carcasses are kept and skinned.

'You'll be all right, will you?' George asks solicitously. You understand why immediately. A truck load of meat includes a newly skinned cow. On the left is the body of a dead fox. Its eyes bulge from the shock which killed it. It is a beautiful bronze and auburn colour. As soon as the terriers see it, they try to worry it, growling. The stiff body of the fox offers only artificial resistance.

'If anybody asks me if hunting is cruel,' George says, taking for granted that I am against blood sports not because the issue has been discussed but because he feels I am bound to be, 'I'd say yes, it *is* cruel. Killing anything is cruel. Cruel is the wrong word. I'm not well-educated enough to find a word which suits it better but there is one. I think abattoirs are cruel. I think they're barbaric because they're so mechanical. I can't stomach them but I can kill a fox with my hands because I consider I do it pretty well. The stupid thing about the Antis is that they will not take responsibility for controlling the fox.

'We hunt vixens in the spring and that's the horrible part of hunting, killing vixens and cubs. We go out on foot in the early morning with the hounds but we never allow a fox to be killed by the hounds tearing it apart alive. That's not according to the rules and I believe strongly in the rules. We use a humane killer.

'Someone said God created the horse and the hound and put the fox there for convenience. I really agree with that – I don't know what else he is there for. Don't get me wrong. I have tremendous respect for the fox.

'The one time I get upset is when I see a fox killed by stupid people in cars or in a fox wire. It's horrible. Antis often say, "How would you like to be chased by a pack of hounds?" The answer is, "I'd be terrified." But foxes have wonderful hearing and eyesight, it's not all one way. The best friend of a fox is another fox.

'It's like a game of tag, they pass scent on from one to another and the hounds run round in circles. I've seen a fox run straight through a pack and none of the hounds have noticed. We had an awful day yesterday because the fox made a fool of us, and a cracker on Saturday . . .'

Blooding, which happened to him when he was six, does not occur often now, at least in his hunt. 'A lot of people come out for a day's enjoyment, not to murder foxes. Digging out a fox is barbaric,' he adds. 'That's when Otter comes into his own. He'll go down a hole and stand back a yard and bay at the fox. We dig them out and humanely destroy the fox and everything's fine. We *are* only talking about five per cent of foxes – and we do have rules,' he adds more emphatically.

'If a fox, for instance, goes to ground and we want to hunt him again, we put a terrier in to bolt him but we pull the hounds back so that he's got some grace when he runs again.'

A few months prior to our meeting, George Hyatt says, he was fined £100 for assaulting two women anti-blood sports protesters.

'We'd had a good day but there were about thirty of them. We'd called the police but they didn't turn up. I was on tenterhooks and slightly annoyed because a farmer had allowed himself to lose his temper with them. I hate what they believe in but I would not want to stop them because one of the reasons why I like Britain is that we are allowed to protest.

'If I believe what I believe, I've got to allow people to protest.' I ask for his views on the Greenham Common women. 'Crazy. You look at nature. The head cow in the herd gets more food because it bullies the other ones. We've got to bully Russia in the same way. "You come near me, I'll hit you".

'I think things have gone a bit wrong because no one knows their place any more. It started to go wrong when the Queen stopped ruling. We need someone who'll say, "*You* do this".'

The assault had occurred when the Antis, George says, began letting down car tyres. A scuffle resulted and two women were punched in the face. He now feels deeply ashamed about the event. 'Local farmers wanted to raise the £100 but I stopped them. I just wanted it forgotten, I was terribly upset that I had hit a woman. I don't hit girls, that hurt a lot. But I got terribly angry and I feel awfully ashamed now.'

At home in the early evening, George Hyatt shows me his diary. It contains no personal thoughts but it *is* a meticulous and beautifully written account of each day's hunt. The descriptions could place the events in almost any century: 'November 24. Sixteen and a half couples. Fair scent, foggy rain. Long draw found old fox in rough near Mr Avenings. Three fields to ground. No bolt so killed . . .'

'November 19 . . . sunny . . . horses: Comedy and Gilbert. Ran well over Gordon Tor down to river crossed to Brimps. Ran locally and well . . . Fox suddenly stopped in Hooper's Hay, fox hard to get . . .'

Debbie writes in her own note on another day, referring to George Hyatt as 'Boss Hogg': 'Boss Hogg made a complete hash of the hunt and marked a badger to ground. A rather disappointing day showing Boss Hogg at his very worst also extremely abusive . . .' George laughs.

He says he has reached a mellow time in his life. He has his best friend, the professional huntsman in Limerick whom he has known since 1978, and he can and does tell him everything. He is 'terribly attached' to his hounds and the hunt seems to run smoothly enough now.

In the far future he probably will become a farmer like his father, but for now all he lacks is more financial security. 'I don't know why, I just feel I need more in the bank. Sometimes,' he adds, 'I wish they *would* ban hunting then I'd have to find something else to do.' It is only whimsy.

He argues that there are advantages in being single. After the hunt, he can come home, have a hot bath, listen to the classics or stagnate in his dirt if he so chooses. He doesn't sound entirely convinced that this amounts to adequate compensation. 'In the end I suppose I just haven't found the right girl – or she hasn't found me,' he says a shade ruefully.

Recently, the Master of the Hunt at home in the Cotswolds resigned. The post was offered to George Hyatt. He refused, but he was very touched by the offer. 'I hope they see me as a genuine hunting character. That's what I want to be. It's something I love. It's something I try and do properly. I think my father now acknowledges I do the job quite well. That matters in a way too. I like to do things properly and I love my hounds.'

At the station while we wait for the train, George Hyatt unexpectedly says, 'I've really enjoyed today, thank you very much. I don't think I've talked in quite that way before. I don't know what you'll make of me . . . I expect I shall worry quite a bit about that tonight.'

David Jenkins *Cardiff*

If the traditional symbol of Wales is the blackened face of the coalminer, it should by rights in the 1990s be the woman worker in the telecommunications factory. By then, in certain areas of Wales such as West Glamorgan, it is estimated that female employees will outnumber male. Land of My Fathers has always been a misnomer. Even now, it could equally well be Land of My Mothers, the Breadwinners.

David Jenkins has a large investment in the changing nature of work in Wales. In 1983, at the age of thirty-five, he was appointed General Secretary of the Welsh TUC, an organisation approaching its tenth birthday. He earns a salary of £11,500. The Welsh TUC has half a million members, one in three of them women.

Women have made a huge impact on trade union membership in Britain, although not on the unions' hierarchy (apart from certain exceptions in unions such as NUPE and TASS). In twenty years up to 1981, female membership in trade unions increased by 110 per cent, more than twice the rate of women entering the labour force. In 1961, men outnumbered women four to one among trade union members, now it is two to one.

Still, women earn only three-quarters of the male wage. Issues such as equal pay, a shorter working week, better childcare provision, an end to the married man's tax allowance, positive discrimination in union appointments, special courses to encourage more female participation, meetings held at times which fit in with a woman's commitments as a mother and wife as well as an employee, are all still considered peripheral rather than central to the agenda of most unions.

A few unions *have* begun to adapt (beginning with the minimum, the provision of crèches at conferences), national women's organisers have been appointed, places have been set aside for women on National Executive Committees, women-only meetings and courses have been organised to encourage more to become shop-stewards, equal rights committees have been set up. Fundamentally, however, the trade union approach is still focused on the traditional male attitude to work – a man earns the money and has little part to play in domestic work or family obligations at home.

In 1980 the Welsh TUC had eighteen women delegates out of 350 at its conference and only one woman out of forty-five members on the General Council. Since he took over in 1983, David Jenkins's main preoccupation, such is the nature of the times, has been less the conditions and pay in work for male and female employees, more the creation of jobs; jobs which ironically largely provide employment for women.

In the 1930s, a quarter of a million were employed in mining in Wales; now the figure is 25,000. Coal and steel still claim centre stage, but today foreign companies employ more than the steel and coal industries together. American companies and nine Japanese companies are involved in the service industries and telecommunications, videocassette production, biotechnology, software, aerospace.

Well over 10,000 jobs have been created but the dole queue is more than 160,000, and while a woman could be lucky enough to find work her partner may not. Some now call it the Hondda Valley (although Honda do not have a stake), the heavy manual jobs are going and the attitude seems to be, female hands make light work – and lower wage-bills.

David Jenkins is, according to his own information, five foot seven; he wears glasses and has a neat greying moustache. He is relaxed, easy to talk to, and the kind of man who may have come far in Valley terms – a white-collar job has always spelled success. But he has not acquired any of the airs and graces contact with London and the big boyos might encourage. In the pub at night, amongst his friends, he is still probably regarded as one of the lads.

He is an only child and lives on a private estate in Llandaff, just outside Cardiff, five hundred yards from his childhood home. His father was unemployed for a long period in the fifties to the point where the family were down to their last half crown. Then he got a job as a toolmaker and finally became a metalworker on continental shifts. It meant working two mornings, two evenings, two afternoons, two nights and then having two days off; a job he hated.

It also meant that David saw little of his father. He remembers his dad taking him to the pictures once, 'an unusual treat'. His first proper recollections of his father's company came when he was old enough to go into pubs. David Jenkins's mother was thirty-six when she had her son and she was, he says, 'very much the traditional Welsh mam'.

'In Wales the mam controls the house. The man of the house has fairly limited influence although he's clearly boss outside. I think one of the reasons why the growth of the Women's Liberation Movement in Wales was very slow off the mark was because the woman's role, essentially home-based, looking after the kids, has stuck much longer. I think there has been a reluctance to give up the control of the house, for a power base, working outside, which is alien.

'My mother didn't go out to work until I was about twelve years old, I suppose. She decided she wanted a part-time job, she didn't have much to do round the house. My father was horrified because he saw this very much as a threat to his ability to earn the money to look after his family.'

In the past, David Jenkins points out, the opportunities for women to work were slender. Once the new industries came in, such as the textile industry, 'women's work' became available. 'Now the male employment scene is particularly bad, there's a strong economic force driving women out to work, whether they want to or not, because the family requires a breadwinner.

'I think there's some evidence that's created tensions,' David Jenkins says. 'The male macho image of the valley man, rugby and heavy engineering, hasn't changed, I think it will in time, but it hasn't yet. Certainly there are tensions, particularly if the man is unemployed.

'In my father's case, for instance, there was limited tension because he felt my mother was insinuating he didn't earn enough money – or he felt the neighbours or his friends might think that. If a man is out of work then it's all the more acute, he clearly *isn't* earning enough.

'Some things have altered,' he offers. 'The concept of the lads' night out for instance. The traditional pub in South Wales isn't really a family pub where a boy can take his girlfriend, they are male places, darts, skittles and so on, but that's been changing over the last five or six years.

'I can remember,' he adds, 'the pressure was always on to conform and be one of the boys. I think what has tended to happen is the bloke falls in love, changes his pattern, but very quickly after he marries he slips back into meeting the lads.'

In the house, David's mother handed out the discipline. 'I don't think it was a strict upbringing. Depends how you define it really. I can't ever remember either of my parents ever hitting me. But I wouldn't say I had an easy upbringing.

'I also had a parent in my mother who would always take me and all my friends down to the playing fields with a pack of sandwiches. There was never a surplus of money of course. I think I find more bits of my mother in me. She was more of a go-getter out of the two, the person who'd take lead positions.

'She'd be inclined to be the secretary of an organisation or the fund-raiser, she was always active in the social scene. She wasn't politically active but I think my desire to be involved, to be in the centre of activity, came from my mother.

'I can't ever remember seeing my mother as a woman, if you know what I mean. My mother was my mother. Having said that, certainly from the Women's Movement side of things, mothers, women, traditionally are often the worst enemy of other women. Certainly I always remember being encouraged to take up *male* activities. It was not to say I was discouraged from doing other things. I was always a good sewer – and perhaps that has encouraged me to take an interest in some things which aren't stereotypically male but the main push was to do things which had a male ring about them.

'I can't remember doing things around the house but that's not to say that I didn't . . . but for girls of my age it would, I assume, be considered part of their normal day to be asked to give a hand with dusting and cleaning.'

David Jenkins attended Grammar School, where he developed a knack for passing exams. Throughout school he was interested in left-wing politics. At eleven or twelve he can remember wanting to be Prime Minister. He tended to be chairman of various committees. His interest in politics has no clear line of origin in the family and is motivated, he says, 'not so much because of caring but out of a desire to see society operated in a different, more equitable way'.

At school, he was also a Scout (when it was U rather than non-U to be one) and his first girlfriend at fourteen was, naturally enough, a Girl Guide. He played rugby, went mountaineering and generally had a good time. He had no ambition or blueprint at eighteen save for the fact that whichever university he attended had to be near enough and far enough away from home. He drew a radius of two hundred miles on the map around Cardiff and eventually became a student at Liverpool University. There he became active in the Socialist Society. It was the era of the occupations at Manchester, Aston, Warwick and, in 1970, at Liverpool in David Jenkins's final year.

Students occupied the Senate. The chosen issue was the alleged racist connections of Lord Salisbury, the Chancellor. Six students were sent down, there was talk of boycotting the final exams which David Jenkins was shortly due to take. He changed his mind, sat the exams and got his degree. The experience of those few months has had a permanent influence upon him, he says. For the next four years, he felt adrift in politics, still firm in his ideals but not sure how they could be applied.

'I think it began in school in the sixties. We had a changed attitude towards authority. We didn't think anybody should be in authority over us unless they were reasonable. That traditional idea, "You will do this because I say so", began to go, things had to be explained.

'I was very, very disillusioned when I came out of university. Looking back, it seems quite stupid. We actually did believe we were on the point of some revolution. We had witnessed what happened in France, although the students had caved in there, we thought that we were at the point of some fairly major changes.

'It dawned on me when the six were rusticated that we were largely defenceless. We'd got into a situation in which we weren't able to defend our people.

'As a result six people suffered quite considerably. I felt there must be something wrong there. I had a very heavy interchange with my parents who reminded me of all the sacrifices they'd gone through and if I didn't sit my finals, I'd be throwing it away on a whim.

'I decided to sit my finals and some of my friends shunned me because I was moving away from the line, I was drifting. I don't think I've actually changed very much now from where I stood politically at the outset. I couldn't change just because I've got a decent car and house and a bit of money in the bank.'

After university, David Jenkins came home and was unemployed for six months. He applied for jobs in Labour research, the Labour Party and the trade union movement, then his mother intervened. 'She said, "I think we've had enough of this, isn't it about time you got a job?" I told her, "I can't get one." "I'll get one for you," she said, and she did.

'She got me a job with a wholesale company in Cardiff where she was working. I thought it was an awful come-down but I had no choice. In those days, I didn't even think of social security so I had a choice of taking the job or being without pocket money. I saw it as a short-term thing but I actually worked there for four years. After a couple of years,

I found that I was actually living my work all the time. I had a full social life but I found it difficult to turn off from the job.

'Then something clicked inside me. I thought, this is absolutely stupid. I made a conscious decision at that stage that I *was* going to have a social life, I *was* going to enjoy myself, work would have a proper proportion of my life, it was not going to dominate every living waking moment of my life. And I did change.

'Now I refuse a lot of invitations because I want to spend time with my family. The invitations aren't essential to the job, they're part of the ego-boosting side, and I know where I'd prefer to be. My work doesn't have any routine. One month might mean being out every evening on necessary official functions, the next month, I could be home every night, but I don't take work home. If I do, then I consider I'm not doing my job properly, I'm not delegating enough.'

After four years in the warehouse, David Jenkins had reached the position at twenty-four of industrial sales organiser for South Wales. He was sacked after a dispute about a management decision. He was happy to go. His next job was as a forklift truck-driver in the steelworks. Another experience which taught him lessons, he says. Not least of which was the ability to lip-read and communicate in grunts, the level of noise was so intense.

'You walk in and say, "Uhhhrh", and the bloke you're talking to replies, "Uhhrh Uhhrh." I still say "Uhhrh" sometimes instead of hello. People would communicate with expressions and gesticulations and that was quite a surprise to me, that people could communicate without words.

'It was a very macho situation in the steelworks. The strongest were on top. I can't remember picking up on anyone being sad or upset, home problems were never discussed, no emotions. About ninety-five per cent of the conversation was about sex. About women, sometimes about wives, but that was more unusual. That was the biggest shock about conversation, the heavy concentration on sex.

'The *pièce de résistance* was, "Did you have it last night?" Everyone did, of course, about twenty-five times. That's the bravado side of it, ninety per cent was made up on the spot. But that was sort of a shock. And of course, you can't stand off, you have to involve yourself, otherwise you're not part of the group.

'It's not just amongst steelworkers. I wouldn't mind betting if you put a group of City men together you'd have the same ribald conversations about what they're going to do when they get home.

'By and large that pressure doesn't exist on women to perform, to appear to be a sexual stud. The pressure on men as to how they should act is so strong. They have to conform in the eyes of their peers. I've never quite twigged whether everyone in the group knows that everyone else is playing the same game as they are. I've always believed that to be the case, so that if I've entered the game it's been on the understanding that it *was* a game.

'That attitude might have disadvantages,' he adds smiling, seeing the irony. 'Other people might think what they're hearing is normal and feel that they're somehow inadequate.'

Shortly after joining the steelworks, someone suggested David Jenkins should try teaching. He did and his first job was in a technical college in Peterborough. He taught young apprentices on day release. He tried to make the courses lively, relevant to their daily work, but gradually gave up disillusioned. He became active in NATFE, the lecturers' union, and found himself spending more time on union activities than teaching.

Just before Christmas 1977, he ordered a subscription to the *New Statesman* for his father-in-law, a Bishop, 'one of the few to support Labour'. He happened to be at his in-laws' home when the first issue arrived. It advertised a job as Research Officer for the Welsh TUC.

At the time, the Welsh TUC was an infant with no staff and a part-time general secretary. At the time also, David Jenkins didn't know that the post made him a natural successor to the position of General Secretary once the part-timer, George Wright, left to campaign for the General Secretaryship of the TGWU.

He took up his research post on April 1, 1978. I suggest to him that, while he has a lot of influence over how women are affected in work, his career appears to have been virtually untouched by anything that's happened in the Women's Movement.

He says he thinks that is true – part of the reason is because of the late development of the Movement in Wales, but also because of his own conflict of feeling. His first contact with feminism was while he was at Liverpool. He attended a workshop on Women's Liberation at the University of Warwick. He says he felt then more or less how he feels now; he could understand the aims being expressed, the pain being articulated, but he was not in agreement with some of the methods being advocated to bring about change.

In broad terms, he believes in helping women within the union movement. He is not in favour of separate committees, conferences or positive discrimination in the allocation of seats on executive committees.

'I think women can argue quite rightly that the Labour Movement is chauvinist. But I don't believe we're ever going to get what the Women's Movement wants until we actually achieve political changes necessary for the whole of society.

'I sometimes think there is a danger of being sidetracked into one issue, unless you recognise what you are seeking can be a wider part of the transformation of society as a whole.' He suspects, he says, that women appointed to committees as part of a quota system 'don't carry the same clout' as some of the men.

'I certainly think unions can do a lot with their female membership to try and encourage women to play more of a role, find out what their problems are and so on, but that initiative has to come from the membership. I don't think the cause is best served by special arrangements such as conferences.

'I know that women's conferences are very much a second-rate affair compared with a proper conference. If you have one the real Executive body tends to feel that it can relax; instead of women's ideas being introduced into the mainstream they become compartmentalised and downgraded.

'Under a lot of lobbying we're under pressure to set up a Women's Rights Unit. I've got certain reservations because I think there will be a tendency to push certain problems towards the unit instead of dealing with them centrally.'

I suggest that special arrangements for women are necessary precisely because certain issues wouldn't be raised *at all* if such arrangements didn't exist. The trade union movement is adept at making promises to women, less efficient at keeping them. In addition, I say, the problem begins when certain issues are regarded in the first place as specifically 'women's issues' when they are common to male and female members.

David Jenkins agrees in part and goes on to contradict himself. A Women's Action Day Conference was recently held in South Wales, he says. He expected about twenty delegates to turn up and a hundred attended. 'It astonished me, it astonished everybody.

'The second thing which surprised me was the really excellent level of debate and the third was the lobbying for a Women's Advisory Committee to be established. I'd taken the view, talking to some women about trade unions, that by and large, this wasn't popular, but at the Conference it was unanimously demanded. So we're now in the process of doing that. I could see a very clear groundswell of opinion in favour of Wales TUC becoming more active on women's issues. I'd always laboured under the impression it was OK in the south-east but not round here.'

In terms of his personal life, David Jenkins says with a grin that he is lucky. He can afford to be quite liberal on women's rights because his wife Felicity (Flick) is willingly 'very unliberated'. They met the year before David went to Liverpool. She was a nurse and the same age as him. They married several years later. David says he thought very, very carefully about marriage before he took the step – he has been waiting for the grand storms of passion to beset him and then realised that long-term relationships endured in more tranquil climates.

He had been waiting to fall magically in love, the kind where you see stars and can't wait for the minute when you set eyes on the object of your affection again. He had also felt a very strong attraction for Flick from the beginning; in the first year it had been 'tremendously strong', then it drifted for a few years but 'for some reason we always gravitated back.

'I suddenly realised that love as you get older isn't that sort of mad infatuation. It may be. I might walk out of here now and meet somebody and have an instinctive mad attraction but whether there's any future in it is quite another matter.

'Basically in a long-term relationship, it's a friendship, a sort of under-standing, symbiotic would be the word. You feel for each other, it's not infatuation, it's different. I think probably in a certain way a long-term relationship is the better.

'Before I got married and I was single, I can remember thinking, am I still going to be like this when I'm sixty? I've always wanted kids but in a romantic way. I certainly never on any occasion wanted babies. We both decided we would like two girls, I don't know why.'

Felicity decided at the outset that when the first child came along she would stop work. It was a decision she took happily, but David Jenkins says a sort of inverted snobbery is practised. The woman who chooses to give up a career is looked down upon by working mothers in his area. 'In fact, I think rearing kids is a highly responsible task as well. It's only that society has devalued the way we perceive the task. I think if we saw it differently, we would recognise the responsibility and the social importance of shaping the next generation.

'Flick has grumbles, particularly if I've been away a lot. But I think she's happier now than when she was working. I know she wouldn't be happy at all going back. I think the activists in the Women's Movement came to assume the goals they wanted to follow were the better goals, they tended to look down on the women who preferred to have kids, stay at home, play a more traditional role.

'I don't see why the two things can't co-exist. I think, unfortunately, the Women's Movement is seen as the woman wanting to go into a man's world. If a woman doesn't want to go down that path, she's a failure to her gender.'

Ruth is nearly four, Gareth nearly two. David sees them for a couple of hours in the morning and in the evening plus weekends if he is not working. 'If I was critical of anything about my job,' he says, 'it's that I spend far too much time away from the children. I would like to spend more time with the family. Certainly, men of my age are far more into that way of thinking. It was unknown in the past for a father to be seen with his kids apart from the special treat.

'In some ways, I think I have the best of both worlds. I am involved with the kids much more. So, when I go into the sweetshop with Ruth, say, and the woman behind the counter tells her, "Haven't you got a good daddy?" I feel as if I've got the best of my traditional role as a man and I've moved more into Flick's domain. In the past, the mother knew that that was her area, she could get all the praise for her efforts. Now, the father is moving in on her patch but I'm not sure he also takes more of the responsibility as well.'

I ask if he resents the extra time Flick has with the children. Does she have more influence over them? 'I think she's bound to have more influence and I don't resent that,' he replies. 'I suppose I could do a different job which would give me nine to five hours and more time but I don't think I'd be as happy in the other half of my life, my working existence. And if that was the case, would I be the same person at home?

'At the moment I'm wonderfully fulfilled because I'm doing a job I really enjoy. I get immense satisfaction and pleasure from the work and that must make me a much more relaxed, affable, happy person for the proportion of time I'm with the kids.'

Could he adjust to a reversal of roles with Felicity becoming the breadwinner? 'It's a fairly abstract notion but I think I would find it difficult. In fact I know I would. There's no rational basis for it, I couldn't develop a cogent argument why I *should* go out to work. But my instinct would be that it would be an attack on my male position. A feeling, quite frankly, that I would not try to deny. I couldn't deny the way I've been brought up, the values, the conditioning.'

Does he feel that, as he is working outside the home, his wife's responsibility is the house? 'To a certain extent, yes,' he replies. 'Principally, she does the cooking, cleaning, the garden, she tends to do the work in the house. Now that's not to say I see it as her job . . . but it's a difficult question. We never sat down and said, "Right, I go to work, what are you going to do in the house?" It has gradually evolved.'

Does he lay down standards? What, I ask, if he came home and found his tea hadn't been cooked? He laughs. 'I quite often come home to find my tea not cooked. In fact, I always come home to find the tea not cooked. Standards don't worry me.' He adds: 'If Flick feels any kind of resentment at all at the moment, it is the fact that she sees herself financially dependent on me. It's small things. She refers to the car as *your* car. Little things we buy in the house, I think she's conscious that it's the money which I earn which buys them.

'Obviously we argue. Sometimes I'm quite joky about it because I can't understand why she views it that way. It's not *my* money, it's *our* money. What we have done is to establish a separate bank account for her. I think she's happier with that arrangement. She does now see that she has personal control over a particular account.'

David says he does help in the house but he has to conform to a standard laid down by his wife. When they first married, for instance, whoever cooked, the other person did the washing-up. Once the children arrived, Flick would cook and he would wash-up. 'I've noticed in the last six months or so that I'm now screened if I'm washing-up.

'I'm not told I mustn't but I am told I don't do it properly. I'm told I don't put things away in the right places. I'm not sure that I'm not being frozen out of washing-up.' He smiles. 'I'm not sure that I mind being frozen out.

'I behave in the same way at work. If it's something I normally do and somebody else does it, I tend to be critical because it's not quite done my way.

'I'm very conscious now too that when I go shopping, I'm virtually an extension of Flick in the shop, buying precisely what she would have bought if she'd been there. I've never been a lists person and she is. When I shop, I drift along, pick up what I fancy, so long as I have a rough idea of what we need.

'I come back and she'll say, "How much have you spent? Why have you bought the spray?" I'll tell her it's for flies and she'll say she hadn't allowed in the budget for that. I can understand Flick's point of view because she's got to balance the accounts . . .'

In politics, he says his wife is 'sort of Labourish', she votes Labour. But she also articulates some views which perhaps indicate why Margaret Thatcher appeared to draw so many female votes in the 1983 General Election.

'She saw Norman Tebbitt on the Terry Wogan show and said, "You should've seen him, he was really pleasant." I said, "Oh, come on." "No," she said, "really, he was completely different." I don't know whether she was serious but she's taking a very consistent line at the moment that Tebbitt did put across this gentle image . . . it's a kind of insidious Tory influence.'

Among his own friends, he says, the role of women is never discussed, sex takes up very little of the conversation. 'All my friends have got a closer relationship with their wives than their parents perhaps had with each other but I still think it's a marginal change of attitude.

'I think the man who allows his wife to play squash one evening a week does it because he sees his wife has a right to her own interests. But whether that actually alters the basic relationship between the two, I doubt very much.

'Certainly, among the people I know, the tendency is that the man is the dominant of the two. It really depends where in the family unit they decide to draw the lines. With myself and my wife, for instance, we don't have demarcation lines. My wife will decide on almost everything which is related to the house, colours of carpets, curtains, even quite big things such as where we go on holiday.

'Principally because I perhaps see those as, not unimportant, but I wouldn't go to the end of the world about the colour of the curtains. On big issues, we discuss it but I have the big vote. That's not to say I can force her one way but she'll tend to give on that and I will give on other things.'

On the upbringing of the children, David Jenkins says his wife didn't set out with any clear ideas but he consciously wanted to avoid stereotyping. 'I've been astonished that there seems to be a clear sexual stereotype almost implanted in them,' he says. 'Gareth spends all his waking hours crashing up against things, falling over. He doesn't worry, just shrugs it off. You can describe him as "a little boy", a real terror.

'Ruth at the same age was delicate, not physically, but doing very precise little things like jigsaws, and she's still the same now. She enjoys intricacies and delicacies. When she was young, she loved to smell flowers and she touched the petals very delicately, Gareth would have the head off in no time.'

At playtime, David Jenkins says, Ruth wants to be the nurse, Gareth the doctor. He's tried to persuade them that a girl can be a doctor and so on but Ruth very firmly says nurses are girls. I think it's probably true that kids *do* want stereotypes. They want to know who they are, how they're going to fit in, what's expected of them. It certainly confused Ruth when I tried to explain nurses weren't necessarily female. She wanted to hold on firmly to her own idea.

'I'm not sure that's a bad thing now but I hope when she gets a little bit older, she'll be able to realise it doesn't necessarily have to be so . . .'

In the first eighteen months of Ruth's life, she suffered acutely from exczma; the problem now recurs only sporadically. At times, the baby's entire body would be a mass of pain so she naturally required constant attention. Felicity Jenkins did not have an unbroken night's sleep for three and a half years.

In the daytime, David Jenkins says, Ruth was content if he attended to her; at night, she only wanted her mother. 'I used to get this enormous sense of guilt for daft things. We used to eat after Ruth had gone to bed. We'd just sit down and perhaps Flick would have to go back upstairs. I'd always wait for her to eat and she'd tell me not to be so stupid.

'In the night, if I did wake up when Ruth cried, there was absolutely nothing I could do. In the daytime, Ruth and I would have hours and hours of fun together, we enjoy each other's company. The moment she goes to bed, she doesn't want to have anything to do with me. Sometimes it hurts to a certain degree. I know it's not rejection . . .'

Does Flick resent the extra burden? 'She doesn't seem to,' he says. 'Sometimes, if she's had a very bad night and it's four in the morning, I'll walk around with Ruth so Flick can get some sleep, but she'll always say she doesn't need sleep as much as I do. "I haven't got to do a job," she'll say, "my work is humdrum." I don't want her to downgrade her role but I know she can muck through the day if she has to. But if I do without sleep, I actually make an absolute mess, I can't think straight.'

In terms of his own future, David Jenkins says he faces 'a very big problem'. He has never been propelled by ambition, things have 'just happened': 'I don't think you can plot a career path but I think that by the time you get to the thirty mark, if you haven't actually started to make fairly substantial progress, I don't think you're going to get very far.'

He says he has no wish to go anywhere else in the trade union movement in Wales, so the next logical step would be a national position and a move to London. He has already lived once in London, and has no desire to return.

He feels he lives in 'a nice place', in 'a nice house' with beaches ten minutes away and no traffic to endanger the children. 'I can't think of a better place to bring kids up, if they'd have to move to somewhere urban because of my career then that's the point where my career and my family come in conflict and I'd defer to my family first, quite honestly.

'Perhaps in fifteen or twenty years time when I'm fifty or fifty-five and the children have grown up, I might consider moving again if the opportunity arose – but by then I'd be looking forward to retirement too. Life is always a compromise.'

Dennis Jones *Wrexham*

Dennis Jones stands on the platform at Wrexham Station: neat blue suit, white shirt, blue tie, short curly hair, big smile. He doesn't look much like a maverick but in his home town of Corwen, thirty miles away, he almost certainly is. In the sixties, Dennis Jones was an outsider, against the trend. Now, he epitomises it. A member of the new right, born of a working-class Labour family in Labour and Liberal Wales – a Conservative with ambition.

Dennis Jones may be built of the same backbone as Margaret Thatcher but he is not one to say a woman's place is in the home. How can he, he asks, when his wife Janet is a part-time clerk in the bank? But more of that later. What Dennis Jones *does* believe, he explains, is that self-help and individualism extends to women too.

We drive to the 'Bird in Hand' in Moss, a few miles away, and pass Wrexham Technical College, a building that in the mist looks like an enormous beached version of HMS *Hermes*. Dennis has worked there for ten years, he earns £12,000 and is now Senior Lecturer in Politics with eight people under him; he is also the co-ordinator of all public administration courses in North Wales and responsible for all the business education courses run from London.

His pupils are mainly civil servants on day release, employees of the DHSS, the Inland Revenue, the local authority: the average age is twenty-five. They know Dennis' politics and the debates are healthy, he says wrily.

The 'Bird in Hand' has low ceilings, timber beams, lots of brass and chintz. Dennis orders steak sandwich and chips and gently chides Jane the landlord's daughter for wearing a scarlet jumper. 'It should be blue, you know.' She smiles. In the last General Election, boundary changes made Wrexham a new and critical constituency. The Conservative candidate lost by only 400 votes. A lot of people told Dennis he would have won if he had been fighting.

He did try for the nomination. He lives in Wrexham, he is chairman of Brymbo branch of the Conservative Association, he stood a good chance as a local man, but a woman, an *English* woman, was selected instead. The selection committee of twenty-five was two-thirds female, Dennis feels that may have had some influence, but he says his perform-ance *was* poor. He didn't deserve the nomination. It is out of character for him to give less than his best, he explains. But it happened. Next time, the candidate should be known in the area perhaps, down-to-earth. Dennis doesn't have to say he is tailor-made.

In 1983 he fought his first General Election in Caernarfon, a seat won by Dafyd Wigley, the Nationalist. Caernarfon needs another ten years and then it will be Conservative, Dennis says. The experience was good training. If the Joneses of Corwen *do* end up with a Tory MP in the family, Dennis's 'difference', which he talks about freely, will, as it were, be finally sanctified.

'I still regard them very much as family,' he explains. 'Whatever's happening, I'm still involved with them but there is an enormous difference in our outlooks. To be fair, we've always come from a freethinking family. We were always encouraged to have independence of mind. The political arguments my father and I used to have . . .

'I've been a Tory since I was at school. I took History and then I took Political History. Perhaps it was a bit of a rebellion against my family but, in retrospect, my teacher was quite a political animal too and perhaps that's where the influence was engendered. In 1964, I formed the first Conservative Union at school which was quite something.

'When I went home,' he adds laughing, 'my father nearly threw me out. You could have your politics but you couldn't do anything like that.'

Dennis Jones is the fifth of six children. His father, a master baker, was a member of the Independent Labour Party. He died seven years ago and for the first time in the 1983 General Election Dennis's mother voted SDP, an event which astounded Dennis. She is, however, a very, very strong woman, Dennis says. It was 'mostly a matriarchal home', but he finds it easier to talk about his father.

'We were very close knit. My mother was led in many ways by my father but she was always the dominant person. My father was often ill so he was home more often than not. All the family live in town and I remember distinctly on a Saturday night the whole lot would congregate in my grandparents' home and my grandfather would tell a story and we'd spend hours listening to him. We were very, very close but as I've progressed, I've grown further and further away from them. Since my father died I've grown even further away because he was always the person I would talk to.

'My mother and I get on very badly. My wife gets on far better with her than I do myself. Perhaps it's just my intolerance. She was very dominant and because all my brothers and my sister had gone out at fourteen or fifteen to work, then the same was expected of me.

'We used to have rows and my father would take a very passive role. He used to say, "Well, you know, he's got the opportunity to go on and do something else . . ." and she could never quite grasp that.

'She didn't read very much herself. I remember reading at the breakfast table once and seeing the book disappear right across the room. The house was very methodically run, we all had our chores. Mine was the washing-up, which I detested. The bedroom was the only place you could go to study.'

At four or five, he says, he lived with his grandparents for two years; something to do with his brother becoming ill with pneumonia. They were both Conservatives and he enjoyed being the centre of attention.

We move from the 'Bird in Hand' to Brymbo Conservative Club. Brymbo is a small grey slate town, dominated by the steel works. It employs 4,000 men and 900 jobs have been lost so far. A number of steelworkers use the club. It is much like dozens of others in the north. A friendly place, lino on the floor, formica on the table, dartboard, snooker tables, telly, a posher lounge and the photograph of Margaret Thatcher which captures her during her blue period in the early triumph of the '79 General Election.

Dave calls in and says hello. Dennis counts Dave as one of his closest friends.

It is not so much a matter of intimacy as the fact they can discuss ideas and politics together. Dennis is Chairman, Dave is Secretary of the branch. He is a salesman who lives locally and works in Stoke-on-Trent. He is married with one child. Dennis says Dave is probably not quite as much on the right as he is.

'I don't think I have a best friend as such but Dave is the one who's closest. He's a very widely read man, that's the kind of relationship I like. I find it extremely difficult, as extrovert as I am, to drag myself down to other people's conversation levels – I'm sorry this sounds terribly snobby – I don't like endless chat, I don't like it at all.

'I do it but I find it extemely uncomfortable and I'm not usually an uncomfortable person . . .'

At the Club we talk of the problems of the outsider in a small community. 'I remember when I got my degree, I was supposed to go back home and not talk to anybody. That's what was expected and that's what I did. I went home and every time I saw somebody, I just completely looked the other way. I had a good laugh to myself about it. I don't think I've built up any defences.

'In the General Election campaign, I obviously went around meeting the *hoi polloi*, there are more traditional old Tories in Caernarfon than here. I visited the President of Abersoch for tea and had little cucumber and smoked salmon sandwiches. I was starving,' he adds smiling, a habit which comes easily to him, 'I could have taken a whole mouthful but I didn't. It's never bothered me, the class system. I just seem to know what to do.

'People keep saying I'm middle class and I ask them to define what they mean. The fact that I'm very much from an old working-class background hasn't bothered me. I haven't let it inhibit me at all.'

Dennis Jones is the kind of person you imagine to be totally alert from the minute he opens his eyes in the morning. The words which come automatically to mind in association with him are: crisp, brisk, cheerful, you feel he is totally unaccustomed to a negative approach towards himself. Hostility, in any case, would bounce off his degree of confidence. He is fluent; ideas logically recorded in conversation as he might present written arguments in the MA in Further Education he is now close to finishing. He seems a man without many doubts; an efficiently friendly person.

We return to the subject of Dennis' mother. 'It shows how dominant she is,' he says. 'Three of my brothers are still living at home, one fifty years of age, one forty-five and the other is thirty-odd.

'I was up there on Friday and she knows to the second when they're expected in and heaven help them if they're late. The dinner will be ready. They come in through the door, they take off their working clothes, they wash and then they sit down and eat.'

One brother works for a firm which makes agricultural trailers, one works in a factory which produces the fertiliser Phostrogen, and the third works in a factory which makes concrete pipes. His mother's relationship with them, Dennis says, is completely different.

'She strains with me, she doesn't know how I think. She knows how they think because most of them have given their thoughts away. My wife said at one time she thought my mother and I both wanted to be dominant. And of course two dominant people together doesn't make for a good relationship does it? My intolerance doesn't help. I'm not normally intolerant, only when it comes down to dear old Mam.

'I've always been able to think far more for myself, maybe it's going to Grammar School. Whereas for my brothers, my mother's always been there to do it for them . . .'

I ask how his father responded to his mother. 'He was a fairly clever chap. He was very passive but if ever a major decision had to be taken, he would take it and do it quietly and unobtrusively and he would succeed. When my mother shouted, you had to look out. The threat was always there. Whereas my father didn't have to shout, he would just speak and people would do it.

'My mother was very much in control. All the money went into a central fund and she was in charge. My father dutifully came home on a Friday and put his pay packet on the table. She would take how much she wanted and then give him what she thought he had to have.

'I only had one sister and very sensibly she got married,' he says. 'I personally think she had a very hard time, she's the eldest and when all the children came along she had to help out. Anyway when she was twenty-one, she took the easy way out and fled. When she married she had to live with my parents for about six months but I think she took the easy course and left.'

I ask Dennis Jones if he can see his mother or father in anything of himself. 'No, no,' he replies emphatically, 'I hope not, anyway. I'm very much Dennis Jones. I'm very much an individual.'

Dennis Jones took three A-levels at grammar school, English, Welsh and History, but left in the final year before taking exams. He moved on to Wrexham Technical College, where he now teaches, and began a course which led to a National Diploma in Business Studies. A tutor persuaded him to try for university. 'If somebody has made an impression on my life,' he says, 'it's Gavin Thomas at Wrexham Technical College.'

Gavin Thomas was thirty-six or so at the time, married, and he and his wife often invited Dennis Jones to spend the weekend. 'We used to go to Rugby matches and just generally talk. He described his days at university and kept introducing me to other people who'd gone to university. It was a deliberate ploy on his part but it worked. I went to the University of Essex and I know it's an awful cliché but if I could relive three years of my life, it would be the three at university.'

The years were 1969 to 1972, he read Politics. At Colchester, at one point, during South Africa week, some students tried to blow up the bank on campus; Dennis went to classes as usual. He joined the Colchester Conservative Association. In tutorials of ten or so he was the lone Tory but he says he enjoyed the challenge. 'I've never been one to be shy and lost for words so it didn't bother me. They knew me for what I was and the arguments in class took on a new dimension because of that . . .'

We talk about his politics now. He brusquely says he is no wet. He is not keen on Jim Prior's 'softly softly approach to the unions'. He doesn't like Sir Keith Joseph's approach to education, Dennis would very much like to see grammar schools revived. He was pleased to see Viscount Whitelaw put in the House of Lords 'out of the way'.

He believes that 'no one owes you anything': 'You go out and fight and you get your reward. It's a very basic and simple approach. I think it's one which until Margaret Thatcher became Prime Minister wasn't heard much, which is nonsense.

'I have been accused of taking very rightist stands on particular issues,' he adds. 'I think they're pretty rational arguments to use.' He gives examples, he is in favour of voluntary repatriation. He feels the trade unions and 'massive inflation' are responsible for unemployment. He would like more discrimination exercised in child benefit. 'Where is the justification for giving child benefit to somebody like my wife and me who simply don't want it?'

Unemployment benefit he feels is too high (although the DHSS's own research figures indicate that more than one in four people were living on the margins of poverty in 1981, a figure which can only have increased).

'I know a lot of people have lost jobs through no fault of their own,' Dennis Jones argues. 'Two of my own brothers have been unemployed but I know of certain people in my home town of Corwen who seem to be screwing the system for every single penny and going about it in the most devious fashion. The welfare system needs a total overhaul. There are a lot of areas where I want to get into the House of Commons basically because I think I've got something to contribute to policy making.'

He has always wanted to be an MP and when he does get in to the

House, he says, he is determined to be more than a backbench MP or even a junior minister.

'If you're not ambitious, I don't really think you ought to consider the House. You have to go in there and make your mark, bring attention to yourself. Make sure you're there at Question Time, make sure you're seen in the Committees, generally go around.'

How important does he think a partner's support is? 'I think it's vital. Now having fought the first General Election, I think my wife's even more keen. She is a political animal, not as vociferous. She's more a liberal Tory. She's always been ambitious for me. She's always been there. We're very much talkers. I've had two good promotions in ten years and she's advised me both times.

'We're talkers, we always talk through,' he explains. 'For instance, there's an opportunity arising next year, the head of Tertiary Studies is retiring. "Fancy it, do you?" she said. "Well, I don't mind . . ." So we started talking about it and the next day I went in and saw the Principal, had a chat with him and gave a little prod. I suppose really that's how I managed to get my promotion.'

Janet and Dennis Jones met at school when Janet was fifteen and Dennis two years older. She is one of two daughters, her father died of a heart attack when she was fourteen and she witnessed the death – it naturally had a profound effect upon her, Dennis says. She is now a member of the First Church of Christian Scientists.

She is a reserved person. Dennis says he would like her to learn to drive: 'I've even promised her a small car but she's lacking in confidence. We're two completely different people. I'm very much an extrovert, she's very much an introvert. She's painfully shy, even over the past five years, the transformation has been wonderful. Because I've been taking an active part in politics, she's had to come out, she's had to go and meet people.

'It's been very tough indeed but it worked. She's had to be in a situation where she's been introduced to someone and I've been taken somewhere else and she's been left but she's come through. It's been perfectly OK.'

Is he the more dominant? 'I think yes. Most decisions are joint decisions but major decisions such as selling the house, she's quite willing to let me get on with that. She's the banker. She takes the financial decisions because I have very little time. I find money rather trivial.' Does he like certain standards maintained. 'Very much so, yes,' he replies. 'Janet knows what they are. She knows to a T and I don't think she goes out of her way not to transgress but she's constantly aware of the fact that I do have certain standards.

'I do enjoy my comforts. I like my house to be lived in as a family unit.'

Janet and Dennis Jones got engaged the first Christmas he was at university. 'We decided that we would get married very soon after so on that basis she decided to get a job rather than go on for more qualifications although she could have gone to university too . . .'

Dennis says he believes in marriage as an institution but they married 'purely and simply' for economic reasons at the time. The travel to and from Colchester and Chester where Janet lived would have been financially crippling. They married at nineteen and twenty-one.

Janet joined in university life and worked in a bank, transferring each time he moved: from Colchester to Huddersfield, where he did a year in a teacher training college, then to Wrexham. 'It was a very good profession for that purpose.

'I think the marriage probably started off on very stony ground and just seems to have got better. I still think it could be even better still. Janet's aim was to have a family – sorry about the feminist ideals! She's got a family now and for the last five years I've been more actively involved in politics.'

The Jones have two children, Sîan, aged nine, and Jonathan, five. A third child in between Sîan and Jonathan was born with no voicebox and died shortly after birth, six weeks premature. Janet took longer to get over it than he did, he says, he can be quite ruthless at times. He decided that fate had taken a hand. 'If the baby had lived she would never have been able to talk, I'm very much a believer in fate. It would have been extremely difficult for us to have coped with a child who is dumb.'

Did that experience sway him on the issue of abortion, which he opposes? 'Not at all. I'm very much a believer in the sanctity of life.'

Sîan, he says, is 'the apple of my eye; Jonathan the apple of his mother's eye. Jonathan is the thinker, very deep', Sîan finds it difficult to concentrate. 'She's got so many things going on in her mind, she's a scatterbrain but when she can concentrate, she's good. She's not dim by any stretch of the imagination.

'People keep saying Jonathan is going through an impish period in his life. Yesterday in my mother's house he was a little devil and my mother came out with one of her wonderful clichés, "Well, boys will be boys" sort of thing. But I think Sîan can be equally impish.

'I don't categorise. Jonathan does quite enjoy playing with Sîan's dolls. I mean I'm not going to tell him off because he does, I know that he's a lad so I know there's going to be no problem there. I think you inhibit a child if you do tell him this is wrong or whatever.

'Equally Sîan when she was four or five was very much a tomboy, always playing with boys and always up to mischief. But she's gone the complete opposite now, she's becoming quite a little lady.

'I have no set pattern, there are no rules as to what they're going to do. I've made provision. If either shows such a degree of brilliance that they want to go on to private education, I've made provision. I think Jonathan at the present time may well be that kind of boy. So you do what every decent person does.'

Janet's approach to the children, he says, is conditioned by her relationship with her own father, who expected a great deal from Janet, the elder daughter, and pushed her 'quite considerably'. 'I wasn't pushed, I was encouraged. I think we've arrived at a compromise with our children.'

Dennis is out most evenings. On a Friday, the couple go out together, on Saturday they play Mah Jong with friends, Janet has one night out a week too. Weekends are for the family and, in the week, Dennis says he never leaves the house at night until the children are both in bed – usually around eight. He takes them to school each morning.

He thinks the father's role is 'vital' not just for Jonathan but for Sîan as well. 'I want to be very much a part of their growing up. We've no routine life at all. We do things very much on impulse. We pack up the caravan and just go. I think for me the paternal instinct is just as strong as any maternal instinct, very much so.'

He says he does a lot in the house – although not as a result of any example set by his father. 'Even though I've three brothers at home, my mother still does the cooking, cleaning, washing-up, she makes their beds. I don't think they even contemplate getting the Hoover out.

'Wednesday is Janet's day off from work so she does everything on Wednesday. I go out and play badminton, I'm teaching all day and I play at night but otherwise the whole week is split very much between us.'

He does the shopping, she picks up 'odds and sods', cooking they share. 'There's been occasions with Janet's career in banking that she's had to go away on courses and I've just taken on board the children and the house. I always enjoy it. I enjoy my family life. I think that the biggest wrench when I do get into the House of Commons, and I *am* going to get in, will be the fact that I will not be seeing the children so much.

'They'll stay here and I'll commute but they'll be ten and thirteen then so they'll be appreciative of the situation. Janet will carry on work, we've always had somebody in the home to help anyway. A childminder or a cleaner, I see no reason to change that kind of situation.'

I bring up the obvious contradiction of Thatcherite Conservatism. Women are entitled to individualism too, yet all the cuts in public expenditure militate more than ever before against freeing them from the home, reducing their 'choice' to a life with only one 'option'. Except, that is, for the few who can earn the top salaries which can buy them the facility to have a family life and a career.

'If you're trying to ask do I think a woman's place is in the home, I don't,' Dennis Jones answers concisely. 'As much as my wife has supported me, I've supported her career too. Everything is thought out between us. When Jonathan went to school, she said there was no way she was going to stay at home and become a cabbage. I said, "Go back by all means, but I would prefer you not to have a full-time job." She said, "Well I don't want a full-time job."

'Except that now, blow me, a possiblity of a full-time job has come along. She's eventually going to say, "Do you think I ought to take it?" At which point I'm going to say no. I don't want her to have a full-time job.

'I'm not saying it's a bad thing that she will be back in a career pattern. But I do believe that the holidays we have together – and I have an awful lot of holidays – are an important part of the children's growing up. If she went full time, it would take that element away. Personally, at the moment I don't want that to happen. I want the family to grow up together, I want us all to enjoy that relationship.'

I ask how he thinks Janet will react to his view. He says he honestly doesn't know, it's the first time the situation has arisen. I suggest that under the present conditions it seems that one partner is expected to make more of a sacrifice. He agrees and says he feels it's 'absolutely inevitable'.

'As far as our situation is concerned, I think there's been a number of sacrifices and every time it's been on Janet's part. But if you look back and see what we've done perhaps you can appreciate why it's had to be

her to make the sacrifice rather than me ... I have every intention of
going further in politics, there's no way I would have done it had I not
had her support.

'I mean I know there are times when she's said, "Is it worth it? Is all
the hassle worth it?" and so therefore the sacrifice becomes even more
for her.'

If the situation was reversed and Janet had an ambition to become an
MP, could he accept the change in roles, I ask?

'I think I've got to say I would support her whatever she wanted to
do. I think I would be a little peeved to say the least but we've got a very
good relationship so it would just materialise in the way things have
always materialised.'

I ask for his opinion on feminism. He says he is not an 'outright'
supporter of 'the Germaine Greers'. 'I can appreciate and accept the role
of women in society quite easily. No, it's all the nonsense, the fringe
element I think within the feminist movement – well, within every movement – which always gives it a bad name. I find the women at Greenham
Common quite horrifying at times to see.'

I put to him the argument that if better nursery and crèche facilities
existed then the resources women possess now could be properly used
for the betterment of all.

'I'm not in favour of subsidised crèches all over the place,' he answers
firmly. 'I mean in our own situation there was no way my wife would go
out to work before the children went to school. I don't agree with
providing crèches at all. Everything is about choice. You've got to make
a choice. Sometimes it's a very hard decision, but insofaras we're
living in a free democracy, you have to make the choice yourself. You
mustn't expect the Government to provide these things just because you
want it.'

Unemployment, he offers, may have had some effect on men's attitudes.
'I am quite amazed at how well the men have adapted to being at home
and the women becoming the breadwinners among unemployed families
I've seen ... The menfolk do seem to have taken it on board quite well.
I obviously don't know what goes on while they're together but from
what I've seen, the men seem to help a bit more.

'In our generation the male/female role is very much one of partnership.
But even so,' he adds, 'I think it's going to be one almighty wrench for
the roles to be reversed and accepted. We've come a long way in ten or

fifteen years but there's still a very long way to go before men *really* accept a change in roles.'

I ask if he has always felt he would succeed. 'I think from the time I passed my O-levels and I realised, My God, I can do something now, from that point onwards I've not looked back. Everything I've done has worked out all right. I saw losing in the General Election as only a temporary setback which can be overcome . . . I don't think there's been anything I regret.'

I ask if he's a contented man. 'Yes, I think I am,' he says and laughs. 'I love being in people's company. I'm not a miserable person. I'm a very happy, outward-going person. I just enjoy life.' Is there anything he envies about a woman's lot? 'I don't envy anything about a woman's lot. No,' he says and smiles again. 'No, nothing at all.'

Chris Martin *Stanmore*

At school, Chris Martin worked it out very fast. If he wanted to survive, he had to join the toughies. He had to join them not as an equal but as something they could abuse. If you're a shrimp at four foot nine, there's not a lot of choice. Besides, Chris had always had this fascination with toughies. It was nice to be respected by those considered tough. If you were with them, you didn't have to spread blood on the streets. People assumed you were like them and they left you alone. So the only abuse you took was from your own lot – like being used as a projectile, catapulted down the chemistry bench. Or hung upside down in the gym. And then the first time Martin decided to mix it, he copped it, didn't he?

'You're all thugs,' the headmaster said, 'and Martin, you're the hardest of the lot.' It left little Chris gob-smacked, really speechless.

What happened was this: the hooligans had decided they wanted a different projectile so they picked a non-cooperating participant, a Jewish boy. Now it's Asians who get the stick in school, then it was Jews.

Chris sat on a stool and watched someone else take the abuse for a change. He's a real little wanker, Chris thought to himself, a mummy's little soldier. He kicked and shouted and screamed and cried while four or five tried to pin him down and it was like trying to pin an eel.

What, are you dense or something? Chris said to himself. What a silly little boy. Don't you know if you just let them get on with it you'll get it over? And then the victim kicked Chris right on the shin. Chris jumped off the stool and kicked him back – but Chris had winklepickers on and the boy started crying something wicked like he'd had his legs snapped or something. And that's how Chris was expelled from grammar school at the age of fifteen.

He learnt lessons though – but very few of the kind he was supposed to learn. From the minute he left school, he never got bullied again. He learnt that it's easier to give a poke in the eye than let someone intimidate you. Give'em a poke and see how tough they are. Most have just got a lot of mouth. From then on he never shied from backing his mouth. It had to do with dignity and playing the game. All this toughness, it's a game, isn't it?

In September 1983, I placed a request in the bulletin of the Multiple Sclerosis Society, explaining that I wanted to include a man with MS in the book. I knew the effects the illness can have and, without causing distress, I wanted to find out how a man copes when the alleged foundations of masculinity, virility, independence, the macho image, begin to subside.

The first letter I received was from Chris Martin. He said he was thirty-four, he had had MS diagnosed at the age of twenty-seven but he could trace the symptoms back to the age of twenty-three. 'I'm not sure what kind of personality you require,' he wrote, 'but I am sure that you have been inundated with replies from like-minded men such as myself who feel that everything, good or bad, that has ever happened, has happened to them personally. If I never hear from you again,' he added, 'I shall not be in the least offended but I shall merely consider it your loss.'

If the letter seemed a shade bitter (understandably in the circumstances), Chris Martin in person demonstrates a passion for life. Since his second marriage broke up six months ago, he lives alone in a ground-floor council flat. He uses an electric wheelchair to go shopping. He lives on £38 a week invalidity benefit and he says he lives quite well. His last job was in 1981; he was made redundant from a garage. Dependent, Chris is not.

He is still small, five foot six. He wears jeans and a jumper, and looks a little like David Essex; he speaks with the same cockney inflection. The voice is soft, and he smiles as he lights up a cigarette.

The sitting-room has two sofas, a television set, an electric typewriter where Chris is now writing *the* novel, and an ironing board up near the table. He is waiting to move into a purpose-built bungalow. On the table there is a box of Valpolicella, empty bottles of brown ale and a Brian Mills catalogue. The records go back to the sixties; Otis Redding, the Best of the Small Faces. He has a couple of copies of a partwork series on classical music. Modern pop is so bad, he says, he is getting into classical: 'It's mustard.' The room makes you feel at ease. On the table are three framed photographs of children; they could be sisters; each has blonde hair, Chris's smile and a different mother. Rebecca is fourteen, Laura eight and Sue is four. Rebecca is the offspring of Chris's first marriage, Laura is the result of a renewed romance with a childhood sweetheart, Sue is the child of his second marriage; she stays with Chris frequently. 'They're all quality,' he says with pride.

In the kitchen, there is ground coffee percolating and the remains of a beef in wine casserole he made for last night's supper with friends.

The phone rings often. Chris visits a local day centre on a Monday and Thursday. The centre is next door to the church where his two brothers got married. Chris was born and brought up in this area and only left at the age of seventeen for six years in the army. He never wants to leave again, he says. This is his manor.

Chris is second of the six. His father and mother were divorced nine years ago. His father has remarried and lives three miles away, his mother and five brothers and sisters emigrated to Australia. His mum asks Chris to join them but he refuses. His mum is 'mustard'. 'I mean there's nobody like your mum is there? That's the end of it. Me mum's me mum, no ifs or buts. But if you've had a little taste of self-reliance . . .'

His father is a printer, and in Chris's childhood worked nights. His mother used to work in the Civil Service, shops, 'anything'. She expected everyone in the house to do jobs, Chris had to polish the copper tap. His parents, in Chris's opinion, never got on.

'They hated each other for years. He was always in his garden, burying his head in the sand. Bit of an ostrich. "I'm happily married." He just kept on breeding children. Getting his bone home once a week. And the number of children seemed to reflect his virility in his eyes. Even though the marriage was an absolute cock-up, disaster, from the time I was eighteen months old the whole thing was a fuck-up, it really was, between him and my mum. But I was son number two, he went on to have six! What kind of doze is that? Why do you keep having children after you know?

'Mum was a bit angry about the last two. I can remember the explosion in my house when the youngest was born. My God! I must have been nearly sixteen years old.'

His mum wouldn't have considered an abortion, he says. He is anti-abortion too – even in the case of rape or when, like his mother, a woman is forced to bear a fifth and sixth child. 'My second wife had an abortion when she was seventeen, before I ever met her. She thinks it's so clever. She's so smug about it. How can you be smug about murder?'

Chris believes his parents' relationship did not affect him. 'I tried to give my old man some advice once. I said, "This really is bad this, your moaning. Why don't you piss off?" I'm totally different from my Dad. He had maybe one girlfriend before he met and married my mum and after they split up, he had one more girlfriend and married her. Three women, that's terribly frugal by my standards.

'He thinks a man's job is to go out to work, a woman's job is barefoot and pregnant, you know the kind of thing. He's full of shit, he really is. He's walking around behind a cardboard image of Clint Eastwood; tall, silent, dark stranger. He's not, you know. He's short and bald and got too much rabbit for his own good. We don't talk much. He comes over, we have a pint. But it's all passing the time of day stuff . . .'

Chris describes his mum as 'down to earth'. 'The problems my mum had in relation to a man are the same problems my second wife had in relation to me. I think my younger sister is starting to behave that way too.

'Initially they're not frightened of sex. They're good as gold, they're mustard, aren't they? And like with my mum and dad I guess she just got fed up having kids and that put her off – put the block on my old man, he weren't too happy about that. And then my younger sister, she was carrying on like some kind of siren with this fella, got in the club and that just knocked her right out, she don't want no more now like, she don't want none of it. And that's exactly what happened to my old lady.'

Chris married his second wife Maureen in 1977. She was twenty-six, they met in a pub and lived together for a year. They were on a trainee pub managers' course and it stipulated couples should be married, so they married.

'Guess what she told me on the honeymoon apart from that she loved me out of sight,' Chris says. '"I'm not going back to that bloody pub." Thank you very much dear, I just married you on the strength of that.'

Six months after the marriage, Chris's MS was diagnosed. He withdrew into himself for two weeks after that, he says, to come to terms with the shock. 'Once I got over that, I turned back and the door was bloody shut wasn't it? I only lasted two weeks but she kept it up for six bloody years. I thought the MS was very unfair on her. It was her I felt sorry for, and it hit her bad, but she turned her back on me.

'At first she said it hurt and I thought, Perhaps it does. "Why don't you go to the Doctor's?" I said. And it kind of just drifted on and suddenly she was in the club and then the door came down, clap, not even once a month any more, "I'm pregnant now, I can't . . ." So, fucking hell, here we go.

'We tried for a baby after I was diagnosed, so it was my idea. I wanted to have a child that I could get close to as an able-bodied person. Should the worst come my way, it would be no big deal, because the child would already love me, I would still be her daddy. No matter how bad I got I would always be her daddy because I didn't start off sitting on my arse. Does that make sense? Something like that anyway.

'As I got sicker and sicker I became less and less inclined to get rid of my housekeeper, if you like.

'It's very hard work to have a marriage with a non-physical side and a non-intellectual side. I mean that was her whole life, the damn TV, it drove me bloody mad. There was no conversation, no physical thing, except when people were here, if there was an audience she was mustard, all over me like – this is the loving wife of the poor little cripple, you know, and everyone was telling me what a lovely woman I've got for a wife. As soon as they'd gone, like, it was back in the chair, turn the telly on.'

Chris says he consciously did nothing in the house. 'In my first marriage, my first wife wasn't very good at things like housework. Who's the donkey that ends up doing the bloody washing and ironing and stuff like that? I swore that was never going to happen to me again. I was getting nothing from Maureen, she was giving me no reason to be an appreciative husband and wash-up or Hoover up every now and again, or anything. She was giving me nothing. All she was supplying was two hot meals a day because she'd still be lazing in bed when I got up for breakfast.

'We kept up a very good front, though. We still do now. If Sue's not here Maureen won't come in on her own, she rather fears for her life.

'She used to say I felt sorry for myself, I nearly attacked her then because I feel sorry for a lot of people but I don't think I felt sorry for me and I resent people implying that I feel sorry for myself. I think that I cope bloody well and it's quite an insult for somebody to –

'If she'd been closer, she'd have had no teeth, and she could have said what she liked through her false teeth.'

On paper, the words sound more violent than they are in delivery. Chris's tone is not so much angry as self-mocking. He brings out a photo album. One snap, fuzzy like a good memory, shows three soldiers and a piece of machinery. Chris was in the Royal Electrical and Mechanical Engineers, REME. He did well at first, 'a golden boy', made a sergeant at twenty-three, 'the youngest'. Then it all went wrong. He was serving in Northern Ireland and he got busted to Corporal. He didn't want to play the game any more, he says; or then again, maybe it was the MS.

The man in the photo with him was a mate. 'We spent all that Saturday really pissed off making that thing work and he went out on the Saturday night to a bomb scare or whatever and he got blown up. The very same day. It's a very poignant photograph, that.'

Still in his teens, Chris began popping pills on weekend leave from the army; black and whites, green and whites. On Monday, back on parade, he'd be on a comedown. On one occasion, he cheeked an officer.

'This Major, he's sitting there with his glasses and looking terribly prim and ex-bloody university and he's telling me what garbage I am and I belong in the gutter . . . I'm on a comedown, it isn't fair. I feel like I'm dying. So I grabbed hold of him and I pulled him over and I said, "Bollocks, bollocks, bollocks." And when I'd run out of bollocks, I put him back and started laughing at him. He said, "I feel there's something upsetting you, young man."

'He charges me a minimum fine, £2. He could've had me in the slammer. The Sergeant-Major marched me out left, right, left, right. I was standing outside and he put his arm around my shoulder. "I've been in the Army a long time son, if you've any problems, you come and have a little chat with me" – which was very touching. And I really blew it. I laughed.

'I felt that big, he just walked away in disgust. I felt wretched really because he was being so nice and I'd laughed right in his bloody face.'

One of the photos in the album shows a young couple, both tanned. The girl is slim with a beehive and an evening dress, the boy has Chris's smile. Julie, Chris's first wife, monopolises all the superlatives in his vocabulary. She was a smasher, magic, the most exciting woman he'd ever met, a toughie, a nutcase, mustard.

They met because Julie used to push pills and Chris was buying. He married her when he was nineteen. Rebecca is the child of the marriage. After six years the pair were divorced, and Julie died later of an overdose. Chris had custody of Rebecca for two years at his parents' house. 'I was mini-cabbing by then but was always there for her bedtime, no matter what.' The maternal grandmother fought and won custody. 'That choked me off more than anything, losing Rebecca. How can it happen?

'I was crazy about Julie. But never once was I sexually jealous. She had quite a past behind her. She was the talk of the town, she was such a goer. But it didn't matter. My second wife, she'd tried it with three or four blokes before she met me yet I wouldn't have trusted her further than I could throw her. You work it out. My first wife was a right little slag when I met her but she never dumped on me while we were together . . .'

At one stage, Chris and Julie spent a month in a psychiatric hospital 'drying out'; Rebecca stayed with Julie's mum. After that, Chris stayed away from drugs but Julie grew more addicted. He was given a compassionate discharge from the army, where if all had gone well he might have become a 'shopfloor engineer'. Sometimes he feels regret at the missed opportunity, he says, but mostly he feels it was what had to be.

At home, Chris gradually did more in the house as Julie's pill-popping grew more frequent.

'If I wanted a shirt . . . There wasn't always a clean shirt so I'd get fed up and I'd do all the washing – I couldn't just wash one shirt – chuck it all in, you know, and it'd go on like that.

'I can never explain that relationship, never. I loved her – or *perhaps* I loved her. She was very affectionate but very hard as well. She'd put her fists up at me. She was a right toughie.

'We never talked about my feelings. I never had any feelings in them days, I was too tough. Tough boys don't have feelings, they . . . I find it easier lately, . . . I almost want to be able to talk to somebody, anybody. Just sitting here talking to you about the whole business is quite a relief to me – just to talk, it might be a load of garbage . . .

'Julie and I used to talk but mostly we were just so in love there was nothing to say. We felt secure with each other.

'In the end it just all went wrong. I wanted out. I was still determined I was going to have the world by the balls. I wanted some of it, not all of it but some of it . . .'

He falls in love easily, he says. 'But I know the difference, falling in love ain't loving somebody, it's different.

'It's the gentleness of falling in love and all that crap that blows your mind. You're so full of shit you can't see what it's all about.' In his day,

Chris says, he would have slept with a woman he didn't like because
'I was always after crumble.' He learnt about sex in Hamburg's
Reeperbahn, and if he had an eighteen-year-old son he'd give him a visit as
a birthday present. 'It's better than learning about it at the back of the
Odeon.

'Sex is something different between men and women. I'm glad it is
because I don't think I could live in the same world if women behaved
as men do. I think for men, it's something to do with dropping the seed
– very heavy stuff really,' he adds, smiling suddenly.

'Like a bloke could come and have a wash and nobody would ever
know the difference but a woman's got to wait twenty-four hours before
she's dropped it all.

'That's what male jealousy is all about. That's what upsets a man. The
thought that another man has come his lot in the same hole as you're
poking. Who's been here before me?

'Can I really be crude?' he asks. 'The women I've known, they don't
want to make love, they just want to be fucked and that's it. They just
want to lay there and read a cookbook and be screwed, you know,
without putting any effort into it at all. Well I used to love all that when
I was younger and it all worked for me anyway. Now I need to make
love before the equipment works. Women aren't really interested in
making love, they just want to be screwed.

'They just like to lay there and have fantasies or whatever women do,
you know, I'm not much of a conversationalist once I get going, especially
not deep conversation, you know. It would all be incongruous. But that's
how I see it, that women just want a man to have them, they want to be
dominated and all that crap. The women in my life have never had no
time for the gentler side of sex, the feeling side of sex.

'I thought that was what women were supposed to be interested in.
But I have got nearly two decades of women and I have never met one
like it and I have been round the block. I've had probably more than my
share.

'The only difference now is that women are a bit more brassy about
the whole thing. You know, they want to talk about it to each other in
the swing park with all the kids running around them.

'We've all got soft spots and nobody denies that we need women but
you only actually need them for a little while . . . the price is too high, it
is for me anyway. I'm sick to death of women. I love going to bed with

women, that's what I need a woman for, for what you call physical release
or whatever. I enjoy sex and I enjoy the companionship of a woman but
that's not good enough for them. They've got to start dictating your
lifestyle to you.

'They tell you which radio programme you're going to listen to, which
television programme you're going to watch, what time you're going to
bed. Oh, it just gets out of hand.

'Maybe women are looking for something men can't be. I mean they're
getting porno pumped down them on the radio, on the TV. All these
fantastic sex lives everybody's got and I don't believe it. I'm sorry, I don't.
I've never experienced it. It's all dream stuff, they're totally gullible. They
get married for the wrong reasons.'

We discuss pornography, which Chris says he finds boring. *Mayfair*
makes him feel 'frisky' but blue movies he finds a turn-off. 'Half the secret
of sex is the secrecy, isn't it? A half-clothed girl really does my mind. A
naked woman, so what?'

Chris recently ended a relationship with Jane, a twenty-five year old.
They still see one another but only casually. Chris felt he'd overextended
himself, 'what with age and MS'. From time to time now, he has difficulty
getting an erection.

'The old chap still works but at the same time he's prone to let me
down now and then. He gets you started. He gives you a little bite of the
cherry and then he runs off. It's very frustrating. I have to break off from
what I'm doing and find another way because there are other ways of
satisfying a woman.

'The most recent occasion was when this girl stayed over the weekend
and we started to make love quite early in the morning. The old chap
failed halfway through, you see, before my orgasm. This happened four
times throughout the course of the day. Afterwards she said, "I don't
care." She didn't need to, she'd had four orgasms.'

I ask how he has come to terms with occasional impotency. 'I don't
believe in impotency,' he says. 'Maybe I should be with a woman whom
I really like rather than a woman who just opens her legs. I'm sure it
makes all the difference.'

At one stage, Chris and Jane discussed living together. He would be
the houseperson, she would continue her career in the Civil Service. He
didn't see a domestic role for himself coming in conflict with his desire
to be seen to be 'a Man'. 'It's knowing what's inside yourself that tells

you you're a man, anyway. You've done it, you've proved yourself. You've never flinched, all that kind of crap.'

One of the people Chris most admires is his friend Billy. He is a year or two older, a veteran toughie now in semi-retirement. Well, of sorts. 'The man was a thug and obviously, as he's got older, he's mellowed and he doesn't walk around the streets being a thug any more. He's making a determined effort to establish himself and make a regular way of life. He was a tough but he's never given me a bad time. He's always shown me respect. That's what happens. Don't ask me why.

'People like Billy acknowledge I've a big mouth but they still give me respect as if I'm a big toughie. As if I'm a bit tasty, a bit special. I love all that.'

Chris has a private joke on Billy. A girl at the pub, aged fifteen, has a shine for him, Chris says. As soon as her sixteenth birthday comes by, Chris is going to lay her – and Billy can't come in any faster. Not unless he wants to be in trouble with the law for having intercourse under the age of consent. 'That'll upset him something wicked, she's a lovely girl,' Chris says.

The effects of MS must have caused Chris to think again about what may or may not be 'tough', I suggest.

'Getting MS knocked the wind out of my sails,' he answers. 'But I can still be tough. I still have the same outlook though with more trepidation. Perhaps that's the right way to put it. But I still admire the same things, respect the same things, have the same feelings. I talk a really good fight, I really do. Show me the tough man that wants a fight with me or wants to bully me. I'll destroy the man.' Has Billy ever shed a tear or really shown his feelings, I ask?

'I think he has, I've seen him,' Chris says. 'I think with men you've got to read between the lines. It's alien to the macho man to show his feelings. Boys don't cry and all that kind of crap.

'A man being macho isn't fighting against other men, it's to impress a woman or the women around him. The woman should know that the man will stand up for her and her children. That's what it's all about. I can't understand why women want all men to run around hanging on the hem of their skirt and snivelling.

'Billy is a married man but a few years back he had this very lively affair with a younger woman and it was me that he confided in because he needed to talk to somebody. It's not the sort of thing you go and shout from the tallest building you know, it's a very intimate thing to reveal to your mate how you feel about a woman. He was head over heels in love with this girl. He went overboard, he really did.

'He's a real man. A man is entitled to have a soft centre. Spit in Billy's eye and see how long your head stays on your shoulders. Ask him to do you a favour and he'd do it for you. That's a man. To me it's to be tough and not to keep trying to shove it up everybody's nose. You are tough, you know it, you've proved it. You don't have to prove it any more.'

Chris says he's become very sentimental of late, 'willing to talk about these feelings I've suppressed or hid or whatever before. I was watching Torvill and Dean win that thing the other day to Ravel's Bolero and I tell you no porky pies [lies], I felt a tear in my eye.

'It was surely the most beautiful thing you ever saw and I thought, Christopher, *what* is going on here? To be so moved is really not the Christopher I've known and loved all these years, is it?'

Has he become more emotional because he feels that is now an acceptable way for a man to behave – or is there some other reason? 'I think it must be the MS,' he says wrily. 'Take that Rocky film, it said something to me about what I haven't got. I think what moved me was that he had love. Love is something I haven't got. Or perhaps I was just feeling bluesy at the time.

'Women don't have to shout about all this Women's Lib stuff,' he adds, 'I don't understand it. They've had it all, all the time. Not on the surface, but behind the scenes. Whose pulling the strings? Bloody women.

'So why do they want to come up to the bar and stand with the chaps? The chaps are the underdogs. I haven't tried to understand Women's Lib because I find it contemptible. When people present stupidity and blame me for it then I treat it with the contempt I feel it deserves.'

I suggest to him that if he hadn't had MS and remained a traditional toughie, never expressing feelings, he would have missed out on something positive. 'All Women's Lib is partly saying is that men should be entitled to those feelings without having to suffer MS to express them,' I add.

'But why,' he replies, 'do you have to be married to a female wrestler before you can feel those feelings?' I ask for his opinion of the Greenham Common women.

'They want to drop one of those missiles on them,' he says. 'What about their children? What about their husbands? What are they trying to prove? It's no longer a demonstration, it's a way of life. They can go through the rest of their lives saying, "I stood up at Greenham Common." Big deal. So what?

'Why did they stand up there? What are you, a lesbian? You don't like your husband? You're sick of the kids? You're fed up with the mortgage? What's the matter with you, girl?

'I'm not against people having those feelings,' he says, impatient with any idea that Greenham Common might be a statement about the need for peace. 'What upsets me is this: they're using Greenham Common under false pretences. They don't give a damn if a bomb's there.

'Disarming would be a bit like me taking shit when I was at school, wouldn't it? I never took shit after I left school. Why? Not because I had a nuclear bomb but because I was willing to stand up and fight. That is the secret. You've got to show you won't take any shit.'

We talk about his ambitions for his three daughters. He would like Rebecca, the eldest, to show an interest in computers but she wants to be a fashion designer. 'It's a step up. At twelve, she wanted to be a Wimpy waitress,' he adds and smiles.

'It's a very poignant moment in my relationship with her. I want to have a little word with her about the Pill and stuff like that. I care because I'm her dad and I think maybe dads care about their daughters because they're jealous. I've tried to analyse it in my own mind and I think that's what it is.

'I don't want her to go on the Pill. It's the easy way out. Go on the Pill and you can screw who you like. All these young girls take the Pill and get cervical cancer by the time they're twenty.

'My Rebecca is a little baby at fourteen. I don't want her to foul up her own life with an unwanted child or an unwanted pregnancy. That would really do my brains in. Then I would have to come face to face with my anti-abortion views. That's really dumping it on my doorstep because for a young girl to have a baby, it can ruin her life. I'm well aware of that.

'Rebecca will fly the nest pretty soon, I think. To a man or her own place or something. I'd like to influence her but mostly I want to be her friend. Whatever she does, she's going to do anyway.'

Given that he's been married twice, didn't Chris feel he might want to suggest to Rebecca that marriage isn't as easy as it seems, perhaps? 'I have to be very wary there,' he replies. 'If I start slagging marriage down, in effect, I'm slagging her mother down, aren't I? I married her mother when she was nineteen. I wouldn't want that for my daughters but I've got to find a clever way of putting it.

'Rebecca is well aware of the drugs but she isn't aware of the men her mother had before I met her. She'd been halfway through the bloody borough by the time she was sixteen. I would just die if that happened to my Rebecca. I really would.'

On the second occasion we meet, it is Chris's thirty-fifth birthday. He has a telephone call from his mother in Australia. He spends much of his time listening, occasionally he interrupts to tease her gently.

In the time we are together, Chris presents a puzzle. While he says he is a toughie, and probably was, he still seems very vulnerable; a shell of sensitivity doesn't seem much of a protective shield. I challenge his views more than with any of the men I meet and he never shows anger. On the contrary, while much of what he says may read as if life has offered disappointments and given him some harsh views particularly about some women, in person he actually conveys an optimism, a decency. Or is that all part of his charm?

He isn't bitter about MS, he says. 'What's the point?' Sometimes, he does feel isolated. He feels luckier than some victims because he is on a plateau. It may be that the illness won't get worse. He has his independence and his humour still. His second wife finally left six months before our meeting. He now says he is better off without her. 'I'm mustard now,' he adds and grins self-deprecatingly again.

A second telephone call on his birthday comes from Sara. Sara is thirty-one and also has MS. In their teens, Chris and Sara mixed in the same circles but never met. The two have known each other for a few months. Sara lives at home with her parents and is much more dependent. She cannot feed or dress herself, her speech is sometimes incomprehensible. She had a course of treatment which periodically eases her dependency, makes her fluent.

She regularly visits Chris, and he laughs as he recites the mini-catastrophes that occur as they try to cope. Sara comes off the phone and the voice of Sara's mother takes over. Chris spends a long time giving her encouragement, support, he cracks jokes and flirts. A skill he has perfected.

After the call, I ask if he has an image of the ideal woman. 'Not any more,' he says. 'I would have young Sara living in my house tomorrow and that can't be for sexual desire. I would give her the rest of my life to make her life a little more happy. That is one of the unfortunates of the world, is young Sara. I really feel for that girl. I would swop all of my tomorrows,' he adds, suddenly serious, 'if she could have just one week of her yesterdays. That makes me sound an unselfish martyr,' he says, slipping back into his sardonic delivery, 'but really tomorrow doesn't hold much of a big deal for me any more. It wouldn't be much of a sacrifice.

'Sara knows about the hooligans I used to mix with and I think she's impressed by that,' he adds. 'I think they're her kind of men. The kind of man I maybe thought I was. I could still be that man with Sara and not have to prove it. She's well aware of the illness but she sees me as that kind of person so with her, I don't have to prove it. She's mustard, is Sara.'

Robbie McGregor *Derby*

Derby Golf Club is functional; red brick and sliding glass doors. But the view from the terrace, decorated with Martini umbrellas, is spectacular. Robbie McGregor orders half a pint of lager, pâté, plaice and chips and pineapple gateau. He is tall and slim with a neat moustache, dark hair, very white teeth and a two-year-old red Alfa Romeo.

He looks like someone you've met before and suddenly you remember. In the sixties, love comics such as *Valentine* and *Romeo* always cast someone just like Robbie McGregor in the role of the tall, dark, handsome stranger. I think he would regard that as a compliment rather than a demonstration of sexism. He is dressed in a grey suit, pale blue shirt monogrammed on the pocket, a monogrammed tie, and his pale grey leather loafers tone with the suit. He is open and friendly, the kind of person others might refer to as 'good company'. He likes to crack jokes. It runs in the family, he says, everyone does it.

The disadvantage is that even if he goes out for a quiet drink, he is expected to entertain. The bonus is that a joker has a visa into almost any company. And Robbie does not like to stay in; in the evenings if he is alone, he will almost always go out – to his local, for a meal, occasionally to the cinema.

Golf is his major hobby. He began playing under his father's guidance at the age of eleven in his home town of Aberdeen. At seventeen, he says, he was considered one of the best boy players in the north. The standard wasn't very high but it was a boost to his ego. 'I was down on the green and people would say, "There's Robbie McGregor." I used to think it was great. It used to make me feel good. Even now since I've been here, I've won two big competitions. Nothing big *really* but big in the club. And I'm recognised as being a good player. That gives me a good feeling too.'

I asked Rolls Royce in Derby if they could suggest a man in middle management. Robbie McGregor was recommended. He is probably considered a high flyer. He joined the company at the age of twenty-four with a degree in geography from Aberdeen University. He also had shop-floor experience in a variety of factories and building sites and he had completed a post-graduate course in Personnel Management.

He is now in a senior/middle management grade, a Personnel Services Manager, at the head of a department of twenty-one. His work covers job evaluation, salary administration and career development for Personnel staff. Rolls Royce do not like their employees disclosing their salary but Robbie McGregor's is high enough to finance the Alfa Romeo, holidays abroad and a detached three-bedroom house some miles from the plant. His next move up should entitle him to a company car too.

At lunch, he spends much of the time discussing his relationship with Kathleen, who also comes from Aberdeen. He and Kathleen, a nurse, have known each other for ten years. They only began to live together four years ago when Robbie McGregor came to Derby. Interruptions have been brought about by Kathleen's desire to travel; she worked for six months as a nurse in Saudi Arabia and in a few days' time she will leave again for several months and a job in Hong Kong. A couple of years ago, the couple also had a long break when Kathleen returned to Aberdeen.

Kathleen is twenty-nine and at one time did part-time modelling. The relationship has the same momentum as a roller-coaster, Robbie says, it has highs and then it dips again. 'We get on really well, then we sink into the depths, then we're OK again.

'I sometimes think we've had so many arguments that we feel Kathleen's going away is a safety valve, it lets the problems drift out of our system. There's no doubt that absence makes the heart grow fonder. When she comes back, it's a bit strange at first, it takes time to get back together but then you start to build again. It's like recharging your batteries.

'When I met Kathy she fulfilled everything that I wanted at the time. She's got incredibly beautiful eyes. She was my fantasy for many years. At first Kathy would do anything to please me, which she wouldn't do now. I just lived in this fantasy world. I could take her out and everybody would admire her and that made me feel great. I expect everybody goes through that kind of thing. At the same time as she grew more secure she became more independent. I know it was a bit of a fantasy and you can't live that way for ever but it would be nice if it came back now and again, that dependency . . .

'When I first moved away from Aberdeen, Kathy would come down every three weeks and we'd have all that pent-up passion hurled into two days. That was fantastic, holidays were good too and it was good for a while when we first lived together.'

I ask whether he would still choose a naïve young girl as a partner or would he prefer an older person who is established in her own right. 'I could go for either, quite honestly,' he says. 'It would be very, very nice to know a young, attractive girl and teach her . . . it's a kind of powerful feeling when you meet someone who's naïve about sex and teach her things and watch her blossom. I suppose it's the male ego but it gives you an incredibly powerful feeling.

'You can only have that for so long. If she doesn't grow out of her naïvety I think you could get bored and irritated. At the other end of the extreme, I've always found older women very attractive too.

'One of the females I met when Kathy was away wouldn't tell me her age but I think it was forty or forty-two, about ten years older than me anyway, but she was almost like a girl in lots of ways. She was very attractive, very sophisticated, the things I would like in a wife, but I didn't think she was as intelligent as I would like my wife to be.

'We had a nice relationship together, she was quite mature and confident in herself, which I liked as well, so it's both ends of the spectrum.'

In a wife, he says, he would like to have 'an attractive person with a nice personality, one that was easy-going, one that you could take into any sort of company. One that was on the same intellectual level as myself, however high or low that is. I'm not saying I'm intellectual, it's just that really nice feeling when you're on the same wavelength.

'At times, I think I don't really like Kathy. She's an incredibly attractive girl, she's got a good sense of humour, but there *are* times when she does specific things and I feel I don't genuinely like her.

'I'm not sure I'd like to tell you what all the arguments are about – a lot of them are very intimate. We definitely have arguments about the physical side. I would like sex a lot more than she does. Her argument is that if I did a lot more thoughtful things then she would respond more too, sexually. It's a bit of a vicious circle. She feels that I ought to do more around the house and things like that . . .'

As Robbie McGregor talks you can see him striving to be as balanced as possible in his version of events – perhaps the reaction of a person who for a time has been forced to become self-critical. The lines seem well rehearsed too – as if they come from a familiar domestic dialogue.

'I wash the dishes, I Hoover, I do lots of ironing and things like that. Kathy hates shopping, she hates housework. My mother's very very tidy and I've grown up very tidy but I used to find that my mother would tell me to Hoover and then she'd go round saying, "You didn't get right into that corner." And well, so what!

'I really resent that feeling with Kathy that I'm being inspected. I hate the house being really untidy but I don't like the other extreme either. Sometimes the house is an incredible mess, Kathy isn't fixated but she gets annoyed because I can leave the mess there longer than she can.

'My brother Gordon and my brother-in-law Jock, they help around the house and do a lot more cleaning probably than I do. Jack, for instance, is a very good cook. Kathy's really disappointed that I don't cook. I refuse to cook, I'm not interested in it. I'm quite happy if you give me cheese and biscuits. You don't have to cook me a great meal.

'In the house we don't have any routine really, perhaps we ought to. I just sort of hate discipline in life. I like to do it when I feel like it. Still I would feel very guilty if the woman did it all. I've been brought up to think the burden should be shared.

'Now, if she was at home all day, I would expect it then, although not if she had six kids, say. I think I should do more than I do. Maybe I'm too lazy . . . I *would* do it, but I don't do it quick enough for Kathy. Does it all sound so petty?' he asks, possibly more out of a need for reassurance. 'Still, as long as the good times outweight the bad times then you're OK. It's when the reverse happens . . .

'It's funny though,' he adds with a smile. 'Once Kathy is away, I even miss the things which irritate. For instance, Kathy likes to talk for about half an hour when she comes homes to get it out of her system. She'll tell me about this patient or that horrible injury. I don't say anything because it would hurt her feelings but sometimes I feel punch-drunk.

'I nod at the right times and so on and I'll try and help her with any problems – she doesn't always agree, of course. But when I come home I don't want to talk about work and she asks why I don't feel the need. It annoys her that she can't give me support in the same way. Now I feel that if I *did* discuss a work problem she wouldn't necessarily be able to solve it.

'Maybe that's being unfair to her because she's quite bright and logical and she sees things very clearly. I just feel that I can work things out by myself. I don't like asking for advice. Even when I go to my manager, what I'm looking for is approval, not advice. I don't like being obligated.'

Robbie McGregor says he *can* talk to Kathy about his personal feelings – and he does to other friends too. 'My closest friend in Aberdeen tells me things about his marriage that I don't think he would tell other people and because of that, I mention things in my relationship as well. But there are some things I wouldn't tell him which I would a woman friend.

'Practically, I can easily manage on my own but I need to have female company,' he explains. 'Part of it's sexual. I don't think I could go for any great length of time without having a sexual relationship with a woman. When Kathleen goes to Hong Kong I will go out with other girls in the same way she will probably go out with other men. I feel that if she wants to travel, I refuse to sit at home and wait till she comes back all the time. So we have an understanding on that basis.

'I don't just like the sexual side of being with a woman, I also like the closeness. You can speak so frankly to a woman you are close to, there's an intimacy which doesn't exist between men.'

If he takes a woman out, he says he doesn't feel right unless he pays the bill. If the relationship develops then it's a matter of sharing. He and Kathleen don't split everything down the middle because he earns far more and he feels he should meet more of the bills. I ask if this doesn't make Kathy feel disenfranchised.

'It comes up in arguments, Kathy *would* like to pay more. It would make her feel more secure because if she was putting more into the house it would be partly hers. It's my house and my furniture because it was my money that bought it all. I just feel that I earn more, therefore . . . and basically she *hasn't* got the money.'

Robbie McGregor says he has no immediate desire to marry or have children. 'When I look at a lot of my friends, I wouldn't want to swop places with them but I think a lot of them would like to swop places with me. If I meet someone new and they've been married before, I always ask them about their relationship. Some are able to analyse it, some don't really think about it but I find it interesting.

'I don't feel the need for children because I've got a big family, lots of nephews and nieces and I've been babysitting since I was about fourteen. I like their company, I know they like me, I do all sorts of things with them so I don't feel the kind of gap that an only child might.

'My family's always on about getting married because I'm the only one who's still single. I tell them, "What puts me off is I've seen all you." It's a bit of a joke but not entirely. My family has a history of unhappy marriages. My oldest brother is happily married. My next brother's married, divorced, remarried, separated, lived with another woman, had a baby by her, split up and is now married to another woman. My older sister is happily married. Mary's married and divorced and remarried. Aileen married and her husband became an alcoholic so she was divorced too.

'I look at so many marriages and they seem to be fairly happy but they seem to lead such *dull* lives. My life with Kathy isn't dull because we're apart so much of the time but there's always a strong bond. We can see other people but the bond is still there. In a lot of ways I feel sometimes that I have the best of both worlds.'

At Kathleen's hospital, Robbie says that he is known by her surname. Most of the time he finds this amusing but it can be onerous too. 'She told everyone she was married because she got so fed up with comments about her living with her boyfriend. I have to be careful on social occasions. On one occasion I said to one girl who is a Sister, "Well, I'm not sure how much I believe in marriage . . ." then I realised. So I said, "Well I always used to think that but since I've been married . . ." I get a bit irritated at Kathy for putting me into that situation but I can understand how she feels. And it only applies to hospital people whom I don't see that often, everyone else knows.

'It's a double standard. If a male lives with a woman, people act as if he's smart. The woman is treated as if it's something wrong, a bit quirky or she can't get him . . . I don't know how Kathy feels about marriage now . . .

'People have this image, "Oh, he lives with his girlfriend . . ." When Kathy and I split up, my boss, who's about fifty and married, asked me to dinner. He's always going on about it. Anyway I took this older woman who was really quite glamorous and he said, "You never know who he's going to take." It builds up an image which isn't really there.

'If I talk to a girl in the corridor at work, they say, "He's chatting another one up." I think men do it because it's a situation they'd like to be in and they fantasise. Fantasise is too strong a word. I don't mean they lie in bed fantasising. I mean they feel that's what they'd like to be – single, young, lots of girls, living with one girl on one hand and going out with others . . . None of it's really true but I play up to it, I sort of joke about it. "Oh I don't know which one I'll choose tonight." It is a joke but some take it seriously.'

If Kathy is away, meeting women is not a problem, he says. He doesn't feel old, so he will still go to the discos he visited ten years ago. He has met other partners at dances, sometimes it happens in a pub over a drink. 'You meet people sometimes and there's a chemistry, a something, a spark. You can tell instantly that there's a potential for some sort of relationship. I don't think you spark with someone who isn't responsive. Usually it's a mutual thing . . . you can tell just by the way they're looking.

'I've been lucky in that I've met really nice women, some of whom have become good friends after, but I have yet to meet a person whom I could have a lasting relationship with – apart from Kathy.'

Later, Robbie McGregor says that while he has no desire for marriage now, he wouldn't like to think of himself as single at fifty. He believes that marriage implies a greater commitment than just living together, 'a commitment to give each other that special kind of security . . .

'At fifty, I'll probably be bald and fat and less attractive by the year,' he adds self-mockingly. 'It will be more and more difficult to draw the kind of woman I like. I just have this feeling I'd hate to be old and single.'

How much do looks matter to him? 'Looks are very important to me,' he answers honestly. 'I sometimes wish that wasn't the case but it is. That's just the way I am.' I ask if he has always been good looking – and he neither protests nor grows coy but handles it – like a man. 'I have my hangups,' he replies, smiling. 'Like that I'm going to go bald. I always think that I've a big nose. Things people say when you're really young hurt you. I used to be much thinner than I am now and it's not nice being too skinny.

'I don't think of myself as being good-looking. I see so many other people who have got all sorts of things that I would like but I just try to take things as they come. I'll be very disappointed if I *do* go bald but there's no sense worrying while I've got hair – it's wasting what hair I've got.

'One think I am very lucky with is very white teeth. It's hereditary – even the dog has good teeth! If there is one attribute that I would be allowed to have, it would be nice teeth. If I meet someone, one of the first things I notice is their mouth and teeth. Especially when you look at some people and think, actually, I could really kiss her . . .'

I ask if, on the days he feels a bit rough, it has an effect on his confidence.

'You feel better if your hair's washed and you don't have spots on your face. You feel better but it doesn't make me do my job any better. I don't have bags of confidence but I think I'm more of an extrovert than anything else. In my job I have to make presentations in front of a lot of people. I've always liked giving them and speeches because I tell jokes. I like making things funny all the time. I mean when I come to work and we go out for a pint I really dominate the conversation a lot with jokes and stories. I feel I've had so many funny things happen to me I've a lot of stories to tell . . .'

After lunch, Robbie McGregor drives us to his office in the Rolls Royce plant, part of a complex which covers several sites in Derby and employs 15,000 in all, making aero-engines.

In the car, a pile of cassettes gives a clue to his taste in music: Rose Royce, Hot Chocolate, Michael Jackson. He says he has been lucky in love. In his last year in the sixth form he began to go out with a girl in the same year. The romance lasted another five years. Once they decided to make love, they were quite methodical about it, taking books out of the library, reading about it and learning together by trial and error. The result was very satisfactory to both.

'A lot of men rely on one-night stands. How can you ever learn how to please someone when you don't even have the chance to get to know the person you're with . . . ? I felt very fortunate that I started in the way I did. I don't feel at all inhibited.' Earlier he had said that while he finds it easy to show a great deal of affection to girlfriends, he finds it much harder to be demonstrative to his parents.

'I just felt that when my parents were going back to Aberdeen after visiting me, I could have easily said, "Have a nice journey," and put my arms round my father. He's getting on, I wonder when I'm going to see him again but I can't do it. I couldn't put my arms around a man because I've just never been used to doing it. I've never been used to showing affection outwardly to any of my family . . . but with a girlfriend I could put my arms around her and give her a great big kiss. I love to show that affection because I like it in return.'

Robbie McGregor's mother is sixty-eight, his father seventy-three. His father was a docker for thirty-seven years and then became a watchman in a hospital for seven years. His mother still works part-time as a fish filleter. 'I grew up with that fishy smell with my mother. My brother was also a fishmarket porter. He'd come home and his clothes also had that stench. I grew up with it so it wasn't so bad. In Aberdeen too there's quite often a smell of fish which invades the town.'

Robbie's mother began full-time work when he was ten, he is the youngest of six – three boys and three girls. His parents married when they were nineteen and twenty-four and have lived in the same council house since 1937.

'We all had jobs. The girls when they were young did the housework. I had to polish the stairs and wash the dishes. We lived in a house with two bedrooms. My mother and father had one and the six of us slept in the other. I have a vision, not very clear, when we were young that I used to sleep between two sisters. We had a hole in the springs of the bed. I remember waking up with my feet sticking out and me down this hole.'

His father has always helped in the house, he says. Each of the children has a different image of him. Robbie as the youngest felt close to him, the girls in particular had a tougher time. He forbade them to wear make-up, and if they weren't home by ten p.m. he would go and find them. 'My sisters had a terrible life.

'I think my parents were happy together. My mother is a strong, forceful kind of character, but at the end of the day it's my father who decides. My mother's always quite happy to be dominated by her man even though she is strong-willed. They've split up, they've been apart, they've all been out of the house at some time except me. I can remember one Christmas, they had a row and my father threw my mother out. I was the only one left and he wouldn't let me go. He was never violent, he would never hit me . . . I can genuinely say that my mother really loves my father and always has.

'I just don't think my mother could have survived on her own. I mean she relies so much on my father. She leaves money and so on up to my father. To a certain extent my father's much more independent and could have survived without my mother but after all this time . . .

'I remember there were times when I was young I used to lie in bed and I would hear noises coming from their bedroom but I was always grateful to hear that. After the good times and the bad times, it was good that they enjoyed each other.'

Has he ever thought his father felt trapped in the relationship? 'I don't know really, because I never had that kind of conversation where I could say, "How do you feel about your relationship with mother?" and things like that. He may tell me, he may not, but I never found I could ask a question like that. It's funny, although we're a close family I think, we don't get into intimate conversations with our parents. Maybe it's because I'm so young, maybe my older brothers and sisters might ask more about it.'

He says that he thinks his older brothers and sisters have a very different view of family life from his own. 'My sisters especially absolutely hated my father. Now, my father is a really nice person. He's got a nice moral sense of values. He worked on the docks for years, he never drinks, never swears but that doesn't mean to say he's very straight. He's quite a hard man, I've never seen him cry. He's got a fantastic sense of humour. He's just a likeable person. Sometimes things my sisters say like, "I'll never forget him doing that . . ." or "I can never forgive him doing this", which I don't think they mean. He *is* their father and now he's as nice as anything with them and all their husbands.

'I like my sisters,' Robbie McGregor volunteers. 'I've got one sister who's very outgoing, quite independent and a good sense of humour. She's probably the type of person that I would quite like as a partner. My other sister is quiet and introvert and I couldn't go out with a woman like that. I like to get a lot of laughs out of life.

'I would hate to have a wife who was just at home. People are much more interesting if they're working and doing a job. I mean sitting at home all day is inconceivable really. What have you got to talk about at night? What do they have to stimulate them? I would really encourage my wife to work.'

Robbie McGregor says his relationship with his mother has always been difficult. 'I would always go further with my mother and get the occasional crack around the ear. I didn't like my father to be annoyed with me because I liked him. It was enough if he got angry.

'My mother and I really rubbed each other up the wrong way. If she said black, I said white. I don't know why. But a lot of my friends say they had the same problems with their mothers. She exaggerated a lot of things. She would put in extra bits if she was telling a story and I used to get annoyed. It's funny because Kathleen gets annoyed with me for exaggerating in exactly the same way.

'My mother used to say I never talked to her enough about my feelings and so on. When I split up with my girlfriend before Kathy my mother really liked her and wanted to know why. It's just that I couldn't explain to her. I didn't feel she was on the same level. Anything I said, she'd say,

"Oh, you're funny, you are . . ." If you didn't see things the same way as my mother, you were weird, you know. I just used to laugh it off.

'I think she's fairly irrational about things, very defensive. I remember when I was a kid and she was going through a bad spell with my father, she could be difficult most of the time. If I brought friends into the house to play, I had to do it when she was out. If she came in and saw them, she'd go wild. I didn't feel the need for my mother's approval because we had so many rows and differences.

'My sisters used to tell me to agree with my mother just for the sake of peace. I used to say, "But she's wrong, she's wrong". I can't agree just for the sake of peace and that's been the source of all the problems. I see now that she's honest and straight and we get on better because I can, for a time, keep my opinions to myself.'

Robbie McGregor says he was always lazy at school, but he was the only one of the six to go to university. Others matched his intelligence or outstripped it but the family didn't have the finance. His mother would have preferred that he left school early. He had the chance of jobs as a fish-market porter or the docks, the equivalent in some people's eyes to a lifelong pension, but he had decided that he wanted to continue his education.

He doesn't know why, he says now. It wasn't a conscious attempt at self-improvement or even the drive of ambition.

'I'd enjoyed school, I'd played for the school rugby and cricket and volleyball teams. I had good friends. I liked the camaraderie. I wanted to go to university because I didn't want to work. It wasn't laziness, it was just I hadn't a clue what I wanted to do . . .'

Robbie McGregor had to do an extra year in the sixth form to get his necessary A-levels. Then he did a fourth year at Aberdeen University when he failed Logic (the only exam he did fail) in his third and what should have been his final year.

'My family were disappointed, I'd never failed before, but I expected it. I'd lived at home while I was at university and really enjoyed the social side of it all . . .'

During and after university, he took a variety of jobs to pay back the money he'd borrowed from his parents.

'The worst job I had was in a fish factory. I had to put fish fillets in vats of yellow dye. I used to go home with bright yellow hands and no one would sit next to me on the bus. One day the water was freezing and I saw some had rubber gloves so I asked the little foreman, quite a nice bloke, if I could have a pair. He said, "Look laddie, a job like this puts hairs on your chest like sticks of rhubarb."

'Another time, we had to lay fish out right opposite the freezer door. Every time it opened, it was like an arctic gale and it hit us all – mostly women were employed. So I asked the production manager, who was also the personnel manager – can you imagine that? – if we could move it all away from the door. His reply was, "If you're not fucking happy, leave".

'That was fifteen years ago, but it hasn't improved that much. My mother, when she fillets fish in the winter, stands in bowls of hot water in her wellies. I mean in this day and age that's incredible but she doesn't think anything of it. It breeds a certain kind of woman who works in those factories.

'The women all used to treat me well. They knew my mother, they knew I'd grown up with the same type of people. You would hear some terrible things, I mean unrepeatable things about sex and so on but you just laughed at it. I would always tell jokes and it was good to work with them, it really was.'

I ask if his experience was the reason why he entered personnel work. Had he a mission to change and improve?

'It would be nice to say I did,' he says with a smile, 'but I didn't.' He didn't want to be a teacher, he felt personnel was the least cut-throat part of industry; so it was a process of elimination.

At first, he worked for Rolls Royce as Personnel Manager at a factory with 2,500 employees in East Kilbride; a job he very much liked. He was twenty-eight and in charge of people twice his age. He sought their advice, he says, but he soon realised the difference between himself and them. 'They just didn't want to make decisions. If they *had* wanted to make decisions they would have gone further.

'I mean when I first came to that job I had managers threatening me. You had to sit back and listen to the guy with a smile on your face. I had one manager on the shop floor who wanted me to do something and I said, "No I can't do it." He says, "I want you to do it." I said, "No." He bent across the table, looked right in my eyes and says, "If you don't do that I'm going to fucking fix you." I sat there and said, "Well it's up to you but I'm not doing it."

'I was just waiting for him to stick a knife right in me at that point. I just thought to myself that it was going to be awful. That's the kind of thing – they try to bully you. This guy used to say to me, "I had none of this kind of trouble with the last Personnel Manager," and I used to say, "No, that's why he's gone and I'm here." I always used to manage to come back with an answer to them all the time and at meetings as well you really had to live on your wits. But I like the challenge, there's a satisfaction in it all.'

Robbie McGregor says that he has never had a blueprint for his career – but he has learnt lessons along the way and, more recently, he *has* become ambitious. He failed miserably at his first round of interviews for jobs. 'I had an interview with British Steel, and again I just hadn't prepared myself for this interview, it was pathetic really. I went in and they said, "What sort of thing would you like to do in Personnel?" It's funny, I just sort of said the first thing that came into my head: "Well, I just want to be in welfare actually." He just sat back and I thought, God I wish I hadn't said that, and one of his friends who was interviewing next door came and he says, "Oh, come in Del, come and meet Robbie McGregor who wants to hand out the Christmas hampers." I felt about that small.

'He was having a good laugh at my expense, but in a lot of ways he was criticising me for not coming in prepared. After that I made sure I did my homework.

'I'm ambitious now,' he adds, 'but I've also been fairly lucky. I've been in the right place at the right time. It just seems to keep happening for me. Every time I've felt a bit fed-up another door has opened. I could have quite happily stayed in East Kilbride but when the job came up in Derby, I thought to myself, well, I'm going to do a job that I'm not going to like as much but I would be crazy to turn down promotion and that opportunity.

'A reorganisation is due within Rolls Royce within the next two years. If I don't get promoted again then, I'd be willing to move somewhere else although Rolls Royce is a very good company to work for – I just don't want to get stuck.'

Robbie McGregor's workplace is basic. A large office with space for a small conference table, potted plants, formica. It has hints of a 1950s primary school. At first he worked all the time, now he does an extra hour or so at night, more in an emergency, but he doesn't work at weekends. He goes next door to his secretary to make coffee. He has three women who work directly under him and more women in the department. I ask if he could cope with a female boss.

'I honestly don't know,' he says. 'If I had confidence in her and she was quite bright and sharp I don't think I'd have a problem. In the end it's not whether they're male or female but a matter of how much confidence you have in a person.

'I don't think the three women who work for me see me as the Big Boss or anything. They see me as a friend. I don't need to wield any authority at all. I wouldn't be slow to tell them if they didn't do something I asked but they're so conscientious that's not necessary. They're very pleasant, I think they just see me as OK as a manager.

'I think because I've grown up with my sisters, I know how women feel about things. I think most of them look on work not as a career but as a supplement to earnings. We've got a lot of career women too but the others look on work fairly differently, they don't take it as seriously. They *are* conscientious but they don't care if they don't get promotion. My secretary, for instance, she'll work for a few years and then she'll probably want to have a family.

'Supervising women, there's no doubt there *is* a difference,' he reiterates with emphasis. 'For instance, two girls I worked with, one had a very strong will and although the other had a great personality, she was completely dominated by the first. The strong-willed girl would simply withhold her conversation for a day and the other would be all upset. It doesn't really happen with men, they tend to be more independent, less emotional. Or perhaps men just show their emotions in a different way – like losing their tempers?

'I do enjoy work,' he says, 'I do feel that I am a somebody at work. I'm a manager and I tell other people, I don't tell other people what to do – I don't want it to sound as if it's a power thing because I don't feel it *is* a power thing – but it's having the position of authority and enjoying it. I mean,' he adds with irony, 'there's always somebody telling me what to do as well.'

I ask if his parents are proud of his position.

'They really are,' he says. 'Rolls Royce is a big name to them. We come from a working-class street and I think I was the only one to go to university too and my father would say at work, "My son in university . . ." and all that sort of thing. I think they feel quite proud of me in lots of ways but I've never done anything to embarrass them . . .'

In the company of friends in Aberdeen, competitiveness is less of a problem than jealousy, he says. He and some friends who work in oil tend to earn much more so he tries to avoid the subject of money in conversation. 'It makes people feel unnecessarily envious.'

He has no plans for ten years hence, he says, he takes it a move at a time, but in his industry you have to keep pushing. He likes to work but if he received enough money to retire now, he would do so – and he thinks he would do so with no crisis of identity. 'I'd want to travel a lot, I'd want to go round the world, but if it came to the crunch, I would probably need to work at *something* . . . if I had the security and money, I'd probably work for myself.

'If I was made redundant now,' he adds, 'I don't think I'd feel, oh crikey, what can I do? It will never be the same . . . I really feel I'd get another job, I may be wrong but I feel I'd get on OK and life would go on. Things seems to happen to me, I don't know why.'

Scott McIntosh *London*

Scott McIntosh comes from good middle-class stock; his father was a merchant banker. Scott was born in Liverpool, raised in Chester and attended public school. He has a degree in History and Law from Cambridge and followed that with a year at Dartmouth and six years in the Navy, which he left in 1979 with the rank of Sub-Lieutenant. He is now a harbourmaster on the East Coast; he spends seven days on duty and then spends a week's free time in London.

He is a compact man with short cropped hair and a moustache; he is softly spoken without a trace of an accent. In check shirt and jeans, the only clue to his sexual preference is his black leather jacket. Hidden by his shirt is the ring through his nipple. If he wishes to dress in full uniform, Scott McIntosh has a black leather cap, chaps, jacket and boots – an investment of around £200. In a striped suit, however, he would made a perfect merchant banker like his father, definitely a high-flyer.

I wanted to talk to a man who is homosexual and has a particular predilection for leather and sado-masochism, superficially such a caricature of what is considered 'macho', 'butch' and 'masculine'. I wanted to discover if his definitions of 'macho' and 'masculinity' *were*, in fact, an exaggeration of those associated with the traditional heterosexual male, or something different. I wanted to find out how the 'butch' connotations of the leather cult fitted in with a person being 'passive' and therefore arguably the 'feminine' partner in a relationship. How did he feel towards himself, towards women and towards other men, both homosexual and heterosexual? Did his intimacy with another man – albeit at times communicated through the language of pain – nonetheless allow him to display the emotions allegedly denied heterosexual men?

Bryan Derbyshire is the editor of *MCM*, 'a man's mag'; he runs a leather club once a week in a London pub and he has an extensive mail-order business. (Like any hobby, a fetish for leather can cost money: black leather wrist restraints £11 a pair, headmask with zip eyes and mouth £20.50, full suspension harness to hang from the ceiling £40, erection trainer with pouch cover £24. In 1979, I made a film about the

civil rights of homosexuals in London (or the lack of them) and Brian
Derbyshire acted as my guide. He took me to the Coleherne pub in west
London, one of the city's Meccas of leather, and introduced me to the
system of semaphore involving keys and handkerchiefs by which some of
the confusion of the heterosexual world is avoided.

Keys on the left or right hip indicate active or passive; a steel-blue
hanky on the left indicates 'cock and ball torturer', a red hanky on the
right indicates a 'fist fucker', a black hanky on the right indicates 'heavy
S & M bottom', an orange hanky worn on the right signals 'nothing
tonight'. So intricate are the details that it is possibly better for the novice
to leave hankies and keys at home, in case his semaphore equipment gets
irreparably twisted.

The *Shorter Oxford* definitions of Sadism and Masochism make use of
the perhaps anachronistic word 'perversion':

Sadism: a form of sexual perversion marked by cruelty.

Masochism: a form of sexual perversion in which one finds pleasure
in abuse or cruelty from his or her partner.

Scott McIntosh gives sado-masochism a more personal definition. 'The
word "pain" keeps coming up but pain isn't it, you see. Pain hasn't got
a lot to do with it at all. I mean there *are* some people who are into pain,
although I think that's more of a heterosexual S & M thing; the woman
in spiked heels with the whip, that sort of thing.

'A friend of mine who's gay but very much into vanilla sex, straight
sex, said to me, "I can't understand how you get pleasure from inflicting
or receiving pain." I said, "I don't inflict or receive it because pain is a
crushing emotion. If you're suffering pain you don't feel anything else. I
can get a lot of pleasure and release out of giving or receiving intense
sensation." I think *that's* the difference.

'The pain is something you go through to achieve something else, like
the pain barrier in running. It's the fantasy and the intensity of it which
perhaps occurs more for a man than a woman. The whole experience of
orgasm is something which is very muscular in one sense. Say, you're in
something like a sling, you're completely relaxed because there's nothing
you can do, you can't move in it. Or, say you're lying on the bed and
you're shackled to the bed legs using some sort of leather device.

'You're stretched to the point which is not agonising but where your
muscles are in distension. At the same time, you have an orgasm, well
obviously the whole muscular contraction is that much more intense. You

could say, "Does it hurt?" Well the first time you have an orgasm it hurts, doesn't it?

'It's the intensity, I think it's about erotica rather than ways of getting rid of inhibitions. In that sense I think men are more physical. I think women would much prefer to have sex – from the women I know – in a nice room and all the rest of it. There aren't many women who get turned on by having it over dustbins in back alleys but a lot of men do.

'The S & M I like is a different thing from what people who are filled with self-hate like,' he adds. 'Some people are into humiliation, they like being kicked and called a filthy little queer but I think it's a very small minority. That really *is* in the way of a perversion. Sex is for pleasure and that's using the tools for some other purpose, a deeper psychological purpose to expiate some guilt you feel caused by something else.

'I've never had any guilt or feelings of a lack of self-esteem. Fear can be an important element with some people. It isn't with me. I'm not really afraid because I've rationalised myself through that. I've talked to myself about it.

'It's deviant yes. But what is normal? The man who lives in Pinner in a semi-detached house with 2.4 children and a Ford Cortina. He probably dresses up in women's frocks at night. I deviate in many other ways. I'm on the far Right and on the far Left on certain issues, I mean we're all deviant in hundreds of ways, that's what makes us individuals rather than lumps of spam. This is just one of my deviances – everybody's got some.'

Scott McIntosh is an only child. He was a day boy at a public school and had a happy childhood, he says. He feels he was probably closest to his father, who died when Scott was twenty-three. 'My father was a very strong personality but he had the strength that he didn't have to show it. In an argument, he didn't have to shout his way to victory, he could always cope, it wasn't a hassle for him.

'We used to have long discussions particularly in the intense teenage stage about the state of the universe sort of thing. I was always treated as an equal. He did lots of leaping on and off trains and planes but he was away only for nights, not weeks. He conveyed the idea of self-fulfilment, he believed a great deal in that. I can remember if I brought home a school report which wasn't so good, mother was usually the one who would say, "Oh, what's he going to do?" My father used to say, "I'd rather he had a decent career but if he wants to be a dustman, as long as he's happy and a good dustman, it doesn't matter."

'I think he had a difficult childhood in his own case – his father died when he was eleven – and although he liked to have the good things in life around him and he had all the symbols of success, he felt that though they were nice they weren't as important as achieving some sort of satisfaction in life.

'I learnt a lot from him. What I missed most when he died, I missed having a damn good friend, somebody I could talk to.' Scott told his father he was homosexual at twenty-two, after he'd left Cambridge. It came up in a discussion about the next step in his career. 'I discussed it with him and it was a case, in so many words, that "if you want to be a faggot be a good faggot". We had a fairly rational discussion and he sort of said, "Well, you don't have dependents but on the other hand, you do miss some things. I've always loved your mother and been happy but it's not something you can voluntarily change. Are you happy with it?" And I said yes because I'd never been unhappy, I've never worried about being gay at all.

'I suppose because I do have a fair ability to rationalise. I had dialogues with myself. I've never felt it was shameful or worrying. It was perhaps something you didn't tell anyone because they might not understand but I felt the problem was not homosexuality but homophobia. This is one of the things, of course, about being a conventional homosexual, unless you've got the full gear on, no one can tell.'

Homosexuality, he adds with a smile, has caused a lot more misery amongst mothers than it has 'amongst faggots'. 'Where did I go wrong?' being the clarion call. His own mother took it well. She knows he wears leather and is gay but she's never talked to him about it. 'She's never approached me and said, "Now sit down and tell me what you do." I think, somehow, she has often wanted to . . .'

On his father's death, Scott says his mother got through sixty cigarettes and half a bottle of gin a day in an effort to join him. She was 'a helluva sight tougher than she thought, she thrived on the diet!'

She coped with the isolation of being single again for three years and then remarried after an eighteen-month courtship. She is now happily married, active on various committees and on the Church Council.

'We had a difficult period after my father died. She depended on me a very great deal because the only other member of her family she has is her mother. She treated me as though I was my father. The only thing we didn't do was sleep together. I had the car, I dealt with the finances and all the rest of it. And also emotionally. It hurt her at the time I think but one day I said, "Look I'm not my father and I'm not your husband."

'I think one of the drawbacks she found after my father's death was the lack of access to male company and I think one of the things she liked was that I provided male company. I think that's something possibly a lot of women, particularly in that social group, do find. They're cut off from Sundays in the pub, all sorts of activities. It's fine when you're with your husband, it looks different when you're sitting on a bar stool drinking gin and tonic on your own, you may look a bit hard-bitten after a while.'

If his father's motivation was self-fulfilment, Scott's mother's drive was for security – at least until her husband's death. 'My parents' formative years were during the war, when the most exciting thing was a khaki uniform and an Anderson shelter. In the 1950s, everyone had a nice little car and a nice little house and I think my mother wanted the same thing for me.

'She sees security as the old upper middle-class thing – property, a field of bricks and mortar and furniture, carpets and curtains to keep the utter chaos at bay. I think my father believed that when I actually had to do something I would. My mother didn't. She did worry a lot and still does to a certain extend that my life is more bohemian than she would like.

'I don't have the bourgeois symbols of success. I think she'd like a lot more of "My son the doctor . . ." That's something she misses.

'I don't believe there is such a thing as security,' he offers. 'I think we skate on very thin ice and when it cracks everything is taken from you. I lost all my savings in a business two years ago and I learnt that I didn't mind. Of course, I have the advantage that being gay I have no dependents, no children to provide for and so on, therefore it's less of a hassle for me if the house burns down . . . but I do believe that cliché, "Freedom's just another word for nothing's left to lose".

'Once you've lost everything in your life, it doesn't seem to matter much. It teaches you that you don't have to carry on doing anything in life if you don't want to. Possessions are nice but if you lose them, it doesn't really matter.'

Scott's mother is in her fifties, her second husband is a year younger than her son. She was reluctant to marry at first because of the age gap. Since the marriage, Scott says their relationship has grown much easier, he sees his mother four or five weekends a year.

'She's become slightly more conventional since she remarried, because he's conventional. I think from what I can gather, they have a very satisfactory sex life but I believe he only had one girlfriend before my mother.' He adds, smiling, tongue in cheek, 'I mean he only wears white underwear because he considers any other sort slightly kinky. Little things like that are a bit strange.

'We get on well enough. He knows I'm gay but he doesn't talk about it. We talk happily about other things. Once or twice I've been tempted to tease him. Except he's not the sort of man who'd say if he saw a pretty girl, "By jove, she's attractive." So I could then say, "I didn't see her, I was looking at the window cleaner."

'My previous affair used to come up with me for the weekend and he would always either call him "your friend" or by his first name. I think he would have coughed, choked and strangled on the word "lover".' Scott smiles, the tone is more one of gentle observation rather than criticism. 'I feel sorry for him. I think he misses out a lot in life. He does have a certain slightly Whitehouse code of morals. If that's how he wants to play his life, fine, but I do feel sorry for him.'

At school, Scott was part of a group of boys who, he says, were academically very bright. This exempted them from the need to excel at sports and excused them from having to display an interest in girls; only those who weren't going to make it into first-rate universities had girlfriends. It wasn't a matter of sexual preference but an indication of intellectualism if a boy stuck to his books – and succeeded.

'One of my greatest regrets was that games and PT at school were presented in such a bloody awful way that you didn't enjoy it. It must have happened at girls' schools – a heap of thirty of you standing on the edge of a muddy field on a wet day in November and you don't really want to be there. They choose the two who are best at games to be the Captains and then they choose one each. You're down to the last ten and those of you with two left feet are always thinking, Oh for God's sake choose me . . .

'One of my friends got away with it by being completely out of this world. He'd wander around the rugby field, ignoring the ball, looking at the clouds. We would not have got away with it if it hadn't been for the fact that we were the intellectual cream of our year. If we had been thicker, we'd have had a terrible time.

'I am one of those wonderful products of the British Education System,' he offers with a wry smile. 'I haven't been educated with girls since I left the kindergarten. Women were for a long time for me fairly queer cattle. I was never quite sure how they thought. Especially in the teen years when they seem to mature faster than boys. They seemed to have a little machine going on in the back of their heads which produced totally different answers to the machine in my head. I enjoyed school. It was quite asexual really, no scandals, it wasn't an aggressively macho establishment at all.'

At Cambridge, Scott McIntosh knew he either wanted to be a politician or an academic. In politics he was a Conservative, not so much because of the party's collection of policies but because, in his opinion at the time, it seemed to offer more to him as an individual. In the intervening years, he says, he has moved from the Right of the *Telegraph* to the middle of the *Guardian*. He was President of the Monday Club, a member of the Union Committee, a member of the Conservative Association. Again there was no pressure on him to display his heterosexual prowess. His sexual appetites remained dormant. The excuses were available: men outnumbered women so drastically most men had a problem finding a mate and there was too much to do to bother with romance.

At university, the Navy became an attractive proposition as a career partly because of his childhood. 'My grandfather used to work for one of the large Charter companies in West Africa. I used to go down to the docks in Liverpool and I always remember, there used to be a building the tram went past at the Pierhead. Along the side of the building in big Edwardian bronze letters were all the places the ships visited. I used to sit on the top deck of the tram and read "Valparaiso, Port-of-Spain", and think, Wow!'

He also felt influenced by two of his heroes, Stephen Roskill, who was his tutor and the Navy's official historian, and Lord Mountbatten, whom he met a couple of times at Cambridge. 'Mountbatten never had any inner doubts. He was a leader. He was very cool and smooth, I like that. He had style, something I think we lack today. I like achievers.'

In considering whether it should be the Navy or politics, he abandoned the latter because he felt the opportunities to rise weren't so sound. He was also aware, he explains, that in both careers his homosexuality would have to remain discreet if not inactive. 'I had a much lower level of sexuality than I have in my life now. It was always a fairly cold choice.

Did I want to screw around or did I want to do a particular job? I decided on the latter.

'You know it's very strange this, but people always say, "Ho ho, nudge nudge, Navy and public school . . . there must have been a lot going on." And there wasn't. In school, there wasn't the interest, in the Navy there was always the threat of court-martial.'

At seventeen or eighteen, Scott McIntosh did have a couple of girlfriends. 'One had a terrible crush on me, God knows why. The other girl, this sounds terrible but I took her off one of my friends just to see if I could, she was a very thin layer of ice over a seething mass of sexuality. You only had to touch her and "Pow!"'

'She looked fairly innocent and pure and you'd start with this innocent kiss just to prove you could actually get a kiss off a girl and you were almost dragged in – slurp! – like a vacuum suction. It didn't frighten or worry me, it just didn't particularly interest me . . .'

In the Navy he slept with two prostitutes, experiences which gave him a feeling akin to the aftermath of a Chinese meal: 'Half an hour later, I wanted something else. It just didn't satisfy me. I didn't feel any pleasure out of it. I certainly didn't feel any revulsion. It just isn't me.

'People think if you love men you dislike women but I don't dislike women. I've always said, I dislike certain men, I dislike certain women. I've had a fair number of dealings with women . . . I had twenty Wren writers working for me, I've worked in factories with women, I had women staff when I had my own business. I can deal with them as people. I don't have the terrible thing that a lot of men have, you know, they've got to prove . . . "I'll take you to bed, I'll give you a good time because I'm wonderful . . ."'

We talk about the sexual competitiveness of men and the locker-room mentality which doesn't exist among women. 'All men are interested to compare the size of their penis. Whether they will be utterly revolted by the idea of touching another man or not. They always do it; to use a quaint Glasgow phrase, they're "willy watchers".

'Dogs do it as well, don't they? The one with the biggest ends up as the boss of the pack. It's instinctive, perhaps it's as basic and primitive as that. The man with the biggest prick and muscles gets the best women. I don't think women feel their femininity resides in the same place – it doesn't reside in muscles and genitals.

'When a woman is aroused it's not so fast and not so obvious. At sixteen or seventeen, you take off your clothes and a lot of people instantly become semi-erect and somebody sooner or later is going to start playing around; some like it, some turn hysterical, some don't bother and some people think, Gosh, this is fun, isn't it?'

Scott McIntosh says he can't recall ever having any sexual ideas or fantasies about women. His first interest in boys could have been around five, but certainly by his teens. I ask him what, for him, makes the male image and not the female image erotic?

'It's similar things which women find attractive. Muscles, a solid muscular chest, body hair I find very attractive. I like the smell of men, not the sweaty smell but the body odour that a healthy normal well-washed person gives off. I like the look of men.

'I like body hair and there aren't that many bearded women about,' he smiles. 'I have positive turn-offs, such as long hair. Even the most wonderful man who's got long hair won't do anything for me. I don't like the softness of women and that's one of the reasons why I don't like young men - they're soft. I don't like the soft, slightly pliable feel of a woman. I like a feeling of hardness.

'Macho,' he adds, 'means something different in the gay world from the heterosexual world. Macho among straight men tends to mean they watch *Match of the Day*, drink beer, spill pizza on the carpet, treat their wives like ratbags. Now that doesn't interest me at all.

'Macho to me, I suppose, means a certain self-assurance. It doesn't impress me if you have big cars and tight trousers and drive at ninety m.p.h. down the middle of the A1. I like coolness and strength.

'One of the most masculine men I know is ninety-nine per cent passive and a hundred per cent gay. I don't think masculinity necessarily has to do with which side you are up when you're actually copulating. I don't know if heterosexual men are missing anything from not experiencing being the passive partner.

'The physical sensation of being sexually penetrated is a different physical sensation from that of penetrating. Apart from the emotional feelings which are different, you've got to accept that for the first time here is somebody coming into you which is a different thing altogether. You're allowing somebody into your intimate body space which I suppose women might sometimes find repugnant if they're with somebody they don't like.

'It is an invasion but there is something else which women must feel as well, the physically pleasant thing about it. The construction of the apparatus you're using is that most of the nerve endings are at the entrance and inside it's relatively dead. At the same time, when it's filled with penis there is a feeling of fullness, of satisfaction which is totally different from the feeling a man gets when he penetrates.'

Does he think having access to those feelings makes him different from a heterosexual man, I ask? 'I think it gives me an insight, possibly it gives me more of an understanding of how women feel sexually. I've had occasions when I've had a bad sexual trip when I've been penetrated by somebody and for no reason I can explain, I've found I just don't enjoy the person, they're imposing their person into you. I can understand perhaps more than a lot of straight men how repugnant that can be for a woman.'

Will he or his partner feel secure enough to act in what is termed a 'womanly' way – not effeminately but being open about their emotions? Does that fit into his definition of 'masculinity'?

'Oh, very much so,' he replies. 'Some people can't do it. Some women can't show their feelings. If you look at my partner and me, I'm the physically bigger one, older, I'm usually the sexually active one but there have been occasions when I've got into bed with Neil and I've cried and I've been able to say those things which all men feel but most men can't say like, "I'm terrified . . ." "What of?" "Well, you know, everything . . . I open the door and there it all is . . . I'm a man and I'm supposed to be able to do certain things and some days I'm too frightened to even buy a bloody tube ticket . . ." One weekend with Neil I was just very very depressed and for about three hours, I just fell apart and he built me up.

'I've helped him too when he's been depressed. Neither of us holds that against each other in any sense and I felt the same with other people with whom I've had meaningful relationships.' Does he think he could have been so demonstrative if he had been heterosexual? 'Probably not,' he replies. 'Jean Genet says in one of his books, "A male who fucks another male is a double male." I don't agree with that but I do feel I'm fortunate in being able to have a really intimate relationship.

'OK, I'm fortunate in one way,' he offers. 'I haven't had a proper loving sexual relationship with a woman, but I don't feel that I'm missing something. If someone could come round tomorrow and wave a magic wand and say, "Do you want to be straight?" my answer would be no. I don't feel any inadequacy or lack as I am.'

It was not until 1979 that Scott McIntosh 'came out' as a homosexual. In 1972–3 he had spent a year at Dartmouth, which he 'cordially disliked'. 'Dartmouth is a case of mind over matter. We don't mind and you don't matter. Rules were totally footling most of the time. But I think it's deliberate.

'At Dartmouth, they found your weak spots and kept poking at them until they hardened and scabbed over – which is sensible, it's got to happen at some time in your life. My weak spots are that I tend to feel sorry for myself. If I think something is stupid, I tend to let people know ... In the end I quite enjoyed the place, it gave me a certain inner strength.'

After six years in the Navy, at sea and on shore, he developed an ulcer which meant he was likely to be landlocked for another three or four years. That and the lack of promotion in sight decided him that he should leave. The Navy, he says, is an 'extraordinary institution', he draws a parallel with his naval experience and the experience of a girl in a convent school. 'It's something that's with you for life, we've all been through the same sausage machine. It's a bit like a secular monastery. It should be a vocation more than a job.'

The rewards of the Navy came, 'the first time you stand a bridge watch on your own, or just the sheer physical job of actually having done something and got it right, great fun. All *Boy's Own Paper* stuff. You've taken the motor launch away and you've done it right and your stoker and three ratings come back and you're tired and happy, it's "Thanks lads, that went well". Those sort of things give you a greal deal of high.'

On the day he left the Navy, Scott had eight weeks of leave before visiting his mother. He rose late – a luxury – put on jeans and a shirt and went to the Coleherne pub in London. 'It was like stepping into a warm swimming-pool, no ripples, no problems, no nothing. It was home. I didn't feel confident, I didn't really care. It was like coming off a diet and walking into a sweetie shop. I made a glutton of myself – wonderful.'

Almost immediately, Scott had an affair which lasted just over three years. The two also set up a printing business together. The firm went bust and so did the relationship. He has now been with Neil for four months. Neil is twenty-four, a cutter for a curtain-making firm. Alternate weeks when Scott is in London, he lives with Neil; whoever has money pays the bills. Neil used to be sexually very active, Scott says, fourteen men in one night on one occasion, now he is going through a phase of wanting a quieter homelife while Scott is still interested in nightlife. At no time, Scott says, has he practised monogamy. He doesn't believe it is necessary or practical in the gay world.

Scott McIntosh usually has sex at least three or four times a week. Sometimes, he explains, sex is a good way of saying hello to someone you've just met; sometimes it's sex with a friend; sometimes it is a one-night stand; sometimes it turns into a longer affair. 'You don't have to take someone out to dinner and promise eternal love for three months before it happens. If you want sex *now* you're going to have it now. No guilt. I don't think about it any more than the average man, say, spends on football.

'Once an affair ended with a person I thought was Mr Right. It was half a bottle of gin and the razorblade time. A couple of people I know, one of whom I'd had sex with in the sense of 'hello', one of whom thought he now stood a chance, rallied around me and gave me an awful lot of support. If I'd been heterosexual, I don't think it would have happened. I'd have gone back into my little shell and hit the bottle.

'I don't believe in monogamy because I don't believe in that kind of security. You can't create a secure bubble which isolates you from the rest of the world. Society, law, history, everything else is an attempt to comb out the knotted mass of hair into a neat pattern but as soon as you let go, it springs back into chaos again. You can't say, "I'm secure. We've paid the mortgage off, we've got the car, we love each other and we don't go out with anybody else," because one of you might go out and step under a bus.

'I don't think I'm capable of meeting all Neil's sexual and emotional needs. The trend at the moment in the gay world, perhaps because of AIDS, is to find a partner and settle down, but I don't think marriage has worked very well for heterosexual people and they've had a lot more practice at it, so why should it work for us?'

If he came home and saw Neil in bed with a couple of men, he says he hopes he'd just go off and make himself a cup of tea. He might get jealous if Neil "pulled somebody I'd been after" but not otherwise, he says. What he likes about having one partner to live with in a non-monogamous relationship is that you can love and try to be selfless.

'If you live for yourself, you don't become a very nice human being. I think all of us if we love someone tend to try and put the other one first and that's good for you.'

Those who are interested in leather and S&M, he says, are like a fraternity. 'There's a surprising sense of community other people don't appreciate. Others think all we do is nail each other to the wall and jump up and down in hobnail boots. But French, German, Guatemalan leather guys all have something in common, we're not as competitive. It's almost like a sisterly relationship that women have, you can talk about everything and you'll always be friends.'

The group also provides a network of communication. If a stranger appears, they will pass the word whether he is 'safe' or not so that risk is limited. Scott McIntosh says his own tastes vary, sometimes he is active, sometimes passive. 'One night, you may want a tall dark man to throw you on his BMW,' he says, echoing what males often consider to be a favourite female fantasy. 'You want him to drag you off to his house and rape you senseless. The next night, you may want to do it to somebody else – perhaps it depends upon whether you've had a hellish day at the office,' he says drily.

'Sometimes if you're with someone you can trust, you say, "Let's go off and have something fairly rough." You might knock somebody about a bit, spank them or twist their nipples. You may use a belt or a whip or a cane but not to the extent, for me, where you'd mark them. Some people do, but I think that's silly. From a practical point of view, apart from anything else, you've got to spend a couple of weeks healing up.

'That's why I prefer to have someone who knows what they're doing. I've known some people who can reach orgasm just by having their nipples manipulated. If you go beyond manipulation to the point of sheer excruciating pain – that sort of pain will stop anyone having sexual feelings.'

Scott McIntosh says he has had encounters which weren't sexually that inspiring but none which resulted in undesired physical harm to himself. I ask how he has the stamina for so much sexual activity. He says, with a smile, it's a matter of training, a build-up for the four-minute mile.

'You often have a code word or something. I mean, "no, no, no" doesn't mean "no" but "rhubarb and custard", say, means, "For God's sake get me down from out of this." There are amazingly erotic parts of men's bodies which some men never know about or understand.

'I mean, when I listen to heterosexual men talk about sex . . . I listen sometimes and they don't know I'm gay. You realise they're not talking about sex at all, they're not even talking to each other. There are five monologues going on about how "I'm a man, I must be a man, look I've got a prick and it works because I can tell you about the six women I've had. I'm a helluva guy, I've had my hand down a woman's blouse." Wow!

'That's what homosexuals like me find silly. They build up how macho they are and in the end they've had the bra straps off or something. That's demeaning to women. It certainly makes the man look like a prick because he's probably spent fifty pounds and four days to get that far and not talked to the woman at all.

'Well, I can go up to a man and I can have his trousers off with his equal agreement and then perhaps afterwards we might say goodbye or have a discussion about Early Minoan Art.

'I think most men are terribly afraid of being considered sex objects. I've never quite understood this. They're willing to treat women as sex objects but any straight man who thinks he is being looked at in a sexual way by another man normally panics. I can't understand that.

'Most men don't touch, except in limited circumstances. If you're a footballer you can kiss people. Men seem to have a great feeling for physical integrity, they don't like anyone to invade the magic circle that surrounds them, I suppose.

'I find groups of heterosexual men talking terribly boring – they only talk about football, the car, the mortgage and women's tits. Gay men are more interesting, they're more open. They'll talk to you about the marvellous time they had last night but they'll talk about other things too.'

Scott McIntosh argues that leather sex and S & M is not a deviation but another legitimate branch of sexual activity. Why does he think more men, gay and straight, do not attempt it?

'We'd all try squid if we weren't socially conditioned to think it's disgusting,' he says. 'Some people just want vanilla sex with the lights off. You know the joke how you can tell a French wife from an English wife? Afterwards, the French woman asks, "Darling was it wonderful?" and the English wife will say, "Are you feeling better now, George?"

'I think a lot more people would try it but we're conditioned into thinking the anus is disgusting. I'm sure you can say the same thing about the mouth if you want to. You throw up through it but you still kiss. It's a matter of choice but not everyone has the courage to exercise that choice.

'People argue that the boundaries have to be pushed further – what satisfied you this year, won't next. That's rubbish. I mean there will always be people who start off with a glass of Wincarnis for medical reasons and end up an alcoholic, but that's their problem. There's nothing inherently evil about Wincarnis.

'A voyeur watching Neil and me would see that most of the time we make love in a very tender, affectionate way and most people would recognise it as making love. Occasionally we do things which some wouldn't recognise as making love.'

Scott McIntosh says he's learnt lessons from being a minority which has comparisons with how women must feel. 'As part of a minority you have to think about *why* you are what you are. It makes you more articulate in your own defence, you think first, you don't just react.

'Who was it that wrote, there's a difference between being oppressed and being depressed about one's social position? There are still occasions when homosexuals are oppressed but I personally won't accept that any more.'

He says that he sees himself in his father. The women in his family despair anyway because all the male children emerge physically and mentally like the men. 'I have ambitions but they don't add up to a career. I don't want to spend twenty years to become Chairman of ICI. I want to go for a walk in the Hindu Kush, I want to see Hong Kong, I want to write a book . . .

'I don't have any urge to see myself in my children, I don't want children. It's one of the advantages of being gay, I don't have a family to support. I suppose one of the things *I've* always had is that whatever I complete, at the end I look at it and hate it. I always feel it's not good enough. I might feel better later but at the time, I always feel, that's terrible. I've always got the urge to do it again, get it right. I think that came from my parents.

'I don't plan for the future any more in any sense. I don't see myself ten years from now because if I plan it that requires manipulation and I'm not interested in manipulation.' I ask the predictable question: does he think he was born a homosexual or is he a product of conditioning?

'It's not something homosexual men spend a lot of time talking about now. Perhaps you know the old gay joke, "My mother made me a homosexual"; friend in reply, "If I get the wool will she make me one?" When I look at my experience it's different from that of my friends. I can't remember being conditioned. I was never one who wanted to wear frocks, I've never identified with women in that sense.

'There are certain physical drawbacks to being a woman which I couldn't stand – facing periods every month, for one! I still think in spite of the advances over the last thirty years or so, women have a rough deal. A man still starts at least five points ahead.

'I'm content. I suppose you could say, if you want to be moral, that I have a slightly irresponsible life. I only have one parent surviving who's no worry or demand upon me. I have nobody else to make demands on me except my lover and he can look after himself. If he became blind and helpless I wouldn't dump him of course. I'd want to care for him but apart from that I don't have any responsibilities.

'I feel sorry for people who think sex is filthy,' he adds. 'I think sex can be so many things – a deep emotional relationship, a nice way of saying hello. O.K., some people can debase sex as a currency, but on the other hand I believe our body is a realm of the senses and we should enjoy it.'

Fl Lt David Morgan   *Yeovilton*

David Morgan flies Sea Harriers, which makes him one of a very small group of men in Britain. A Sea Harrier costs £7m and looks like a very expensive portable razor. It is stubby in shape and different in performance from any other aircraft. It lifts off vertically; it moves at eleven miles a minute; 'viffing', it can decelerate and change direction in seconds in mid-air like a malevolent gnat; it can drop up to eighteen feet on to a target when its power is cut.

Its versatility at speed naturally means that it devours pilots who do not give it total concentration. It takes five years in all to acquire the skill necessary to fly it, and yet still pilots die. David Morgan sees it as ten tons of steel, the pleasure of which he finds difficult to describe. He can make it draw graffiti in the sky.

On Saturday April 3, 1982, David Morgan said goodbye to his family; his wife Carol and the two children, Elizabeth and Charles. The children knew – insofar as children can have that kind of knowledge – that they might not see their father again. It was not an unfamiliar situation.

For the previous four years, Flight Lieutenant David Morgan had been in Germany in what is termed 'a permanent state of readiness'. Given the odds, that meant a permanent state of readiness to die. At any time, day or night, at least once every month, the hooter would sound. It might be practise, it might be real.

The men would put on their war kit, listen to the war briefings, prepare for the sorties. No comfort came from the macabre equation which told them if it *was* for real, it wouldn't last long.

In six to eight sorties a day, the expected loss rate is up to thirty per cent. After three days, only a small number of aircraft are left. After five or six days, it is hardly worth taking up the remains. Average life-expectancy in wartime for a front-line Harrier pilot: five or six days.

The mathematics are so functional it makes it easy to forget that it is the incalculable which is being discussed; loss of life; grief; degrees of fear and pain. Much of service life seems to be conducted in this impersonal vocabulary – 'strikes', 'hits', a pilot is 'lost' or 'spears himself'.

In the Falklands, it became the vocabulary of those who showed courage – recognised perhaps whether you were for or against the war. In peacetime, however, the euphemisms seem to me to be the Esperanto of those who are either brave or foolish or who lack imagination, perhaps all three. I wanted to find out, so I asked the RAF if it would suggest a man who had been 'a hero' in the Falklands and who was still active in the service.

I wanted to ask him about the nature of courage as he saw it. I wanted to ask how it is possible to live constantly with death and why it is necessary to have a career which pulls you away from home so much and involves such a high degree of risk, in or out of war.

Is the motive the pursuit of some idea of manliness? Or is the spur the camaraderie of all all-male society, a sort of Masonic league of the air? Or is it simply an overriding passion for flying?

Even if I received no answers at all I knew only a man could recount the experience, because it is one which, rightly or wrongly, is denied to women in Britain today.

On the Saturday in April David Morgan said goodbye, he returned home again the same day; his aircraft was unready. He set sail, a member of 899 Squadron, on HMS *Hermes* from Portsmouth two days later. In the Falklands, on May 1, for the first time in his life, he flew in combat. Three days later, the first Sea Harrier pilot was killed, Lieutenant Nick Taylor. Three more were to die.

The Sea Harriers in the Falklands were outnumbered six to one by the Argentinian Air Force but the latter was unused to flying over sea and much more vulnerable to radar detection. In addition, the Sea Harriers carried Sidewinder missiles.

Seven days a week for six weeks, David Morgan flew two or three times a day. Routine seems a bizarre word to apply to the experience. The pilots would get up, get into flying kit and wait for up to two hours on twenty-minute alert. Flight Lieutenant Morgan would read up the latest intelligence reports, try to solve the Rubik Cube, write letters home occasionally if he could find something to say.

Next, he would sit strapped into the cockpit of his plane on deck for maybe two or three hours at a time. It is the mundane which made itself felt. If you wanted to pee, you could 'frig' it. Unstrap, jump out of the cockpit, pee over the back end and jump back in again but you still had to be airborne in five minutes.

If something came over the horizon while you were having a leak, you had to swallow your pride, get a wet flying suit, and fly for an hour, maybe an hour and a half. You turned for home only when your fuel was so low you had no option. If you were lucky and it was late in the evening, they might keep the bar open so you could have a pint.

Taking off was achieved from a 220-metre flight-deck often swinging like a seesaw and a 12-degree ski-jump for a launching ramp; none of these details being supplied by David Morgan. On deck, strapped into the cockpit, he felt safer than below decks, he says.

'It's your natural habitat, sort of thing. You're Lord of the World when you're in your aeroplane. You can do anything and you know bloody well that if something happens, the first thing they're going to do is launch you. Once you're in the air, you know, the world is your oyster.

'The only time that I personally felt fear . . . was when I couldn't do anything about it. When I was on the ship and under attack. Then I was actually looking for somewhere to hide. But once I was in the air, I was never ever frightened except maybe for one half-second. That was the very first time I saw people firing at me and realised that I was actually going to have to fly through all the crap that was being thrown at me.

'I actually had several extremely good friends who were shot down. But the reaction to that really is just "Oh damn, not him" and then a few minutes later it's dismissed and you get on with the job.

'It wasn't a sense of unreality. We were aware the whole time what was going on, it's just that the death of colleagues is something you get used to in the flying order anyway . . . I've lost count of the number of close friends I've lost in plane crashes. It must be thirty plus and the reaction is . . . it doesn't ever get any easier. It's just that the reaction doesn't last so long. You feel a sense of frustration for maybe an hour or two and then it's past.

'Every month or so, you see a little notice in the paper, another chap's gone, like the display pilot who crashed a couple of months back. It happens from time to time and everybody accepts it. If you can't accept it then . . . If a good friend spears himself then you usually have a few beers. But it's very rare that there's the mammoth piss-ups there used to be in the early days because we can't afford to do that any more.

'You can't actually afford to take the whole squadron off, get them absolutely blasted and then not fly the next day. The job's still got to be done. You haven't the flexibility any more for that sort of thing.

'On a couple of occasions I've got back and sat down and thought, Christ, that was bloody close.' The occasion he remembers most clearly, he says, was in Germany when he almost flew himself into the ground. A few days later, he developed a psychosomatic problem. He felt something was at large all over his skin. He looked for bugs and then realised it was his skin crawling. It continued for a week before it cleared up. Did that affect his nerve?

'Not really. It didn't make me want to stop flying, it just made me go a bit cold every time I thought how close I'd been. But when we were really in the thick of it, I never got that feeling at all. I was always –' he searches for a word '– not *happy*, but certainly on top of what was going on.'

After his final action in the Falklands, David Morgan says his hands shook for three hours 'like this' – his hands waver like the hands of a man with Parkinson's Disease. It was the result not of fear but of adrenalin pumping for two minutes. 'Life was like that: a lot of semi-boredom punctuated by moments of enormous high.'

Royal Naval Air Station Yeovilton looks like a beached liner; all the accessories are there, only the sea is absent. The sense of unreality continues. Able-bodied Seamen and Wrens salute and march and direct the traffic. It is as comforting as an early Ealing movie. Everyone knows their place; the unpredictable is removed so you feel secure, but you can't help but wonder when conformity becomes claustrophobic.

David Morgan comes to meet me dressed in the air force blue trousers and jumper of the RAF; he is on a three-year secondment to the Navy. He is only one of two in the RAF who specialise in 'electronic warfare techniques to negate the enemy's use of radar and radar-controlled weapons'. As part of 899 Squadron he helps to train four or five pilots at a time, some from overseas, sent to Yeovilton on courses.

He earns a yearly salary of £14,000 for a working week which runs for five days; eight to six on two days, noon till late at night for three days when night flying is required. David Morgan spent weekends the previous summer as a one-man display team, taking the Sea Harrier to shows and exhibitions in Britain and abroad.

On those weekends, he says, he missed the family desperately if the company was poor, not so much if it was good – and he had time off in

s going to leave me she's actually going to leave me and I can't
y more."

ok at it from the Services point of view to start with. It's our
ke him an effective part of the team and if he's got a problem
eans he can't be an effective part of the team then you've got to
ut somehow. In this case we actually said to him, you know,
er out, get rid of her." And I think that's just the final thing which
im do just that and he's a much happier guy now.'

d Morgan says he himself has a 'particular buddy' who runs a
ron at Culdrose.

e known him for many, many years. He was my best man. He's a
amiable bloke, we both enjoy good food and good wine, he's got
most outrageous sense of humour, and we've always been good
ds. I wouldn't say he's my best friend because I don't have best
nd's but he's certainly somebody that I'm always happy to see.'

ertain standards are expected in the Services, David Morgan says and
t includes a code of behaviour in the treatment of women: '. . . when
ing's exhausted, then birds usually come up. We don't talk about
rsonalities and names. That's definitely not on – or very rarely any-
ay.

'It's sort of a general appreciation of people either in the area or people
you've known. You usually find several people know the same sort of
circle of friends. I suppose you tend to get more lecherous as the beer
flows . . . but it's all very gentlemanly. You don't actually bitch . . . We
would all be fairly upset if someone took a girl for a ride because it's,
you know, one of those things which are frowned upon.' 'They aren't
cads?' 'Well right,' he replies, smiling.

Carol was nineteen and David a couple of years older when they
married. He had never thought about marriage much, he says, it just
seemed the right thing to do at the time. Carol does not come from a Service
family, her father is an engineer, but she enjoys the mobility of Service
life. They have moved ten times in twelve years of marriage. At the outset,
the partings helped them to adjust to each other and defused some of the
eruptions. But she regrets the effect constant movement has had on her
career as a teacher.

David says he wishes she did have a career as she always seems happier
when she has a job. This is a Monday night and Carol's keep-fit lesson,
so we leave the naval station in time to baby-sit.

David Morgan

lieu. The attraction was 'professional satisfaction'.

David Morgan's conversation is only lightly spiced with the kind
of language you might expect an RAF pilot to use; his car is 'the
wagon', women are occasionally 'birds', men are 'guys' but otherwise
he evades the favourite stereotype; no handlebar moustache and false
bonhomie.

He is medium in build, blond and quietly spoken. The accent is
neutral. He appears to be quite shy but perhaps it is just that his
instinct is to hold much of himself in reserve. Later, at home, a
beautifully restored fourteenth-century cottage in a small village, he
becomes much more animated as he shows his own work; the cupboards
and shelves in the eaves of Elizabeth's room; the fitted cupboards in
his and Carol's room.

His passion is flying. You feel it is a passion he keeps private even from
his family, sharing it only with other pilots – an impression he
confirms later. He is modest and mostly admirably austere about his
descriptions of his work; you feel bravado would suit him as comfortably
as a boil on the backside.

At Yeovilton, we enter 899 Squadron's headquarters. We walk
past the Mae Wests and into the squadron's common-room. One wall
is dominated by a series of caricatures by Tug Wilson, the naval car-
toonist. Others have added stickers and captions. 'Green Meanies' reads
one, a present from the US Marines. '899 Are On the Piss Again' and
'We Want to Wee Wee' are among the other messages which catch the
eye.

David Morgan was brought up in Kent. His father was a pilot in the
Fleet Air Arm during the war and became a teacher. David's sister is two
years younger but his father could only afford to send one child to
boarding school; so his son was sent to a school in Sandwich, which he
enjoyed, at the age of twelve.

At five or six, David decided he wanted to become a pilot. He supposes
his father may have been an influence but 'it was just something that got
in the blood'. At fourteen, his parents were divorced. David's mother had
been a nurse in local factories. 'My mother did the traditional thing, she
ran off with the lodger. It left my father to bring up the kids which he
did bloody well.

'He was more of a friend to me than a father. It was more like a brother
relationship. Later whenever I brought girlfriends home to stay the

weekend, he would always move out of the double bed and give it to the girl friend.'

For eight years David made no attempt to contact his mother. Then he needed information for his application forms to join the Navy. Since then, they have kept in touch but they have never discussed her departure or the missing years.

'We gradually drifted closer again after that and now we've sort of got a normal relationship. I didn't feel rejected, I just felt extremely let down that she'd disappeared and left us to it. My father explained all the whys and wherefores, I suppose, when I was a kid.'

Both parents are remarried with second families, ten years younger than David and his sister. His sister married at nineteen after secretarial work.

Until the divorce, David Morgan says it seemed 'a perfectly standard happy family life' with neither parent exercising more influence than the other. 'It obviously does affect me now in that if I ever thought of rushing off and leaving my wife and kids, I would have to think twice because I know what sort of pain it can cause. Still I don't think it would actually stop me if I decided that that was what was *really* going to happen. I think it's a sort of cautionary tale.'

At fifteen, David Morgan applied for a Naval Scholarship. A medical revealed that he had a massive hole in his heart. Up till then he had been active playing rugby, cricket and hockey for the school. He needed six months to recover from the surgery.

'It was a traumatic period in my life because there was an awful lot of discomfort and quite a lot of pain, most of which I've forgotten, luckily . . . My father came to see me the day after the operation and tried to make me laugh and it bloody nearly tore me in half. I never played rugby again for the school but I managed to play hockey.'

He subsequently failed A-levels but fulfilled his ambition and joined the Navy. After two years training on helicopters the Navy decided he wasn't good enough and offered him a transfer to air traffic or submarines. David Morgan decided to leave instead and six months later, at the age of twenty-one, joined the RAF; the latter didn't have enough pilots while the Navy had too many.

He spent four years on helicopters going backwards and forwards to Northern Ireland. In 1973, he was promoted to Flight Lieutenant and sent to Germany, where for nearly four years his job was to find alternative sites for the Harrier force. At the same time, he lobbied and cajoled and

persuaded others to give him ex[...]
Harrier trainer.

'I wanted to fly the Harrier. Ha[...]
more impressive than watching ten[...]
yards of grass stretch in the middle o[...]
That's what I wanted to do. All I nee[...]
Force that it actually wanted me to do [...]

'So I wrote lots and lots of letters and [...]
final experiment to get people from helico[...]

He came back to England for two ye[...]
Germany in 1978, having come second in t[...]
trepidation or failure about leaving the Nav[...]
bition was so strong. 'I knew then there was [...]
I could do and that's fly. I didn't want to sta[...]
because I knew I'd be frustrated.' In the Harrie[...]
enthusiasm almost manages to convince you that [...]
on the runway has a soul of its own. 'It's the mo[...]
ever flown. The most demanding and the most f[...]
there aren't superlatives to describe it. It's fantastic.[...]

'I enjoy flying,' he says again later, 'I'd need some[...]
take the place of flying. Even if I won a million pou[...]
didn't have to work, I'd probably stay in the Service[...]
know what it is, it's an intangible thing.'

Get a group of pilots together, he says smiling agai[...]
about the loves of their lives; aviation and women.

'Aviation first really. Feed them beer . . . Americans, Du[...]
all pilots talk about the same thing. We have this great b[...]
terribly boring to others.'

In a squadron, he says, the bond extends to discussing per[...]
lems – for practical reasons.

'If you've got a problem which you can't share with someb[...]
it means that you will not be performing very well. At the [...]
trip the Formation Leader debriefs the sortie and goes round th[...]
and says, "OK, have you any points?" If the guy you've been [...]
with thinks you screwed up, he will stand up and say so. And [...]
talk about it.'

'We all have a mentor and guys will come up to you and say, "L[...]
I've got a problem. My wife has just decided, after three or four years[...]

saying she[...]
take it an[...]
'You l[...]
job to m[...]
which m[...]
sort it [...]
"Kick h[...]
made h[...]
Dav[...]
squad[...]
'I'v[...]
very [...]
the [...]
frie[...]
frie[...]
[...]
th[...]
fly[...]
p[...]
w[...]

At the cottage, Charles, aged six, propels himself towards a bath – more or less. Elizabeth, eight, changes into her Brownies' uniform. Carol has left tomato soup, cheese, ham, bread and fruit for David's supper. She has written a note suggesting he make quiche but he rarely cooks. 'Tomato soup will be fine.'

He does housework 'as and when', he says, and adds that Carol would probably say she does it all. Carol later expresses surprise when he says he would have no objections if a woman was allowed to fly a Sea Harrier.

Later, he writes to explain with a certain dry humour that they had never discussed equality in the RAF before and his views took Carol by surprise. 'I think she thought me more jealous of my male preserve than I actually was.'

In the kitchen of the cottage, tomatoes ripen on the window sill and the pine is honey-coloured. The rest of the downstairs is pine and stone with a Welsh dresser and some antique furniture; dried flowers; a pile of Argentinian tin helmets under the stairs and Carol's collection of Victorian leaf plates on the wall.

The only other visible sign of military memorabilia is the *Sunday Times* book on the Falklands War and a canister from Mount Kent transformed into a flower vase. The resurrection of the cottage is Carol's doing.

After three months in the Falklands, David Morgan's homecoming was confused. It was uncertain whether he would fly back or arrive on the *Hermes* so the family decided to wait at home. David says he can't remember much about the first few hours 'but we probably drank several bottles of wine'. In the time he had been away, life in Somerset had changed.

Carol and the children had moved into the cottage; they had acquired a dog. I asked David if missing pieces of family life is one of the negative sides of his job.

'No, I don't think so. Carol would probably disagree. We had signed the contract for the house two days before I went and so I just gave her a Power of Attorney and disappeared and she moved into this ramshackle old fourteenth-century house, with water running through the lounge and the wiring which the Electricity Board refused to connect because it was dangerous. She got it rewired, replastered, redecorated, damp-coursed, everything done without any reference to me. The letter cycle was taking about three or four weeks so she just went ahead and did it. She worked bloody hard and did a super job of it. I got a bit of stick when I got home because of that, you know, because she'd been working so bloody hard. She told me before I got back, "Don't you dare question anything I've done with the house because I'll wring your bloody neck." Then I disappeared off again a few weeks later and she got on with building a double garage and extending the kitchen and all the rest of it.

'But I don't think that was a negative side of things. Had I not gone then I would still be up to my eyeballs in trying to re-do this house, trying to save money and do it myself rather than just blow the savings and get it done.'

But did he have difficulty in explaining to her what had happened? Was it easy to talk about it or not?

'No, it's not. If people haven't been there it's very difficult, no matter how interested and concerned they are you can't really know what it's like unless you've been in that situation, and I do tend to talk too much about it because it's a very important part of my life. Carol thinks I ought to forget about it and let bygones be bygones.'

Is he trying to analyse what happened?

'I do that as well, I kept a diary when I was down there, for the first time in my life. It just seemed to be a good thing to do, I had a feeling it might be an important part of my life so I kept a diary. It's an old exercise book and I put down maybe half a page a day.'

The diary is mostly details of factual events with some personal thoughts. One promise David Morgan made himself for instance was never to worry about money again. 'It lasted until the first bills came in,' he smiles ruefully.

In one of the celebration pamphlets put out by the Directorate of Naval Recruiting at the conclusion of the Falklands War, is the following statement: 'Sea Harriers flew over 2,000 operational sorties and achieved 23 kills of enemy aircraft in air-to-air combat.' Four of the 'kills' were achieved in one sortie by David Morgan and his partner, Dave Smith; two Sea Harriers flying together as was customary.

It was at the debacle of Bluff Cove, the pilots could see the punishment the Scots Guards were receiving below.

'I was sitting over Bluff Cove shortly after the second raid hit them. I was sitting at ten thousand feet, just trying to keep the heat off them and I saw a Skyhawk running in on one of the small landing craft as it was coming along the coast.

'I just yelled at Dave Smith, who was with me and dived down on this guy. He was about five miles away, and as the speed increased I stuffed the nose down really steeply, to get down to his level. I saw him attack the landing craft and miss, and then a second one came in and hit it with a bomb and disappeared after the first one. Then a third one came in and missed, I thought, OK boy, this is going to be your day, I was just about to go for the third guy when a fourth one came past and it just so happened that my dive actually took me out right behind him, so I released a missile off at him and took him out fairly effectively. Then took out the one in front of him with the other missile and then my gun sight went unserviceable, all the magic green writing disappeared. I lost all my weapon-aiming, which was a great shame. So I closed on the lead two Skyhawks and fired two hundred rounds of cannon at them. I didn't actually see any hits but we were down about fifty feet over the water at this stage.

'Dave was behind me. He heard me shout and saw me disappear down into the gloom and then lost me and just saw the missiles coming off, and the explosions. He saw the splashes on the water from my guns and saw a guy flying through the splashes, and he didn't know whether it was me being fired at, or me firing at someone else. I ran out of bullets and just pulled it up and vertically climbed out of the way to let him get a shot, and he took out the third guy with a missile.

'Dave still had a missile and his guns, I had nothing but we were desperately short of fuel. We had about thirty-two minutes' worth of fuel remaining at cruising speed when I first saw the Argentinians, and we used a hell of a lot of fuel in the two minutes of the attack. I was full power, everything I could get, going down, I was round about the speed of sound when I actually got into the fight, going like a train, and of course, you know, all thoughts of fuel just went out of the window. And when we got the three and lost sight of the fourth one we both pulled up. I pulled up and then Dave pulled up and found me on his radar and joined up with me and we discovered we would both be lucky if we got back to the ship, we had so little fuel left. In fact I landed with about two minutes' worth of fuel, and Dave landed with about a minute's worth.'

Did he feel anger when he attacked?

'Oh yes, blazing anger, because I'd just seen them actually hit one of our landing craft and I knew they'd got somebody and there was no way they were going to get away. They'd lost a lot of Guards and that was obvious from the air, you could see the ships burning. We felt that we'd actually helped to level the score a bit.'

Did he worry about that whole side of death and destruction or was it just part of the business?

'No, it didn't worry me at all. Death doesn't bother me and the only time in which I worried about others, for a short period of time, was the very first aircraft I destroyed. It was a helicopter and I just flew very low over the top of him and threw him into the ground. There was a bloody great explosion and little tiny bits all over the side of the heather. I didn't feel too hot about that – especially when I heard that it might have been carrying one of our guys who'd been shot down – I didn't think that was too great but for all that, you know, you pay your money and you take your chance. I subsequently discovered, in fact, that it was loaded up with mortar bombs. So I've got no qualms now at all, and certainly that was the only one I ever had the slightest doubt about.'

I ask if as a result of his score of four out of four, people have tried to appoint him a hero?

'Yes, that really does get on my nerves. That word hero really grates because heroism, bravery are terms which are only used by people who haven't actually been in that situation. When you're in the situation you don't actually sit down and say, "Right, I'm really going to be brave, I'm really going to do something heroic." You just go and get on with the job and whatever happens to happen at the time you go and do what you've been trained to do. It's only when it's all over that people say, "Hey, Christ, that was bloody brave," which probably means it was stupid.

'I don't know what courage is, actually. I don't think there's very many people who actually sit back, look at it, and say, "This is going to be a brave thing to do" . . . I mean you do it because, you just do it.'

Did it set him aside now, being one of the people who went out there? Was there some camaraderie still, or had it dissipated?

'No the camaraderie is certainly still there and you still have the odd get-together. Earlier on this year we had the 1st May Raid get-together, guys on the raid on 1st May, just a few beers, a few dozen beers. There's certainly a great feeling of camaraderie between the people who were down there and there's a lot of very hacked-off people who couldn't actually get down there although they wanted to go.

'It doesn't cause very much friction. I certainly would never dream of saying, you know, "Shut up, you weren't down there, you don't know." I've met one or two people who think in the opposite way, who keep badgering me, saying, "You're bloody lucky getting down there. I wish I'd been down there. It's all right for you".'

I ask if the experience in the Falklands changed him in any way.

'Yes,' he says instantly, 'I've thought a lot about it, obviously, and it certainly did change me. The first thing I noticed is that I lose my temper a lot quicker. I got back and I was absolute hell to live with. I found it very difficult and it annoyed me intensely if anyone asked me to make a decision on anything that wasn't a matter of life or death. For quite a long period, a couple of months at least, the only decisions I made were decisions of life or death and to have to make the decision of what I wanted for tea or something like that used to make me really annoyed. I was absolute hell and I still have to be very careful to control the temper.'

Is the degree of anger out of proportion to the offence?

'Oh usually, yes, totally out of proportion. You know, there's no half measures, I'm either absolutely calm or I blow my stack completely. It happens quite quickly, and I'm trying to control it and it's getting better.'

I ask him if that is just at home, or in work too.

'To a lesser extent at work because normally the decisions I have to make at work are decisions to do with flying and therefore have an importance of their own.

Did he feel a terrible sense of anti-climax when he came back?

'A great sense of relief. Terrific climax when we actually came in on *Hermes*, that was absolutely amazing, tears streaming down our faces.

'Since then I've become a lot more aware of the little things in life. I think my family mean, if anything, more to me now than they did before I went. I was obviously extremely fond of my family before I went, but I'm very conscious of the fact now that if I don't sit back and enjoy the family to the full then I'm actually wasting something. I was certainly very much aware of that down there. But I don't think that there's anything else that's changed dramatically.'

Nobody among his colleagues enjoyed the war while it was on, he adds, but when they responded to a challenge successfully and proved themselves, *that* was what was worthwhile. He is pleased that he had the experience.

'If I had come back early or not gone at all, I'd have been as sick as a pig now. Having actually gone through it and come back from it, I wouldn't have missed a single day.'

Barry Nuttall *Hull*

At nightfall, the camp is quiet. A Cortina with red doors, white wings and blue body, a symbol of patriotism, stands guard accompanied by a man in khaki. In the distance there is a flickering – not the movements of the enemy but the animation of a dozen television sets visible through curtainless windows on the estate beyond.

On the dirt track, two W-registration army lorries are parked before two large camouflaged tents. Around the tents a line of bricks traces a different pattern. It looks like a magic circle. Inside one tent three or four 'privates' sit somewhat incongruously on the remains of a three-piece suite and chat softly. The chief is in his quarters. A man salutes smartly. 'Sir,' he says to the chief, Barry Nuttall, 'do you fancy anything from the chip shop?'

The chief's quarters are compact, two 'rooms' in one of the military vehicles. At the far end is the study. It holds a desk, two chairs, piles of files, a heater, a postcard of Prince Charles, three briefcases, a small portable television, a radio, a toy tank used in miniature battles, a potted plant and a military peaked cap embellished with two stars.

The predominant colour is brown. Barry Nuttall, a large man, sits comfortably in the main chair. He is not in uniform today. Instead, over several layers, he wears a Marks and Spencer cardigan. The second room holds a bunk, a small stove, buckets of water, cupboards. Kerry is cooking Barry's tea. They take turns because Barry likes his gravy thick enough to stand a spoon in and Kerry makes it as thin as lemonade.

In front of Barry is a book of cuttings; a logbook, as it were, of the exploits of his 'army', formed ten years ago. There they were, darts, dominoes, pissed every weekend, bored out of their heads with one army jeep between them intended for use as a breakdown vehicle in Barry Nuttall's garage.

A bloke told them of a gathering down south of 150 owners of restored army vehicles. Barry has always been interested in World War II. He is, of course, totally opposed to all war – but he likes the *detail* of it. They went down south, they were accepted, class barriers dissolved, Barry says, the uniforms appealed to some. Four formed what became the Allied Axis Society. Blokes who had been in the army and returned to civvy street found the comradeship again; blokes who were without a job could at least glean status as they climbed the ranks of Barry's army. It may have begun with four but now there are 100 plus – fifty of them 'hard core'. They meet regularly; organise mock battles; display themselves and their military vehicles and their guns (properly licensed) in the name of charity.

The Allied Axis Society raised £30,000 in 1983, Barry says. At the outset, he was voted Chairman, President, whatever top rank he happens to hold, in whatever uniform he chooses to be wearing at the time. That is the significance of the name Allied Axis Society; they are keen on American, British, but forget the Nazis and he has nothing to do with the National Front, he says categorically.

'Bloody warmongers,' a man called Barry Nuttall at a charity show one day. 'If you'd known the war, you wouldn't bloody well be doing this; fake bodies and death and bang, bang. Toy soldiers. War is horrible, a bloody waste of time and life. Why are you doing it?' 'For entertainment, for charity,' Barry politely explained, 'it's not *real*, is it?'

Barry, ex-bouncer, garage owner, brickie, renovator of houses, is full time Commander-in-Chief. 'I often think to myself, What the bloody hell am I going to do next? If I hand it over to the next one down the line, it would make such a hole in my life now, I don't think I could.

'It's not a hobby where you go fishing and it's "I'll see you then, Bert" at the end of the day. It's a way of life. I haven't just got myself to consider, do you follow me?

'It takes a very special person to run a society like this. I'm not just bumping myself up. You've got to be cruel to be kind. We've had a few who've tried to be General Pattons and I've had to throw them out. When you've got the public out there, you've got to be polite and respectful. In this society I have people from every walk of life . . . one lad's an accountant, well-off; another's never been further than where the society's took him and I'm their boss.

'The lad who's been nowhere tells the accountant what to do basically because he's better in the society. I often chuckle to myself, I can't weigh it up half the time that I'm where I am. But I do enjoy doing it.'

Six years ago, the society took on a real battle; a battle symbolic of something in a lot of people's lives in a lot of cities. Barry says that's why old-age pensioners used to send over supplies for the troops, apple pies, soap, bread and milk. That's why they had an eighty-seven-year-old man wearing a row of medals, sleeping alongside the lads at the barricades each night. Worried them all sick, he did, in case he did himself harm.

In the event, there have been no mortalities yet, only badly battered pride and a community on which savage wounds have been inflicted; and the loss of two homes. Barry Nuttall and his father moved into the two three-bedroom houses in Melbourne Grove in 1968.

Melbourne Grove is five minutes from the centre of Kingston-upon-Hull and the headquarters of Barry's foe, Hull City Council. The Grove is one of a thousand small streets which, like a tangle of streamers, spin off from Hull's main roads, or rather it *used* to be; now it is a wasteland, intended as a car park – or is it a factory site?

Hull was once described as a city with 'hairs on its chest'. Philip Larkin suggested that only relatives and travelling salesmen visit Hull. Certainly the trawlers don't call any more.

Hull was once a port which outstripped London: when the boys were home, everyone was in the money. Shops now halfheartedly offer goods which echo the era of instant cash; lavish plastic cocktail cabinets, cheap Japanese stereo units, fake fur coats, elaborate party frocks like miniature crinolines for little girls – and dozens of pubs.

Once the men went away, the money spent, the women had a hard time to manage again. Now, those hard times are perpetual. In 1980, the last two fresh-fish trawlers went out of business. Four-fifths of the jobs in the fishing industry – and consequently most of the jobs on land which serviced the industry – have been wiped out.

The Council is now one of the main employers, as is Education, 'industries' which have few places for the craftsmen, the fishermen and the unskilled.

Light industry tries, and a yacht marina has opened, but in 1983, 30,000 were unemployed and the number has risen since. Even the Humber Bridge, the largest single suspension bridge in the world, appears less of a feat of engineering than a gesture of futility. Promised by a Labour Government, allegedly so it could win the Hull North by-election in 1966, it has cost over £188m. Interest rates a day in 1983 amounted to £62,000, while the toll fees are little more than a sixth of that. The bridge is supposed to limit Hull's isolation; so little is it used, it only serves to underline it. Add to all that the sense of dislocation felt by so many in the city.

'Trash, that's what I am,' some people will tell you with irony. TRASH stands for Tenant Ready to Accept Substandard Housing. In Hull, not only is there the customary housing waiting list of crippling length, there are also the refugees from the massive redevelopment schemes. The city was devastated by bombing and later by the planners' good intentions.

People have been decanted from the capillary-like streets to satellite areas such as Bramsholme. Barry says the Council doesn't realise a basic fact: you can't turn city people into country folk just by moving them out and giving them new bits of bricks and mortar. Barry's history has paralleled that of the city's.

Barry's father was a fisherman who came to Hull from Blackpool when Barry was five. He and Barry worked hard on their respective homes in Melbourne Grove. Barry spent £3,500 installing a shower, an inside toilet, central heating. 'It wasn't the best house in the country,' Barry says, 'but it was mine. It was me home.' Then one day, the Council came along and stuck a piece of paper on the door of his father's house 'like something out of medieval times'.

It told the Nuttalls they had a week to get out or be forcibly removed; this was the climax of years of negotiations. The Council had placed cumpulsory purchase orders on the row of houses; while others had conceded, the Nuttalls refused. Barry was offered £2,400; his dad £1,000. What could he buy for that, he says? Why should he move to a council house at £30 or more a week when there was nothing wrong with what he had?

It wasn't just the house, it meant the end of the Allied Axis Society. Barry needed a drive to keep the vehicles, no council housing could provide that. So Barry fought not against progress but, he says, for his rights. He fought first to keep his home, then for adequate compensation, finally, now, for a decent size council house. The Council says it is trying.

The other houses came down but the Nuttalls' two houses remained. The men of the society barricaded themselves in; reinforcements came from local volunteers – some of whom had lost their homes but saw a chance to vent some anger, regain a bit of self-respect. The siege lasted for five years, more or less.

In May 1983, the siege ended. The Council moved in. The ninety-year-old houses took two hours to demolish with a digger. 'They really were solid,' Barry says as if in respect for old veterans now deceased. But even once the Council had finished, the battle continued.

The Allied Axis Society etched out the foundations of the C-in-C's home with bricks, pitched tents and has been in occupation ever since. Barry spends most nights in his truck, he won't move until he gets what he wants. It's not his battle any more, he says. 'What do I say to my blokes? What do I say to the two thousand who signed the petition? Or to the OAPs who kept us in supplies? Sorry, they've won, I quit?'

This, however, is not just the story of Barry's battle. It is also the chronicle of Barry and Anne; Barry and Cathy; Barry and Cathy's sister; Barry and Alyson; Barry and Kerry and Barry and several other women whose names are not mentioned. First, the wedding.

A photograph in the cuttings shows Barry magnificently costumed in the full-dress uniform of an American Major-General, complete with several rows of medals.

On his arm, dressed in white, is his bride Alyson Finch, aged twenty-eight. The date is September 3, 1983, the anniversary of the outbreak of World War II. Also in attendance are the lads in uniform, some majorettes and the four children from Barry and Alyson's twelve-year relationship (or is it thirteen?) and two children from Barry's first marriage. That marriage, to Cathy, took place in a registry office fourteen years previously. After the reception, Alyson went home to her council house and Barry went back to camp. Now, he spends a couple of nights a week at Alyson's and Kerry helps to look after him at headquarters.

Silently, Kerry makes constant cups of tea. If Barry's cup, half full, grows cold through neglect, unbidden she pours a replacement. Kerry is like a daughter, Barry says. They met when Kerry and John lived next door to Barry. Kerry was pregnant with her son, now aged five, when John met her and the two lived together for a time. They split up a few months ago. 'Kerry didn't know what she wanted,' Barry says, 'did you, Kerry?'

'He was trying to make me into the perfect woman,' she says mildly. She is tall and slight, nervous but very friendly. It seems as if, if she's given any attention at all, it is more than she expects. 'You didn't want him when he was here, now he's gone you want him back.' 'Yeah,' she replies, 'it's a funny thing really.'

'The trouble with Kerry is that like most women in her position, they get jilted with a child and latch on to the first available male, like she did with John,' Barry theorises. 'Then they end up in the club again. She could have gone on the Pill but once she was pregnant, he didn't want to know. I'm old-fashioned, I think the bloke should've stood by her. I don't think he should turn around and say, "Well, she's as much to blame as me, I'm not bothered . . ."'

Kerry looks as if she might be in her late twenties, early thirties. She says she is twenty-two. She lives in a council house with her son and she is frightened. It is attacked by vandals and drunks. She has been secretary of the Society since she was sixteen. She says the members give her protection, something to do, a sense of belonging. She often sleeps in the camp because she feels safer. She goes with the society on holidays, on mock battles and she attends the meetings.

'Kerry's as good as any man,' Barry offers. 'When it comes to it, she'll stick to her guns. Look at the Russian women in the war, they did bloody marvellous. I don't put women down. I like an army woman, do you follow me?

'I don't say everyone's got to be like that. I don't say to Kerry she's got to be in the kitchen. Believe me, when she goes away with the lads, she mucks in. There's no preferential treatment for women. And I'm a chauvinist, a Victorian, I can't help it. My mother made me that way.'

I say it must be hard with a child, no job, pregnant and living on Social Security. Kerry smiles broadly, she speaks only when Barry invites her into the conversation. 'You get used to that,' she says. 'I mean my mam had nine children. When she went in for her seventh, I had the other six.' 'How old were you then?' 'Oh, about ten I reckon.'

Barry addresses himself to Kerry: 'When you and John were arguing and falling out all the time, he'd be in bed and you'd give him a right earache. Eventually, he'd get out of bed and there'd be a row, you'd end up with a clout and wonder why. What I'd turn round and say to any woman if a bloke gives her a clout is, "Stop and think why?" I'll bet he's only done it because he cares.'

'What if the woman clouts the man?' I ask. 'Fair dos,' Barry replies. 'We're talking about a situation where the woman is wrong. I suppose the answer you're looking for is: "No woman is going to bloody hit me and get away with it."' He smiles. 'She probably *would* get a clout back, human nature being what it is.' Kerry makes yet more tea.

Barry talks about his past, as he sees it, in rich detail. 'I've a colourful life,' he says. 'You could write my memoirs, only I think it would be unbelievable.' Judge for yourself.

Barry Nuttall's father came from a Romany family, Grandma Nuttall was a bareknuckle boxer in the fairground. She weighed in at twenty stone and Grandad Nuttall was half her size. Grandma was drowned in the Fleetwood floods, her husband was devastated. Barry's father was in the Royal Navy and met Barry's mother, a Blackpool woman, in World War II.

The two never married because Mrs Bennett was a Catholic and already married to Wilf, by whom she had had two children. Barry was her third child, the offspring of the Bennett-Nuttall relationship. Barry's parents separated when he was six. He changed his name to that of his father when he married at nineteen because he felt 'it was the proper thing to do'. And besides, all his life, he says his mum, in fights, had made a point of claiming, 'You're a Nuttall, we are Bennetts.' His step-brother committed suicide at twenty-eight, his step-sister lives in Australia. His mother has moved back to Lancashire.

Twenty-five years ago, when Barry was nine, his mum adopted a black baby girl. The girl has now become a woman and a mother; Barry's mum looks after her two children. On his mother's side too, there is a touch of the unusual.

Grandmother Bennett, he says, was raped. The child was Barry's mother; she was sent to live with her Auntie M, who had twelve sons. She spent her childhood on the Lancashire moors amid males; 'She was like a lion, no wonder she could be hard,' Barry says. He speaks of her with a little reverence, some admiration, a good degree of wariness. He says she has been a big influence on his life.

'If my mother said to be in at eight, she didn't mean five past. She was a real character, as hard as a brick, that's where I get it from. When she said "No" she meant it, I inherited that. She would strap you, she would. She was caring but very, very strict. She fought bloody hard to keep us all together. She was very strong-willed. You couldn't get very close to my mother, I'm very much like that. I shut the doors a lot, no one's got close to me.

'She could do anything; weld, brickie, mend, paint, decorate.' At eight, Barry recalls a time when he was lying on a fur rug in front of the fire, playing with toy models he had made. 'Me mother picked me up and gave me such a clout. I went flying. She says, "Don't bloody lie like that again. You're not a poof, you're a bloody fella."'

In the early years, Barry was frequently in hospital, first with fluid on the lungs then, after injuries caused by a fireworks accident, for treatment to his leg. His mother moved homes often. 'Perhaps that's why I fought so hard to keep my own home.' The two sparred constantly. At some point, Ronnie, a taxi driver, joined the household. Barry says he is a decent fellow but he only really saw him on Sundays. 'We didn't go to football or fishing or anything like that . . .' He saw his own father at Christmas and occasionally in the holidays.

'I've always been a scrapper,' Barry says. 'Lads fight anyway. That's how you're brought up. Johnny's better than you, he'll start picking on you, if you back down, that's it. I rebelled and fought back, I earned money that way. I left home when I was young. At fifteen I used to spend the summer on the barges, it was marvellous.

'Once I left school, Ronnie got me a job in a factory working on a conveyor belt. The whistle went at seven and wallop, you stand there thinking, What's going on here? At nine, the whistle goes again, stop dead, cut, tea. And then they'd talk about the holiday they had last year, where they're going next year, football . . . I can't stand football.

'I stuck it for a month. I had bloody nightmares. I'd go home, I'd be laid out on the couch, wake up and look at the clock, half past seven. I'd say, "Bloody hell, I'll be late for work."

'"Calm down, you daft sod," my mother would say. "You've just come from work, it's night-time." It got me that bad, I couldn't stand it. I got myself the sack. I felt terrible because my stepfather had got me the job. I carried on pretending for a week, going to work.

'My mother was a shrewd old bag, she knew. In the end I told her. She said, "Bloody lazy bugger . . ." and all that. All the usual things.'

Eventually Barry Nuttall worked as a doorman in a succession of clubs. 'I'm talking about backstreet docks. In those days, you carried a knife. If I had to hit a bloke, I would've hit him, I was doing a job, but nine times out of ten, you never had to. Those kind of people, be it seaman, prostitute or anybody, they knew that if you were on the door you were more than capable of handling yourself.

'A man only feels pride in fighting when he's shown up. The time when you feel another bloke is saying, "You're nothing, you're a mouse." For instance, the first time I saw my first wife and her boyfriend, as a man I felt threatened. My pride was hurt. I could have gone and knocked his block off. In the old days I might have done just that but I ignored them and walked off.

'Some men will go out and fight for the sake of fighting. Half a dozen drinks and they think they're God. But I think women are the worst causes of fights. Nine times out of ten, in a club, a woman is always the cause of a fight. She goes out with one man, eggs another one on. Next minute of course, her partner's playing bloody hell.

'I think basically she eggs on a stranger to see if her man loves her. "Look how much my man loves me." A lot of it goes back to the caveman and stuff like that. That's why I like mock battles. Man gets a lot of hang-ups today about his identity changing. I was thinking about our mock fighting the other day.

'I thought to myself that it was bloody stupid, grown men playing cowboys and indians. Then I realised it's about putting back something which is missing today in man, his way of hunting, his survival instincts. Do you follow me? the good thing about us all going away together on a weekend for our society, is that you can just close the world off, the world doesn't exist any more.'

At seventeen, Barry met Anne. He also a little later met Cathy, three years younger than himself. Cathy temporarily got his exclusive attentions. Then Anne's sister came to tell Barry that Anne had had a little girl. 'I said I wish somebody could have told me beforehand. I went to see her and arranged getting married. It was the right thing to do at the time. I was young, what do fellas know about love at that age? I was a pretty mixed-up kid. I was happy, I wanted a child. Cathy, Anne and I sat down and talked and agreed it was the best thing to do.'

Barry and Anne lived together for a few weeks, then Cathy began calling. 'She wouldn't leave us alone.' On one occasion, Cath brought *Please Please Me*, the Beatles album, as a gift. Anne walked into the flat, saw her there 'and decided she'd had enough.'

Barry tried to call to see her and explain but he didn't see Anne again until she visited a club where he was working as a disc-jockey. The 'baby' was then seven and asking after her father. Now Barry sees his daughter regularly and he says he and Anne are good friends.

Two years after he and Cathy met, they married. She was pregnant but Barry wanted to marry anyway. 'As far back as I can remember all I ever wanted was a wife and kids. Most kids would say they wanted to be an engine driver, I wanted a wife. I was passionate about Cathy. I worshipped her. I still do.'

Two months after the baby arrived, Cathy left for the first time. The details on subsequent history get hazy but in Barry's version at least it seems she left many more times. Occasionally, she would go to her mother, at least once she went to a battered women's refuge. She would apparently leave without warning and return in the same fashion. Barry served two short sentences for hitting her. He will regret the death of the marriage to his dying day, he says.

Each time Cathy left Barry cared for the children, eventually winning custody of Barry, now fifteen and Deborah, fourteen, when the divorce came through a year or so ago. 'Cathy spent a lot of time in a children's home. Her father was a fisherman and got killed, she had a hard life too. Maybe if she had had a different upbringing and I had, we would have been all right. We loved each other, we just couldn't get it right.

'We used to fight every day when we first got married. I was so bad tempered in those days. I could never weigh her up. Jealousy that's what it was. If she went out, it was the classic thing, where have you been, who with, why? . . . Cathy was a marvellous mother when she was at home. She would play with the kids and sew them things but she could turn off like a switch.

'I could go to work, we'd be happy, I'd come home – and nothing. The kids would be at school and she'd be gone and I wouldn't see her for ten months. Things would get on top of her and she'd just go. Eventually, I'd see her again and she'd come home straight away. She would always say she wanted to come home but she just couldn't. I took her to the psychiatrist.

'I don't know what happened there. Apart from frightening her to death, I don't know what he said. She couldn't talk to me about how she felt. I used to sit for hours trying to get her to but she wouldn't say. Just as even now, I'm trying to get her to see the kids this Christmas.

'I used to try again and again for the kids because I didn't want them to have the kind of upbringing I'd had. Barry ran away to his mum once for six months. I told him if he wanted her back, he'd have to ask her himself. He did ask and when she stayed away, he came home again. I don't know how it's affected them but I think we're close. Cathy lives quite near now with another bloke. In the end, I used to say to her, "If you're going to go, stay gone. All the coming and going, you're killing me inside."'

I ask if Barry resents the power Cathy appeared to have over him. 'I don't think she did have any power over me, love, I don't think anybody has,' he replies. 'I'm a very adamant person. If somebody told me, "You're going to do as you're told," there's no way in the world I'd do it. I said to Cathy the only way you'll get anything off me is by playing the game.

'We've got to pull together. I had four businesses and I'd just get them going nicely and she'd be gone. I have very strong ideals about family life. I believe the wife should be good in the home, not work when there are kids, give me a rollicking when I'm not doing my share. A bloke's generally messy but I like things tidy, so she should clear up, keep things in their place. The man's role is the backbone, the breadwinner.

'The only thing I resented Cathy for was that half the time, the times when she went away, she was trying to turn me into a male/female.

'I've got a weak stomach as it is and when you're changing nappies on two children, with one on each arm, you don't know whether you're coming or going. It might sound awful but I was going out with Cathy's sister. I mean you're living in an environment like that, you don't know whether you're on your head or your feet. It's easy to get involved with someone else, especially somebody who's willing to change mucky nappies.' How does he think women manage then, I ask?

'I think women manage because they're indoctrinated to it over the years. It's something I suppose they accept.'

I ask if he would mind being kept by a woman. 'I would never allow it,' he says emphatically. 'I wouldn't feel a man, definitely not. If I thought a woman was feeding and clothing me, certainly not. What really annoyed me when I was alone with the kids was that I was classed more or less as a woman by the Social Security.

'I had a helluva time over that. I nearly flattened the bloke in Social Security, I was really annoyed. I thought he was trying to call me queer. I think even if you're unemployed, the only time you feel less of a man is if you sit back and do nothing. The fundamental thing in war is that the war is never won until you stop fighting the battle. You may keep losing, but you carry on fighting.'

I ask if he ever hurt Cathy. 'Hurt her? I'd have bloody killed her the way she was messing me about. I can't explain to you how I felt then. *I* was very hurt. Cathy is five foot and weighs six stone. I was big then too. She was the "poor thing", so sweet and innocent. It used to infuriate me because although she was small, she was more strong-willed than I could ever be.

'She could turn on the charm so well, everybody believed her. I was the big bad wolf, she was the poor little thing. I've seen me come home from work and say to her, "Please no rows." Then she would do something like shift my cup and I ask her why. "I ain't shifted it," she'd say and that's how a row would start.

'It would build on that for two or three days and then boom, all hell would break loose. It used to kill me when I fought her, I used to be very upset. She didn't hit me that often, I can't say she did. But it was my temper. It used to build up to such a pitch, it would take maybe a week. It would be niggly things but I never hit her serious enough to put her in hospital.

'I hit her across the face,' he says, 'She went and told the police I'd hit her for six hours. On the last day she went, I sneaked home for a cup of coffee because I was driving for the Council at the time. She was all lovey-dovey, she wanted sex, I am not joking. Anyway we had sex, I went off and when I came back, she'd gone. In the end I just accepted it. The kids would come in, "Where's mum?" "Don't know."

'Even now I say where did I go wrong? I got sent to borstal and Cathy used to write saying she didn't go out at nights but then when I came home, one of my mates said he'd seen Cathy coming home one night at two in the morning. Of course, I went up the bloody wall.

'She was seventeen then, she'd just had Debbie. I went absolutely crazy, I was very, very jealous. Ten minutes after I hit her, I'd feel regret. I'd make love to her all bloody night. Buy her anything. I think sometimes she deliberately goaded me into violence. I told her she must be doing it on purpose, otherwise I couldn't understand the way she used to behave as she did.'

I ask if he would hit her once or for a period of time? 'Oh, I don't know. I'd clout her and if she carried on, I'd clout her again. But in the end, I just said, "That's it, enough. I'll never hit you again." She looked at me as if I was joking.'

Did he think Cathy was frightened of him? 'How could she be? If she'd been frightened, she wouldn't have carried on. She weren't frightened of man nor beast. I never did hit her again. I've had me fights with Alyson. I'll give her a clout but I'll never *hit* her if you know what I mean. Even with Alyson that was a long while ago. That was because of Cathy.

'At one stage I was running two families. I was torn between the two. The good thing about Alyson was she never said, "Leave her, come with me." If she'd done that at the beginning I wouldn't have bothered with her at all. But the thing was, I needed somebody else besides Cathy because I never felt secure with my first wife.'

Alyson was fifteen when they met but told Barry she was three years older. He was nineteen. Their first child, Kirsty, is eight and Barry didn't know Alyson was expecting until well into the pregnancy. The last two, twins, were conceived when Alyson was thought to be on The Pill.

Barry says Alyson loves children, she would like another. She is 'a marvellous shoulder', interested only in the children and him and the home, she doesn't bother with friends or going out. What do you talk about, I ask.

'It's a problem,' he says. 'It's a problem I have to get over with Alyson. I went around to the house the other night and told her, "You hardly ever talk to me." She said, "I know." She doesn't really talk, she never presses me. If I leave, she doesn't say, "When are you coming back?"'

'Another thing is, she trusts me so I never bother with other women. I did have other women with Cathy because I never knew where I was with her. Alyson makes a fuss of me. She takes my shoes, washes my feet, puts clean socks on. So did Cathy. I don't say they've got to, they just want to. They know that me, being the way I am, it's an acceptable thing – do you follow me?

'I dare say Alyson gets jealous. I mean if there's no jealousy, there's no love. I don't know, she doesn't show her feelings a great deal. Sometimes we have an argument because I think she spends more time playing with the kids than getting on with the housework. I tell her to get her finger out. Then again, I'm glad that she does play with them because it shows she cares.

'I have the greatest respect for Alyson,' he adds. 'She knew that if the wife came back, I'd go back to Cathy. She went through all that. I've never wrapped anything up with Alyson or lied to her. It's not as if I've said, "I want you and love you" and all that. I haven't. The funny thing is, I told her I loved her the other night and in my own way, now, I do.

'I'll tell you this for nothing. When I was with Cathy, we would have sex every night. Alyson, it's not the same. It's not so often but I'm getting more to love her every day. In another six months or whatever, I'll feel the same towards her as I do to Cathy, I know this.'

I ask Barry what he thinks women see as attractive about him. 'He's cuddly,' Kerry volunteers. 'Alyson says he's cuddly.' Barry says he knows he is fat, 'I'm big boned anyway. But I cannot understand it. I personally don't like fat people. I would never go out with a fat woman. Jesus Christ no. Sometimes I go to the sauna to try and get my weight down and Alyson will play bloody hell with me. Cathy used to try and feed me up too so I wouldn't be attractive to other women. She liked me big. A strange creature is a woman,' he laughs.

He volunteers that he is 'hard' but he can be quite sentimental. A tear will roll down his cheek watching *ET*. 'If I watch a soppy story and feel a tear, I think, Bloody hell! I don't believe men who boast they never shed a tear. What's wrong with being sentimental so long as it doesn't get out of hand?'

Barry's son, a reserved, quiet boy, is now a sergeant in the junior section of the Allied Axis Society, 'the apple of my eye'. Barry explains he is strict with all the children but as long as they stay within the guidelines, all is well. He wants both Barry and Debbie to go to college. He says Debbie wants to be a career woman, so he is steering her towards secretarial work. 'If I was a woman today, I'd want to be a career woman too. Let's face it, it's not bloody easy being a housewife.'

Does he now feel he is closer to fulfilling his childhood ambition of settling down with a wife and family? He says not exactly, not yet. He has a wife, the children but not the security. All he wants from life now is a council house to accommodate the eight of them, a drive to keep his military vehicles, a small business perhaps, more opportunity to fund-raise for the Allied Axis Society. In short, a victory or two.

What would he do now if he discovered a member of the society was hitting a woman, I ask? Would he condone it? 'I wouldn't agree with it,' he replies instantly. 'I didn't agree with what I did to Cathy then, I don't agree with it now. There was nobody more sorry than I was. Just before we finished, I told her that you can guarantee if a man is hitting a woman, he bloody cares about her.

'I'm not talking about the man who goes to the pub and has a few pints and comes home and beats his wife. I'm talking about a bloke who gets upset enough that he'll clout her if she doesn't play the game.

'In a way I feel a man has a right to clout a wife if she messes about. I decided to stop hitting her and she took that right away from me, in a sense. I used to ask her if she left because she didn't love me or if she regretted getting married or she fancied somebody else, she'd say, "Oh no, certainly not. I love you, I don't want anybody else." So I'd say,

"What is it?" And she'd tell me, "I don't know, I just get depressed."
She'd never talk. This time, hopefully, I'll be all right. All the problems I
had before with Cathy, have never arisen with Alyson. When I look at
this,' he adds, making a gesture in the direction of his camp, now lost in
the dark, 'I think for a back-street kid who used to be a scrapper, it's
unbelievable.'

Frederic de l'Orme *West London*

At twenty-one, Frederic de l'Orme had an ambition: he wanted to be the best producer of music programmes the BBC had had the privilege to employ. He had a job in the gramophone library at Television Centre, he had been on a few courses, he had a casual girlfriend, a good social life. Then, one day, he was sitting at his desk and an unexpected dialogue took place inside his head; a dialogue which frightened him considerably.

He began to think about what he was *really* going to do with his life. Did he *really* want to see his name on the credits? Well, why not? He was mixing with people of talent, gifted, intelligent people. On the other hand, there were the more unsavoury parts of the life.

In terms of *really* being useful, he grudgingly admitted to himself, a Catholic priest was probably overall the most helpful to people. And suddenly a voice said, 'Well, why not be one?' 'No way,' Frederic replied, literally breaking out into a sweat.

He had been born into the Catholic faith but he now was an irregular visitor to church, only going at all because he enjoyed playing the organ. He had a normal interest in marriage and sex, an average ambition to earn himself some material comfort.

'No, not me,' Frederic said to himself emphatically. 'Well, why not?' came back the voice. 'You're young, you're reasonably intelligent, why not give the priesthood a try?'

The tone of the voice struck a chord: if you don't try, you won't be happy. For the next few weeks, Frederic de l'Orme became a social hermit. He walked for miles, he sat in pubs over solitary drinks and all the time he was thinking. Eventually, he came to a decision. He attented a vocations meetings. It put him off quite decisively. The priesthood, thank God, was not for him.

Eighteen months later, still at the BBC, the voice came back again. The pull towards the church had grown stronger although his practical commitment to Catholicism was still weak. He had begun to think, It's no good fighting this. I'm going to have to give in sooner or later so I might as well spare myself the agony. He had already sorted out the question of celibacy.

Frederic de l'Orme went out with his first girlfriend in the fourth form at the London Oratory. He was fourteen and it was a matter of prestige. She was a girl all the other boys found attractive. He was shy but he dared to ask when the other others held back. He took the two of them to the cinema on the six shillings a month he earned waiting on the teachers' table. The fact she had said yes boosted his standing considerably in the class.

Since then he had not had carnal knowledge in the fullest sense but had had fairly deep relationships with a number of girls. He found women sexually very attractive. Yet at the same time the thought of sex with someone he didn't love he found somehow frankly degrading.

Celibacy he could see was necessary as part of the whole question of a priest's commitment to the church. He decided he couldn't cope with being a priest and having a wife and family so celibacy made some logical sense; a necessary sacrifice. Frederic de l'Orme had become accustomed to sorting out matters of faith and sin and commitment unaided.

Earlier, in his teens, he had to unravel for himself the mystery of masturbation – was it evil or a natural act? The first sentence of practically the first article he read pronounced, 'Masturbation is a mortal sin.' A devastating piece of news for a Catholic youth, even for one who was an indifferent participant in the faith. The image of purgatory is vivid.

Then Frederic read more enlightened books. 'Who's right?' he wondered and never had the courage to ask a priest or approach his mother. In confession, the closest he got to the dreaded word was to say he had been 'impure'. Eventually, he resolved the issue for himself; he no longer felt a sinner. Not at least on that matter.

On the second occasion Frederic de l'Orme tried for the priesthood he was more successful. Some friends reacted with astonishment – there were absolutely no clues to indicate he might take such a step. Some said it was a waste of a life. He was summoned for an interview before Cardinal Heenan and fellow priests.

He went into the interview at twelve twenty-six and emerged three minutes later. Cardinal Heenan asked if he felt ready the second time around. 'Well, as ready as I can feel at this stage,' Frederic replied. 'That's good,' Cardinal Heenan said. 'I'll accept you for the Diocese.'

Frederic went to a Seminary in Hertfordshire. A year into the six-year course, he decided again that the priesthood was not for him. A few days after he left, he remembers thinking to himself, Well, here I am. I don't have to embrace celibacy any more. I've got freedom. I'm all right. I can get on with being a successful man. Six weeks later, he knew more strongly than ever before that he must be a priest.

This time, Cardinal Heenan instructed that Frederic should wait a year. He worked in an Assessment Centre and left because he felt the regime was heartless. He took up a post in Orpington Children's Home and left within a few months, sure it didn't suit him. He drifted for a time and then rejoined the BBC in a temporary position as a clerk on a TV series called *Europa*.

A year later, he had his second interview with Cardinal Heenan. This time, it took much longer. The hardest question to answer was why he wanted to try again. All Frederic could say was, 'I know it's a vocation and that's what I've got to do.' Cardinal Heenan seemed to understand.

In October 1973 Frederic left for Spain, where he spent six years in a Seminary. First he learnt Spanish, since all instruction was given in the language. He still had phases when he thought, Is it really for me? Once, he took an exam and it was the only exam in his life he really enjoyed, he says, because he had decided that immediately after he would tell the Rector he was leaving. But the voice intervened again.

Frederic was ordained in 1979 in his home territory of White City, London. He remembers he sat down in church ten minutes before the Ordination and tears streamed down his face. It might have been relief, it might have been happiness. My god, I've made it, he thought. And this time no voice made itself heard.

Five years on, he says he has had many moments of frustration and anger and annoyance with people trying to tell him that the priesthood is what it isn't. He dislikes being seen as a member of the professional class, akin to a doctor or a businessman; the priest as the original white-collar worker. In his view, a priest is not the power in the community but a servant of the people. 'Professional' and 'eminent' seem words out of place when you think of Christ hanging on the cross, he says.

He has had these moments of frustration but he has never had a single regret. He has no ambition to hold a prominent place in the church hierarchy. He says he just wants to do the best he can and let the Lord take care of the rest. By nature, he is a plodder. In the five years he has been a priest, he hasn't had a single moment of unhappiness. Not one.

The road in Isleworth, Middlesex, looks like a semi-industrial area in any part of suburbia. Drive through a discreet set of gates, however, and suddenly it is the country. A white stone Madonna is surrounded by green lawns, in the far corner are the red brick buildings of a Catholic school. By the entrance is a modest house, the West Area Centre and Frederic de l'Orme's work base.

The West Area covers four boroughs, Hillingdon, Ealing, Upper Thames and Hounslow, a total of forty-two Catholic parishes. The Irish Catholics arrived around thirty years ago when building on a large scale, including Heathrow, was taking place in West London. The Polish Catholics came after the war and settled in Ealing before it went upmarket. The few Catholic Asians arrived in the sixties and seventies. In all, the Catholics probably make up twenty to thirty per cent of the population.

In October 1982, Frederic de l'Orme was appointed co-ordinator of the Marriage and Family Support Programme, responsible to the Bishop of West London. Before that Frederic was involved in parish work and a hospital chaplaincy. His present role is a totally new one in the Catholic Church in Britain. Basically, he works with all elements of the extended family; single people, engaged couples, married couples, young people. He encourages groups to hold monthly meetings where they, as lay people, can talk to each other and discuss ways in which they can be helpful within the community. 'The idea is to make membership of the Church more meaningful in an active way. So that lay people no longer simply see it in terms of mass on Sunday.'

It is not, he says, primarily a problem-solving exercise. One group begun in Hanwell has two couples who discovered they each had a child about to marry, so they spend time discussing the issues involved. On another night, he has a group of three married couples who are being trained to prepare engaged people for marriage. Another group meets for Scripture study. A fourth group recently split up, some are now organising a support group for parents of handicapped children, some are preparing to do family counselling.

His post initially has a three-year lifespan. It means a working day which begins at nine. In the afternoon, he may take a couple of hours off to read, play the piano, walk, sleep, rehearse with a quartet, Just for Fun, which for three years now has played rock 'n' roll and country and western at church functions. Sometimes, Frederic sees friends.

He used to take Fridays off but that has been swallowed up by the pressure of work. In the evening, he always has a meeting. He has his own bedroom and sitting room in a Presbytery in Feltham which he shares with the parish priest and the curate. A woman comes in to cook a meal once a day. Frederic de l'Orme's salary is £2,000 a year plus board and lodgings. In the position he holds in forty-two parishes, he is lucky, he says, he has an embarrassment of riches; a constant flood of invitations to join parishioners for meals and so on.

He makes coffee in the Centre's spartan kitchen. The nun responsible for Pastoral Care to the Bishop of West London comes down for coffee. She is dressed in mufti, a wedding ring on her finger. Only a small, silver cross, pinned to her dress indicates a religious connection.

We sit and talk in a room similar to a university common-room; low chairs, coffee table, posters on the wall. It is devoid of any visible sign of God. Frederic de l'Orme, called Father Fred, is of medium build. He wears rimless glasses and has grey flecks in his hair. A woolly can be seen under his black priest's shirt. He is open, friendly, relaxed. Cuddly, some of the less reverential might call him, not in the sexist sense but almost in an asexual fashion; a comforting presence.

What entices some people to the priesthood, he says, is the power it can hold; the control you have over the lives of others. It is a power that he does not enjoy but finds, instead, 'a quite terrifying responsibility'. It is a power he nevertheless exercises each time he takes a group of teenagers, advises engaged couples, listens to the confession of women who are guilt-ridden about their alleged inadequacies as mothers, or men who may be unemployed and fear they are failing as the traditional breadwinner, the 'man' at the head of the household. What kind of direction does he give?

Frederic de l'Orme works in a scheme organised by the Catholic Marriage Advisory Council. He, the parish priest and a trained married couple, offer four sessions to engaged couples as a preparation for the practical and spiritual side of marriage. I ask him what he thinks a couple's expectations of marriage should be.

'First and foremost, support for each other,' he says. 'A growth in love. That obviously means different things to different people but I think a growth in understanding and respect in the other person, the dignity of the person and the spiritual development of the person. It's really mutual development on an emotional, physical, mental and spiritual level.

'Still, some prejudices exist. Some people see the primary role of the woman as in the bedroom and in the kitchen. They see her sexuality in terms of childbearing rather than considering her dignity as a woman. We have a lot of men too if they're unemployed, especially when they're preparing for marriage, who feel they can't be the breadwinner and support their wives and they feel angry or confused. You also see some people who feel that the partner is simply an aid in their career rather than a proper partner. I've known that mostly in men, only in the case of women perhaps once or twice.'

I ask what he thinks the role in marriage for a woman is. 'I think it's a question of complementary partnership,' he answers, carefully choosing his words. 'I think the woman is still very much a homemaker because it comes naturally to a woman. Usually they do it much better than men.

'Now that's probably made me sound like an out-and-out chauvinist but in practise with the engaged couples I'm working with, having seen them after marriage and baptised their children, it transpires that they fall pretty well into what might be considered traditional roles anyway.'

What advice would he give to a woman considering marriage who was anxious to continue her career but had worries about how that might conflict with having children?

'I would explain that in terms of nature, usually a woman's role is as homemaker. I would try to explain that the stresses and strains of having two career people can be a disaster for marriage. But a lot depends upon the approach of both people, their level of maturity, their understanding. More often than not, a man's work is far more important to him than a woman's work is to her, certainly after the age of thirty.

'I think I would explain that it's probably better to understand that for a certain length of time in her life she will probably be regarded as a homemaker, as a mother. Could she adapt to that or would her career come first?

'If she says her career comes first, I would ask what her expectations of marriage are? Is it to bolster her career? Or as a means of starting a family? Or a means of supporting her husband and his career? I think you'd have to explore different sorts of angles.

'Experience tells us that many marriages, if not all, break down on the basis of lack of communication in the final analysis. Most of the engaged couples are surprised we get them to question each other and talk about things before marriage. They see the sense in it but whether they do it or not is their business. We don't crack any whips. We don't say, "Unless you talk about this, you're not getting married."

'People don't seem to make the effort to talk to each other because there's so many things going on. A lot of it is the fault of the telly or maybe it's the couple's fault that they haven't got the discipline to turn if off,' he says.

'Some of the couples are already living together when they come to us. We have to point out the morality of what's right but then it's up to a person's conscience. We can only advise. They have a responsibility to themselves.'

On contraception, Father Fred advocates NFP, Natural Family Planning, in accordance with the teaching of the Church. The arguments he puts in its favour he expresses as being arguments which are 'pro-women'.

'It's to do with the dignity of the person, especially the woman, because the Church is far more pro-woman than it's given credit for. It's to do with mutual respect, the question of sexuality being seen as the involvement of *both* partners in the development of their sex lives.

'If the Pill is used it is only the woman who is involved in one sense. It's her responsibility to take the Pill. Coitus Interruptus is totally against the teachings of the Church because it's really not the complete sexual act. We're talking about dignity and mutual growth.'

I suggest there is sometimes little dignity for a woman having her sixth or seventh unwanted child.

'Absolutely,' he replies, smiling. 'I have spoken to couples, doctors and tutors who tell me that with NFP you can plan a pregnancy as well as avoid one.' What of the high rate of error? 'The rate of error is when NFP is used partially or misunderstood. It's a question of motivation and understanding and preparation.'

NFP may be practical for a couple prepared to work together, I suggest, but it is difficult for a single woman, for instance, who may have sexual desires. Sexuality in any case must be a difficult issue for him to tackle, particularly when, irrespective of the morality involved, sexual appetites at the present time seem so easily distorted by commercialism. The immediate sensation – or satisfying it – holds far higher profits than the development of more refined feelings, so how does he approach the issue of sexuality?

'With great difficulty,' Father Fred says instantly and gives a small smile. 'The young especially are under such intense pressure from the media, from people who are making an awful lot of money out of the bestial side of sexuality, those who make millions out of it without any regard for the dignity of the person, especially in terms of pornography.

'In realistic terms, the saturation bombing by the media about sexuality outweighs the support we can give. I think young girls are far more sexually aware now but frightened. The level of insecurity is so much greater. Many girls – outside the Church too – have asked me, "What is sexuality?" They're frightened because its portrayed really from a selfish point of view. The only important thing is self-gratification. They're confused, they're frightened. They think, Well, if I get married is that all sex is going to mean to me? They're terrified they're going to be a disappointment to their husbands who may not feel gratified.'

'What about their own gratification?' I ask. 'That's obviously important,' he answers. 'I forgot to mention that. First and foremost I try to say that it's not just the sexual act, that sexuality means seeing the person as a human being, not just a body from who you take your pleasure and leave. The respect is mutual, the person who's having sex with you will hopefully see it in the same context. It's very difficult because we're telling them one thing, the media tells them another and they sit in the middle and say, "Who's right?"'

'I would like to think that all people like sex,' he adds. 'It was created to be enjoyed in its right approach. We certainly don't say to girls that you shouldn't enjoy sex or love play – we say enjoy it in the right context.'

'Obviously we would rather people waited until marriage. We say we understand they're under a lot of pressure but we talk a lot about peace of mind and peace of spirit. We ask, "What is going to give you peace of mind, self-respect and respect for other people? Is it going to be having casual sex or is it going to be seeing sex as part of love?"'

I ask if girls don't tell him that the onus is unfairly on them? That if they try to remain virginal boys will continue to try equally hard to get their leg over?

'I think basically it *is* unfair,' Father Fred says. 'It is still very much a male-orientated world. It probably always will be. Teachers like myself at school explain that the physical drive in men is much stronger than in women, that women look for emotional security in sex more than men do.' I suggest that that view is now strongly being challenged by scientific research.

'Yes, but women who are sexually active of no particular faith at grass level would perhaps say differently.' How do boys respond to his arguments? 'There's quite a large spectrum. Some boys will say, "Well, a girl is just there for us to enjoy." Others will say, "Well, you're saying this which is fine but I can't wait until I'm twenty-three. I'm going out with a girl and I fancy her like mad and I know she fancies me, what can I do?"

'I have to say the final decision is with them but I can only point out what is morally right. The highest point of commitment between a man and woman is marriage and the highest expression of love between a man and a woman is the sexual act. Or it should be. Some will understand that and accept it but some will say it's a load of hooha. "Thank you, but no thank you."

'I went though the whole thing of the sixties myself as a teenager,' he adds, 'when the subject of sexuality just exploded really, it was admitted as the social norm. Friends who were non-Catholics were always boasting of having a girl and so forth. They would say, "Oh, I had a great time with Linda or Susie last night." Somebody would say, "You going out with her?" "Oh no, it was just a one-night stand." Almost always the response would be "Well done Johnnie or Well done Bill." Somewhere along the line someone would ask how they felt about it and almost always there was a great big But . . .

'I think there's been a great deterioration in the portrayal of the human being,' he continues. 'Since the early sixties, the tensions and pressures have increased to such a vast extent that the human being is regarded either as a money-making machine or as a sexual machine or as a servant of the State. The whole question of this fantastic creation we have in the human being is laughed at.

'In the time of Flower Power, the people who dropped out were considered oddballs all because they rejected materialism. Perhaps they didn't reject the sexual side but they certainly rejected the animalistic and selfish approach to sexuality, I think.'

I ask where he believes the present trends he has described will end. 'I think because of groups like the Peace Women, the women against abortion and so on, people are stopping and thinking, Well now, nuclear war, materialism, bestial sexuality aren't good for me, so what is? They're starting to think about the kind of world they're living in. They're asking for leadership, they're asking for people to speak out with courage and determination. I think there's a natural law of goodness in people.

'In reality and in fantasy, we have this terrible dehumanising of people. Might is right; the strongest is the best. The person who is gentle and kind and considerate is looked on as being a fool.'

I suggest that what he has described is often seen as synonymous with male characteristics. 'Very much so,' he agrees. 'It's a male world and it probably always will be so, as I said before. I have a friend who is a genetics expert and he says a lot of the high-powered career women have a lot of male characteristics. The desire for dominance . . .'

Conditioning must also play a large part, I say. Would he regard, for instance, the popular image of Jesus Christ as that of a fairly 'feminine' man?

'Yes. A lot of people would say that for instance, because of the depth of his love. It's considered effeminate to show love in a man in the sense of being tender and compassionate. It's considered effeminate to be forgiving and to care for people.

'I personally find that masculinity and femininity are tremendously attractive understood in the right way. Now, by masculinity I don't mean brutality, because some of the most masculine men I know are incredibly tender people.

'I would say that a masculine man is first of all a man who enjoys being a man. He enjoys activities in sports, he enjoys his own worth. He doesn't have to be six foot two and fifteen stone of solid muscle. I think it is a man who is well-mannered, who's got self-control, intelligence, educated in the wider sense of how to treat people. That's what I would call masculinity.

'Masculinity isn't necessarily equal to basic aggression. I would regard Jesus Christ, Gandhi, people like that as incredibly masculine because of their qualities.

'I think there is an artificial standard of masculinity laid down by the media,' he offers, 'which says a man is only a man if he is butch. It creates a sense of inadequacy or failure in some men.' It is that, he says, which sometimes prompts men to take such terrible revenge on women in the form of sexual abuse.

How then does he define femininity, I ask? 'Again, as in a man, it's the ability a woman has to recognise in herself the female qualities.

'I think a woman is more inclined to show her feelings than a man. She is not afraid of tenderness and gentleness. Women aren't afraid either to show their vulnerability. their partnership with mankind. They don't feel inferior or superior; they don't desperately try to do what a man does and avoid doing what a woman does. They enjoy their femininity and their partnership with males.

'I think there's a maternal instinct and a paternal instinct,' he adds. 'Social conditioning had made it difficult for the paternal instinct to develop. It's such a rat race to make ends meet now. A man has to work himself into the ground. Time and again, men have said to me that they would love to spend time with the wife and kids but if they don't work, the kids don't eat or they don't get a holiday.

'They're torn between obligations and loyalties. Sometimes the wife is driving them on, perhaps she is more materialistic or she wants a husband who's in a higher management level.

'Many men would love to enjoy their children as much as women do. Again, fellows have said to me that after work they may refuse to go round to the pub because they want to get back to the family. The response from friends is often, "My wife doesn't tell me what to do." It's nothing to do with anyone being told what to do, the man certainly loves his wife and happens to enjoy her company.'

I suggest that some of the 'feminine' qualities he has described aren't always necessarily to be found only in the stereotype 'feminine' woman. 'Yes,' he replies, 'femininity isn't necessarily being completely docile and subservient and all those things which femininity conveys to some people. I think in every human being there are male and female qualities.'

Given the female qualities he has described, women's alleged willingness to 'give', would he be in favour of women priests? At first Father Fred says, 'No.'

'Being a priest requires an outlook that is perhaps – I say *perhaps* – more prevalent in men than in women. The emotional demands are so great I wonder if women are built to cope with it.'

I suggest that from his own description they seem to have exactly that reserve of emotions on which to draw. 'Well, that's right. But I think there's also something to be seen in the question of a man being regarded as a leader and a woman as his partner. Again, there are exceptions such as Mrs Thatcher and Mrs Gandhi, but by and large a man usually emerges as a leader of a community.

'At parish level, the majority would like to see a man as the leader of the parish community.' I suggest that there seems to be an absence of social justice in that view. Isn't it the kind of logic which once upon a time said married women weren't fit to own property or cast a vote?

'With respect I'd like to disagree,' Father Fred argues back. 'In my own personal judgment, I know women who would make very good priests. But many of the women I talk to would rather be involved in the decision-making rather than in the priesthood.

'The priesthood is mistakenly seen as the institution which holds *the* power in the community when, to my mind, it should be about service and support.

'Many men try for the priesthood and leave because they have a rude awakening in the Seminary. It's a sheer slog of service. If women saw it as a means of service then I wouldn't seriously object to their entering the priesthood. I know some women who would be natural candidates but I can't see it in my lifetime.'

We talk of Father Fred's own background. His father was French; his mother is Burmese. The couple married and lived in India where Frederic was born. When Frederic was two or three, they came to Britain and moved on to the massive White City estate in West London. A year later, at the age of forty-seven, Frederic's father died. Frederic remembers very little about him except that he had one arm and worked for the Post Office.

Frederic's mother was then thirty-seven, she had three children; a daughter aged eight, Frederic four and another son of eighteen months. She had had little opportunity to make friends, and acute asthma made it impossible for her to work. The family lived on Social Security and grew up close to poverty.

Frederic says his mother was – and is – 'a woman of great determination'. She was a devout Catholic, 'very very puzzled as to why God had taken her husband from her'. They had been married for eleven years.

'From an early age I can remember a stock phrase of hers was, "You're big and ugly enough to take care of yourself and get on with it." I think in retrospect it was her way of saying, "You're the eldest boy so you've got to take care of yourself."'

His mother is five foot, weighs seven stone and kept 'quite fiercely' strict discipline with the help of a coat-hanger. 'I think by the time we were thirteen or fourteen we were beginning to laugh when she hit us. She wasn't particularly cruel, it was just the first thing which came to hand.

'In all honesty,' he offers, 'I contributed very little to the running of the home although we were all supposed to have our own chores. I hated housework. If I was asked to do anything I always did it badly so that in frustration, she would do it herself or just leave it.

'I think she was ambitious for me because she had seen all the violence and social problems of living on a big estate and she didn't want me to live in that kind of environment – if that doesn't sound too snobbish.

'I think she reacted with great surprise when she knew I wanted to be a priest. I think possibly with some sort of disappointment, which sounds strange for a woman who is basically very religious. I think she realised I would never be able to give her financial security of any kind.

'She had a terrible life when we were young. She had her asthmatic illness, three children and a very low income. I can't ever remember her buying a new dress, it was always things people had given her.

'I can often remember my mother putting one beefburger on the table for my supper because that's all we had. I had friends who had both parents working who came home to sausage, egg, chips which as a kid was the height of the culinary experience,' he says, smiling.

'I had mostly secondhand clothes until the age of fourteen or fifteen when I started to earn money by playing the organ so I could buy my own clothes. She used to shell out two bob for half an hour of piano lessons which was a fortune at that time but she always managed to find it.

'Lack of money had a stigma attached to it. In school you had to say, "Free school dinner, Sir or Miss," and that was always embarrassing. We used to go on holiday with the Childrens' Country Holiday Fund. I remember kids would ask where you were going and when we told them it was a holiday for kids without mums or dads, they'd say, "Oh," in a very knowing way.

'There was no point in hiding our background because everyone knew on the estate anyway. It's taught me that there can be dignity within poverty. Poverty can be self-inflicted, there are different kinds of poverty. There's poverty of life, money, spirituality, poverty of education.

'It did prompt me at times to say, "I'll never be poor again," until I started to meet people who were quite well off. They didn't strike me as particularly happy. Until then I'd believed that having money could only bring *happiness*. Now I don't have much myself but I do feel content.'

Did his mother present him with a very vivid image of Sin? 'I think so.

The biggest sin that I can remember as a child was the sin of being disobedient to parents. She used to say, "God will be very angry if you don't do your housework."' He smiles, 'I can also remember thinking, Well, I'll risk it. Or I'd pull the blankets over my head and hope that perhaps He wouldn't be angry after all. My attitude, that God was the God of Love, was stronger.

'I knew other children's parents used to go out to the pub and my mum never went anywhere. I can remember her in shabby dresses all the time when others flaunted new clothes. We couldn't afford a telly until I was eighteen and I went through a period of feeling ashamed.

'In one's limited view of life as a child, I'd think, Why can't she work? Everybody else's parents work. I overlooked the fact she wasn't physically capable. She tried, she really tried. She was trained as a teacher but she couldn't hold a job down because of the asthma.'

As the middle child, Frederic says, at times he felt 'desperately lonely'. His oldest sister was close to his mother, 'being the only girl in the family', his younger brother was the baby.

'I was quite relieved in some ways that my sister *was* close, I felt that meant she would be asked to do all the jobs. I felt as number two I might get a bit more freedom. I thought my brother was a bit spoilt because he was the baby. I tended to bully him and make life a bit unpleasant, maybe through jealousy. But now, hand on heart, I would consider him one of the kindest and one of the most Christian men I know, although he doesn't go to church.'

Frederic's brother works for the Post Office and lives in Bexley. They see each other perhaps three times a year but he, his sister and brother are still close. He has no worries about his relationship with his mother. she is more financially secure living on a widow's pension than when she had three children to rear, he says. She still lives at White City. 'I visited her twelve times last year and she was only in four times. She is very independent. We thought she might vegetate once we left home but she's out almost every day. She goes to a convent three or four times a week and does the old folks' hair, writes their letters, reads to them. I thank God she's enjoying her freedom. It's been a long time coming and good luck to her.'

Frederic says he constantly felt the absence of a father as a young child. Friends would say, they were going to see Queen's Park Rangers with their dads, his mother wouldn't let him go alone and he was too shy to ask his mates if he could join them. 'I think out of pity a couple of dads took me along with their boys to soccer matches, out on Sundays, things like that.

'I thoroughly enjoyed the company of men. They were obviously interested in football and things I was interested in. One obviously couldn't expect one's mother and sister to talk about that sort of thing.'

He had no experience of racism until the age of around eleven at the beginning of secondary school. Until then, children bred on the estate were curious rather than vindictive about others born elsewhere. Then West Indians began to arrive, and Asians, and the racism became pronounced.

'I was called nigger and wog and things like that and I couldn't understand it really. It hurt but I couldn't understand it. I didn't remember India, I didn't remember anything except the White City. Basically, I had to handle it myself. I did what the West Indian kids did. If they were told to go back to their own country, they'd say, "Well, White City *is* my country."'

We talk of friends. Frederic de l'Orme says he has a few good friends, some of whom are married, husbands and wives. His best friend is a woman whom he has known for fifteen years, with whom he can discuss anything. He also has a Spiritual Director; a person he is allowed to choose. They have only as yet met a few times so it is too early to tell how their relationship will develop.

I say that being a priest must be a very vulnerable role to play at times. Some women must see in him the 'perfect' partner; an easy target on which to pour love, real or imagined, partly perhaps because he is technically out of reach and partly because of the priestly mystique; a surrogate love affair with God?

'I would be very worried about the priest who says he doesn't get sexual urges,' he replies. 'If young people challenge me, as they often do, and ask me what I know of such things, I say I grew up in a family as they did, I visit families and learn a lot about life, above all I'm a human being just as they are.

'The fact I'm a priest doesn't make me any less of a man in the physical sense. I still enjoy being in the company of women I would find attractive. I'm not frightened, I'm aware of it all the time. I have to constantly remind myself, both out of respect for the other woman and for myself, that the relationship can't develop into a love situation.

'It is also the case that sometimes a woman will get involved in Church work because she hasn't got a completely satisfactory marriage and she doesn't feel particularly fulfilled. She sees the priest as the man of the parish, she thinks she falls in love with him and its very, very difficult. The priest has to be careful not to hurt the woman who may be seeking support and emotional security. She wants love and the area where she thought she might find it isn't forthcoming.

'You have to be careful not to destroy her faith. And the priest has to be careful for himself because celibacy is a frighteningly difficult thing with which to live. It happens to every priest, it has happened to me, thank goodness only a very few times.

'I had to be frank and honest and the women concerned responded to that.' I ask if that kind of attention doesn't boost his ego. 'Yes, but you've got to be careful not to be selfish. You've got to say, "Well, this may be boosting my ego but where will it lead six months from now?" If everything's in a hell of a mess will I still feel my ego is boosted? What's going to happen to the woman?

'Many people, usually women, have talked to me about their sexual lives and the problems they have and this again makes me vulnerable. Some have effectively said that they think I could satisfy them sexually, many other priests have had this too.

'You have to say, "Well, it isn't going to happen so forget it," as gently as possible.'

Doesn't he regret not having made love to a woman at least once before becoming celibate? He answers in terms of sex within marriage. 'Not necessarily,' he replies, 'I think it's this question of total commitment. For me personally, my commitment to the priesthood would not stand up if I also had a commitment to a wife and children. And I wouldn't visualise sex outside marriage.'

His decision not to have a family has entailed some sacrifice he says, especially as his brother and sister both have children. 'You think of the women who would have made a good wife and so on but then you've got to make up your mind what sort of commitment you're going to make. I think in my case I'll stick to it because I spent a lot of time thinking about it before.'

Virility – and being seen to be virile – seems to matter very much to some men; had it caused him any confusion about his own 'masculinity'? Had he been challenged at all about his capacity to be a 'real man'?

He says he draws his sense of his own masculinity from the kind of love he receives from people and yes, he has been subject to abuse. 'Some married men have called me queer, a poof, they say the only reason I'm a priest is because I couldn't cope with marriage.' He smiles. 'Obviously it hurts but I just tell them, "I respect your opinion but I disagree." I've found that those who say it are men who themselves feel inadequate.

'They vent their fury on someone whom they can attack without fear of being attacked back. The men who are mature and fulfilled recognise that there can be different paths to masculinity.'

He says he feels the priesthood is most definitely a vocation. 'I couldn't have survived otherwise. If I did this for anything other than vocation, for money or power, I'd be crackers.'

He has had to learn to cope with grief and death, for instance, with 'great difficulty'. 'I've come to accept it's a part of life. In peoples' lives there are areas of grief and areas that give great joy. It's very difficult not to get emotionally involved because the people you see, for example, wasting away with cancer are often the people who have worked in the parish and you've grown to love and care for. You do think, What's it all about?

'The only conclusion I can come to is that at some time in the world there must have been no suffering. I don't believe a God of love could have created something imperfect. We've got this question of free will, someone or somewhere mankind has chosen and evil has developed. Conversely, the vast majority of people are full of goodness, so there's this battle going on between good and evil.

'I think everyone knows people who are just struggling through life to be good people, irrespective of whether they've got faith or not . . . The evil is more public, or the fantasy of the evil is more public, but thank God, we have a silent majority of goodness in the world,'

His own reward as a priest, he says, 'is sharing people's lives at a very deep level. I see that as an incredible privilege really. It's being able to offer support to those who are struggling through married life from one who isn't married. But one who is saying, "Look, I care, I'm not up there on a pedestal because I'm a priest and celibate and so on. I recognise your worries." I do feel content,' he adds. 'Fulfilled as a man?' 'Yes,' he says emphatically.

Michael Proudlock *London*

Michael Proudlock, 'restaurateur, reformed Bacchus, tennis-mad extrovert', lover of 50s rock 'n' roll, comes between Anthony Price, the clothes designer, and David Puttnam, 'the British film industry's Moses' in Compton Miller's *Who's Really Who*, a directory of 400 names in the hoi-cum-pop-polloi of café society.

Inclusion in the directory is extended only to those who possess the 'X factor of excellence and social notoriety'. Michael Proudlock is also credited in *Who's Really Who* for his 'after-sales' service at Foxtrot Oscar, the Chelsea restaurant he has co-owned since 1980.

'Table 17 by the mirror was great fun,' he is quoted as saying.

The restaurant is cork and brick and potted plants. The food is good. The menu on the blackboard links the East (satay) with the nursery (liver & sage) and New York's Upper East Side (eggs benedict). Its position in the Sloane zone means the clientele is a mix of Hooray Henrys, businessmen, a number of acquaintances of Michael Proudlock and models as thin as fettucini.

During his first marriage to French model Corinne, known professionally as Pamplemousse, and before his second marriage to Lena Villiers, an astute Swedish knitwear designer, Michael worked hard on table 17 and, by some accounts, on all the other tables too. In *Fear of Flying*, Erica Jong created (or rather christened) that meeting of like libidos, 'the zipless fuck', a coupling uncomplicated by commitment or even a degree of fumbling. Michael Proudlock's reputation is such that he is said to have lent this exercise the same qualities to be found in nouvelle cuisine; a satisfying experience without being too heavy. In theory, the essence of the zipless fuck is that no one should become involved and therefore no one is hurt.

In *Who's Really Who*, the symbols above Michael Proudlock's name indicate that, nevertheless, he is considered 'a heartbreaker', but he has other qualities too: 'stylish' and 'funny'. And he is successful at his business. Since 1980 Foxtrot Oscar seven days a week, lunch and dinner, has been exceedingly busy.

219

On a grey Friday lunchtime, Foxtrot Oscar is full. In a corner by the bar, sorting out an order for champagne, in between saying 'hello' and 'goodbye' to customers, sits Michael Proudlock. He is slight with longish hair and wears jeans and a jumper. He orders a Bloody Mary. His humour is dry and appears frequently in his conversation. He smokes Silk Cut fairly continuously.

He says he was born in May and shares his birthdate with a famous Hollywood siren, 'two tarts on the same day'. He is a Gemini by sign and by nature. He may look casual, he explains but actually he is a closet crispy. 'A crispy is someone who wears crisp suits, short hair and is really basically traditional . . .'

What he wants from life he now has: a job he loves; a family (his daughter Laura is ten months old and he says he is besotted with her, he also has two stepchildren aged six and ten); and enough money to get by.

He is usually in a state of cash-flow crisis. He says he spends about £20 a week on himself, rarely bothers with clothes and has a daily routine which doesn't demand much cash. He works in the flat above Foxtrot on the books in the morning; supervises and greets at lunch, goes home in the afternoon and returns at nine to the restaurant on alternate nights. He also works an alternate weekend, splitting the duty with his partner, Rex.

Security is important to him, he says, that's why he keeps getting married. His second marriage is now two years old. Lena Villiers is thirty-six and was once a part of Edina and Lena producing expensive knitwear. Now she is setting up her own company.

Michael says he doesn't look for a highly domesticated housekeeper in a wife, he wants someone who will keep 'the mystery' alive.

'Till the day you die you have to play games. Most relationships die of boredom, nothing more, nothing less. If other men or women come along it's because you're bored.

I mean that's why Erica Jong's zipless fuck is so fascinating. It's the mystery of it, you don't know anything about that person. As you get to know people they become less fascinating. There always has to be that certain air of unattainability to retain interest.

'Lena stimulates me because she's got a great deal of get up and go. She is developing, she is growing the whole time . . .' I ask if he isn't fearful she might grow so much that she outgrows him. 'Absolutely,' he replies quickly, 'but why should that be a fear? That's the joy of the tightrope ride . . . If you're complacent all the time, you've already got the seeds of boredom creeping in because then you're feeling automatically she's never going to catch up with you . . .

'I feel secure in myself – I mean it sounds very cold-blooded – I don't really give a toss about anything. I don't depend on anyone else really for anything. No that's not what I'm really trying to say. I depend on Lena in a different sort of way.

'I depend on her because she stimulates me, she's fun to be with, she creates a nice atmosphere in the house, which is very much a home, there's a beautiful baby she's produced that I'm very keen on . . . But put it like this, if someone said, "Look, Proudlock . . ." and implied emotional blackmail, "Unless you do this then I'm going . . ." I could always survive without.'

Even without Lena? 'I could survive,' he answers quickly, 'she could survive without me. You should always hold a bit of yourself back . . . if people know they've got you a hundred per cent under their thumb you become boring.

'If Lena walked out of my life,' he adds later, 'I'd be very upset but, you know, life would go on. So I don't suppose you could say it's an all-consuming love like you sometimes read about in books. I've always kept a bit in reserve, I mean that's instinctive really, it's more a defensive attitude. I remember in my teens and twenties, all my friends being hurt by women. Although I suppose in honesty women have been hurt too . . .'

Michael Proudlock says none of this in bitterness, anger or defiance. He doesn't appear to speak as a man bruised by experience. Instead, he sounds a shade distanced; like a cartographer mapping out familiar territory.

'I find women much more interesting than men,' he offers. 'I enjoy the company of women. I do need to be stimulated. I find that even the stupidest woman has a low animal cunning, conniving, scheming, devious mind that no man can ever match. It comes from centuries of being the so-called underdog. Men are very predictable. You know what men are like, at least I do. Women I will never understand.'

Michael Proudlock claims he is basically lazy. He can work hard but only in response to a challenge. Part of his sense of security comes from recognising his own lack of ambition. What he wants is to have fun and make enough money to pay the bills while he is doing so. He has seen too many people who have allowed money and/or work to take over from their families: '. . . and what do you make money for if it's not for your family?'

His lack of competitiveness, he says, makes his life easier than some.

'Lena for example will never be really totally content because she is very ambitious and if she's not doing enough she says, "God, I wish I was doing more." When she's doing a lot like she is now, she says, "God, I wish I could have a bit of peace to myself."

'She's ambitious for money – I mean in a nice way. Don't get me wrong, this isn't a grasping woman, she isn't at all, but she does want to make a lot of money. She doesn't want fame as much as she used to. I think she's gone through that now.

'She can never reach the equilibrium. I mean it's a question of sort of positive thinking.

'I very much departmentalise things. If things are going badly which quite frequently they do, I just block them out because I know perfectly well in a year's time I'll be able to look back and laugh at the situation . . .'

A few years ago, he says as an example, he lost £50,000 on a magazine which folded. 'It's all relative, you know. Whenever I've got disasters I think about what I've got rather than what I haven't got. Right so I've lost all my money. Big deal. Start again. So yes, I'm happy. I'm very happy. I always have been actually.

'I mean so many people are unaware . . . unaware of other people's feelings . . . unaware of what's happening around them. I mean all this shit about the trees and the sky and everything. It's difficult to be aware of the beauty of them all because you're so used to it.

'It's like familiarity breeds contempt. It's like relationships . . . unless you're aware of what you have, you just accept it and then boredom sets in and it loses the edge.'

At two thirty p.m. in Foxtrot Oscar, a group of half a dozen begin to assemble at the bar. Each wears a pink scarf. This is the Girls' Club. The most frequently used pronoun is 'she'; the membership is exclusively male. Michael Proudlock is the founder member and chairWoman, as it were.

The club has been going for some months. Each weekday, the members, who vary from day to day, come to eat lunch at Foxtrot. The majority are restaurateurs and/or chefs so this is, in a sense, their works' canteen.

The conversation is often shop talk, sometimes politics, a bit of sex, a lot of joshing.

On this Friday, the members include Martin, who is in printing but who also 'does' antiques. This morning he sold two Victorian whips for £750, a profit of £400. He orders a seafood cocktail to celebrate. He has had to skip some Girls' Club lunches recently and he has suffered withdrawal symptoms. Today, he plans to have his starter at Foxtrot then move on to a Wandsworth wine bar for his main course and some business. He finally leaves at four thirty.

Patrick Gwynne-Jones, owner of Pomegranates and Tapas, is also present, looking rather like a mix of Errol Flynn and David Niven and with the same sense of panache. He enquires very courteously after the state of my sex life; it is so gracefully put he could be discussing the state of my petunias. Brian, the chef from the Capital Hotel, calls in and orders a capuccino; Roddie, an old Etonian, looks a touch morose, though whether it is because he is the only teetotaller (a temporary condition) at the table or because he will be away for a month and absent from the Girls' Club is not clear. Rex, Michael's partner, is also present and orders a hamburger which he highly recommends.

The conversation, inevitably affected by my presence, turns to men and women. Rex does a quick check round the table. Everyone present, he decides, is a lady's man rather than a man's man. That is, they hate pubs and would rather be in the company of women. Rex's wife, on the other hand, is a woman's woman. 'She loves to talk to her girl friends . . . she goes on and on.' Rex is suffering a tiny trauma. He has a sports car, his wife has a Golf, she wants to swap them both for a four-door family car. Half-mockingly, Rex wonders what this will do for his racy image.

Rex is thirty-three and has been married for three years, with a year-old child. He says he is relieved to settle down; the stress of being single was causing wear and tear.

Martin is in his second marriage and is quite happy to be dominated, he says. He needs someone to give him orders. Roddie tells how at a recent party Martin, in joke, had said to someone, 'At some point I'll cease to be my wife's doormat.' His wife standing nearby commented, 'Not until I say so dear.' Martin smiles. 'It's true,' he says cheerfully.

Martin recites the kind of conversation he can have with a man. 'You ask how he is. "Fine," he replies. You ask how's business. "Good," he replies. Two weeks later, you find out he's died of a terminal illness and his business has gone bust. Men exchange information but they don't tell each other much. We're too competitive to confide.'

Michael Proudlock explains his theory about the master/servant relationship. From the outset, he says tongue in cheek, you have to train your parents, the nanny, your teachers, your work colleagues, your partner who is the master and who is the servant. 'I still haven't got it right.'

He says he believes every relationship is about a balance of power. One person is always dominant: 60/40. So far, he says when questioned, he has always been the dominant one.

Rex disagrees with the theory. In his opinion the balance of power alternates. It must or the relationship will suffer. Michael says that he doesn't have close friends, nor does he want them. He prefers acquaintances, his 'muckers'. If you have a confidant, it only makes you dependent and obligated and vulnerable. 'I don't think anyone really knows me,' he says. Martin agrees.

It is one of those afternoons which happen at the Girls' Club now and then. The time slides by as Bordeaux is followed by Kummel and a few bottles of Schlitz. 'I like the Club,' Michael says, 'it's informal, it's interesting, someone's always got something to say, if you feel a bit down, you can have a laugh. They're good muckers.'

A few days later, I go to Michael Proudlock's house in Kensington. It is huge and explains why he is described in *Who's Really Who* as 'stylish'. Nine bedrooms, a playroom, two studies. It is on a scale you usually associate with the embassy of one of the smaller African countries. It is said to be worth close to £1m – Michael's main asset should a cash-flow crisis grow too tough.

Michael is holding Laura, who smiles and shows off her four teeth. He plays with her in the morning and at night before she goes to bed. He suffered morning sickness during the pregnancy and says he's only got a month and a half of post-natal depression left to get through now. Laura warms to the joke.

'I loved it all. I was there at the birth too. It was lovely. I was so sure we were going to have a boy, I suppose my initial reaction was – I wasn't upset, it was just unexpected.

'My father had three boys, my uncle had three boys and I thought I was going to have a boy. Now I'm so pleased she is a girl. She's absolutely adorable. I think girls look after their old dads much better than boys do. Every night when I put her to bed I say, "You look after your old dad".' Michael smiles and so does Laura again.

I ask if he will bring her up differently from the way in which his parents treated him. 'Yes, because part of the thing is that with girls you can afford to show your emotions more than with boys. I remember when I was a boy I never kissed my father from the age of eight onwards because that was always considered very sissy. I was terribly close to him but I never kissed him at all.'

Michael Proudlock is the eldest of three brothers; he was born when his father was twenty-two. His father came from a family which had money but he began again when much of the money was lost. He went into films and then built up his own engineering company. The family lived in London until Michael was twelve and then moved to Harlow. At eight, the boys were sent to boarding school near Abingdon, which Michael says he used to dread returning to each term.

In childhood, the boys had a nanny. Nanny Blanchflower stayed for five or six years. 'She would tell us wonderful stories of India and the Far East.' Every evening, bedtime was six thirty but they were allowed to listen to 'The Archers' for fifteen minutes through the open door. 'She had a lot of influence.'

Discipline, he says, was provided by public school. 'It's the classic sort of cop-out, you get the discipline at school so it means in the holiday you can be spoilt rotten.'

His father would see the boys in the morning and at weekends; his long hours at work meant they were in bed by the time he got home. His mother, Michael says, 'is one of those people who's never worked and would probably be incapable of doing something normal but seems to be doing things about eighteen hours a day. She does voluntary work and I suppose coping with us wasn't easy . . .'

I ask who was most influential, his mother or his father? 'It's very difficult, my mother was especially devious. She would always bring my father's name into things. You know, "Your father wouldn't like you doing that . . ." My mother is what I would call a very typical cunning English mother. I think we're very much a matriarchal society. The English woman has a wonderful way of infiltrating.

'It was a very warm family, very warm,' he adds. 'We always got on well . . . Everyone who knows my parents absolutely adores them. They're more in love now than when they met.' He remembers that his mother used to say that if it came to a choice between the boys and her husband, she would choose her husband. A decision Michael endorses.

'You have a different love for your children than you do for your mate but you really have to put your mate first.

'I often feel if I can do half as well as they have in their lives, the way they've brought us up . . . I mean they really are very popular. I don't know anyone who could dislike them . . . they contribute a lot and they're great fun . . .'

Michael was sent to Eton. He was never very good at anything but always just good enough to get away with it, so he had neither 'the piss taken out of me' nor was he 'mercilessly bullied'. At games, however, he was 'never great . . . It was a source of disappointment to my father that none of us were any bloody good. He was a very good cricketer, first choice for the Eleven for Eton.

'The two things that Eton taught me is that one, you get punished for being caught so you learn to be quite devious,' he explains. 'Two, it taught you the art of delegation. I remember there was always one person in the class who would do the work so you would go in a quarter of an hour before and go through it with him and bung him a milk shake once a week. I suppose you could say that this is where all the corruption comes from in high places.' He laughs. 'What it does do is teach you to get the best result with the least effort.'

In 1973 Michael, who had spent the years since leaving school working for Dormeuil, an upmarket textile company, joined his father and uncle in a new branch of the family business. In a few years, the business was successful enough to be sold for £½m. They all worked hard, Michael says, it was 'great great fun', but it doesn't diminish his right to claim that he is 'lazy' by nature. 'It's the challenge I respond to.'

Michael Proudlock finds it difficult to recall when he first grew interested in sex but he reckons it was around fourteen or fifteen. About that time, he was given a terrible reputation for necking at parties. He slept with his first girl at around sixteen or seventeen. Since then he has regarded women as his hobby. 'It used to be my problem, like other people have a drink problem,' he says, only semi-serious. He has reformed since his second marriage but during the first, at eleven p.m. or so, he would fairly frequently receive a phone call at the restaurant from a woman asking if he'd like to drop in on the way home. Quite often, he did.

He says the frequency of his liaisons (he counts Lena as his only affair) was not due simply to a sexual urge; the excitement of the contact came first.

'You can go through all the seduction jingles and everything like that but a look can tell you far more than any verbal. You can walk into a room and you can catch someone's eye . . . you know perfectly well that neither would have to say much and you could go to bed with each other. I never particularly looked for it. I never went out saying, "God I must get laid tonight".

'I never did it for ego, I never did it to prove anything, I mean I did it because I actually enjoyed it.'

He believes firmly that every woman he shared a bed with understood and agreed with his terms; it was only in fun. Always, the main motivation was the company. Sometimes it would be a friend, sometimes it would be a natural conclusion to an evening, but he says he never tried to get his leg over when he was drunk just for the sake of it – and if an evening out didn't end up in bed, it wouldn't bother him unduly, the company would be sufficient compensation. Well, most of the time.

I ask if, in spite of the clarity of the rules, some women didn't want involvement; didn't some perhaps feel one night might lead to 1001?

Michael Proudlock says he thinks not. The Women's Movement has helped the change. When he was eighteen or nineteen, a man who screwed around was 'quite a lad', a woman was a slut. 'I think what's happened now is that girls can pick and choose what they want without anyone thinking they're a slut. All right, they won't leap into bed with anyone but if they want to go to bed with someone they'll do it. They don't have to say they're mentally in tune with that person or say they're in love or whatever . . .'

Proof that he has never hurt anyone, he says, is that the clientele of the restaurant has remained faithful – no dissatisfied customers, as it were. And he has never been badgered or pestered at home by someone who misread his motives.

In his early twenties, Michael Proudlock spent four years in New York. At one point there, his sexual appetite caused acute indigestion. He withdrew – so to speak – and spent three months in celibacy. 'I went to bed with so many people I was bored. I was bored with listening to my line. I was bored it was so predictable . . . But then luckily I got over it.'

He professes monogamy now. One motive is that he has no desire for marriages three, four and five. 'I do like the security of a family. You look at single people and get terribly jealous, being able to go out with any woman you want to . . . The only thing with age is that you know what happens, you don't take life by the minute, you have a much longer view. Every single man I know wishes he was married and every married man I know wishes he was single.' He shrugs. 'That's the way it is.'

Michael Proudlock says in spite of his sexual curiosity he has never had a homosexual experience. He has no curiosity but neither does he feel threatened by it. Some of his best friends – or rather muckers – are gay and he likes to be quite camp at times himself.

'I suppose the only time you could resent it strongly is if you have a son and he has a gay master. You could feel threatened by that . . . in case he tries to convert your son.'

The financial position of Michael Proudlock and Lena Villiers means they can afford to avoid some of the friction imposed when one person has to take on the role of housekeeper as well as an outside job. An independent woman is also the kind of woman Michael says he needs for stimulation so she is hardly likely to make him feel threatened. I ask him if he thinks that the changes in relationships between men and women have come as far as they can – or is there more change possible?

'The excesses of Women's Lib have allowed the happy medium to develop,' he replies. 'If it hadn't been for the sort of people like the Greenham Common women, your middle range of career women wouldn't have got so far. They would have presented more of a threat. As it is the dumb schmucks at the top think they're quite feminine by comparison to Greenham Common . . .'

Some women will continue to fight against being the underdog, he says; some men will continue to insist that they have a housewife rather than a career woman at home . . .

'That is right for some men because they would then feel threatened. Men who haven't got the minds or the capabilities to understand that this isn't a challenge to their masculinity . . .

'What you *do* need is people to do what they want and not really be held back at all. I've always basically believed if people have the mind and inclination to do it, they will anyway . . .'

What he wants for Laura, he says, is a life rather like Lena's; to be her own boss, to have a career, some independence. He thinks she will go to boarding school, partly to teach her the self-reliance their household demands.

Lena tends to leave early in the morning; Michael has a main meal at lunch at the restaurant. Lena refuses to cook. 'We tend not to eat at night, unless we go out.' On free evenings he comes home and goes to bed with Lena and the video at eight. 'I always really look forward to coming home actually, I must admit I do like cuddling up when I get home. I'm very cuddly. I do like the security.'

I ask if he will worry about how much time he spends with his daughter. 'No,' he replies, 'because I wasn't with my parents that much and we have a very good relationship. I can be flexible too. Some days I may decide to take her to the zoo for instance . . . or I can take a day off when I like . . . I've more freedom.'

If he had a second child and it was a son, I ask if he feels times have changed sufficiently to allow him to show more affection. Is that, in any case, what he would want to do?

'I don't think I *would* necessarily. You see always with my parents, we've never been that demonstrative but we've always had tremendous feeling. I think if the feeling's there, you don't necessarily have to demonstrate it, it's something rather private between you anyway.

'I mean in our family we demonstrate our feelings by taking the piss out of each other the whole time. The worse fate anyone could have is coming to family lunch,' he adds laughing, 'the whole thing is one non-stop thing of putting each other down. It's great fun and we all love it.'

We talk about disappointments and loss and he says he has never really had a hard blow in his life, nor has he ever had an experience or experiences which have seriously made him question his sense of self-esteem. 'Not experiences that I'm actually really conscious about. One is aware that we all have weaknesses. You might, for example, meet some incredibly successful man but you happen to know that he likes to be tied up and have the shit beaten out of him.

'However successful on the surface, we all have our limitations.' What are his?

'Oh, I don't know, I have a lot. I mean I'm not very pushy, I'm not very ambitious. There are times when I could definitely take more interest in the children. If I come back from the restaurant and I'm feeling absolutely awful I don't want anything to do with them.

'I suppose there are times when I won't make enough effort for other people when I should do. I know the only thing my parents used to criticise me for was not thinking enough about other people. I do try now but I must admit I don't always do it. I do often do what I want to do rather than what other people want me to do. Otherwise,' he adds in jest, and smiles broadly, 'I'm perfect.'

Andy Rashleigh *Manchester*

Andy Rashleigh is an actor. He is also a director and playwright. He is the kind of actor who gets cast as the Detective Sergeant or the geography teacher, he says, character parts. Unusually, he earns a reasonable living in his three crafts – reasonable by the rest of the profession that is, around £9,000 a year. When Andy describes his father, you get more than a description, you are given a cameo performance. Andy's accent is neutral; his father's voice has a touch of the West Country:

'He's five foot seven, very jolly, great sense of humour, great raconteur, talks like this: "Andrew, we'll all go and do that now will we." He's been in London thirty years now so his accent's not so strong. I was scared of him as a kid and yet I can't ever really remember him hitting me. I can't even remember him shouting but I jumped when he said jump.

'My relationship with my father reminds me of his relationship with *his* dad. His father was a Petty Officer Cook in the Navy and he had six children., When he sat at the dinner table nobody said a word. My father could talk but he was very formal on occasions, I think he felt there was a certain way we had to be brought up, he was always warmer with my sister Viv than me.

'If he washed us in the bath as opposed to my mum doing it, it was not a loving wash. It was very much, "That's your wash and that's it." It was very *formal*. His formality was the thing which was very peculiar.

'I think he was warmer to Viv, because she is more like my mum. She was much more emotionally free. If she wanted to cry, she'd cry. If she wanted to laugh, she'd laugh. If she didn't like something, she'd say so. I wouldn't. I was as quiet as a mouse all through school. I don't think I strung a sentence together until I was about eighteen.

'My dad had very clear ideas about the sort of things men do. He was very strict about things like that. I knew what was expected by osmosis I suppose. I just knew when I pleased him and when I didn't.

'I remember I used to be good at maths until my third year at Secondary School when I came about thirty-third. This really upset him, he went to see the teacher. My dad took me aside and I just bottled up and cried. He tried to say, "Look, this is easy, this is simple . . ."

'He didn't have the capacity to allow me to discover how to do it and I didn't, by then, have the capacity to accept him teaching me . . . My reaction was . . . "I can't do this, I'm a failure, oh God, I'm going to burst into tears . . ." I just clammed up. I always do if I'm nervous.

'I think his approval was important but he didn't betray emotion. He was the one who went to work and I felt secure at home with mum, then he'd come back from work, smelling of man, and I just didn't know how to react.

'I had confidence in certain circumstances when dealing with one or two friends, groups of less than three, but within a classroom with a teacher, an old fascist who would bash you over if you didn't get it right . . . I had no confidence. I was terrified of authority for years and I still retain it a bit. I was hit through Chemistry 'O'-level as far as I can remember.

'I didn't dare tell my father because he would have thought I was . . . I don't know . . . soft, I suppose. Although I'm sure he wouldn't have thought it. He was a suppresser of emotions in himself, so was my mother. It's something I suffer from, it's an ability to keep from the surface everything so you don't look as if you're nervous or worried or upset. You bottle it up. It's only recently I've begun to lose my temper. I've begun to think, Well, why *should* I always be Mr Nice Guy? Why should I be charming and pacific?

'There was no weeping and raging in the family but there were demonstrations of affection between my mum and dad. I mean she showed a great deal of affection towards us, openly in front of him too, but there was more support for each other. I always knew that my father's priority was my mother. If there was ever a decision between what we wanted and what she wanted, it was what she wanted. I haven't any idea whether that's right or not . . .

'Really my dad's a great bloke, it's difficult to explain. He's very jolly, he'd never hurt her. I never heard them row. They seemed the happiest couple I've ever known. I'm sure,' he adds, smiling drily, 'that's screwed up everything else since. I supposed I'm looking for something similar. I think if I was forced I'd have to say that I've never seen a relationship as extraordinary as that.

'My mum was overawed by my dad. Overawed is the wrong word.

She was a wonderful mimic. She could have been the dominant one in the family, I think she was typical of her generation. She was very talented but she spent forty years working in the home. She's where I get my acting talent from. She used to run the Sunday School – she was teetotal and a churchgoer – but she would always hold back a bit.

'My mum didn't subordinate her personality, she subordinated her chance of being professionally successful, but I don't think that occurred to her. They used to go out independently sometimes, but we never had babysitters. They were usually both there all the time supporting us.

'They controlled us with love really, that's why when Viv and I didn't get into university, we both felt guilty. My mum being overawed is the wrong word, it was something in my mum's relationship with my dad. When the two were together, father was the head of the household, simple as that. She didn't want her children to behave in a way that would upset him. Viv could, because she was a girl. I don't think I could, this is me now reading a lot into it, but I have a feeling I didn't somehow fulfil what they wanted.

'What they wanted was someone to do boyish things and I didn't, I submitted all the time. I went under. If they said, "Don't get dirty" I didn't get dirty. I mustn't to this, I mustn't get into fights, I mustn't behave as boys do, I mustn't come in with snakes in my pocket – and I didn't. If I stayed out and they shouted at me, I never stayed out late again.

'I was so anxious to please. My dad didn't ever sort of imply, "I'm going to bollock you but you know it's because I like you." To me every day was a new challenge about getting approval.'

Andy Rashleigh says he has begun to unravel a few of the skeins which make 'a childhood' an apparently neat pattern of contentment for some, a nightmare of tangles for others. If his words make him sound embittered, one of the wounded, in reality he appears congenial, composed, a large, comfortable, untheatrical man with a dry sense of humour and an unusual honesty about himself. The most difficult influences to understand are those which come camouflaged in affection, concern, protectiveness – as they often do in families. He broke the mould, he says, when he went to Jamaica for three years in 1973.

Until then, he was fulfilling his parents' expectations. At twenty-four, he was about to be promoted as Head of the Drama Department at a comprehensive in Ilford. He resigned and went to teach in a school in Jamaica, also acting on radio and in television. 'Jamaica changed me in that it got me away from a life in which I'd made no decisions. It made me independent. Since then I've worked out a way of living which is probably my own way,' he says. 'It is a combination of all the things which have happened but it's certainly not the way it was fifteen years ago, when it was the way of my parents' son. Now it is the way I go.'

Andy Rashleigh works through a co-operative actors' agency. Eighteen actors, six of them women, set the agency up four years ago. He has his own terrace house in Todmorden near Manchester. He spends time there and in London where his girlfriend Maggie co-owns a house. She is also an actress, in her mid-thirties, and a founder-member of a feminist acting company, Mrs Worthington's Daughters. The two have been together for almost two years.

Among the plays written by Andy Rashleigh is *The Hellfire Club*, about the Falklands War, and a version of the Prisoner of Zenda. He had a small part in *The Ploughman's Lunch* and has appeared in a couple of feature films for Channel Four, plus episodes of *Brideshead Revisited*, *Hinge and Bracket*, *Coronation Street* and *Affairs of the Heart*. He has directed, among other productions, *Epsom Downs* and *A Midsummer's Nights Dream* for the Contact Theatre in Manchester (where he works regularly), and *Oh What a Lovely War* for the Nottingham Playhouse. At our second meeting, he is appearing at a pub theatre in South London in *Where the Wind Blows*, a play based on Raymond Briggs's book about the aftermath of a nuclear war.

Teaching was his first career, acting has become his second. On his return from Jamaica, he did some supply teaching – at one time in a school in Dagenham. Then, he eventually got a job in Nottingham with the Theatre Education Team working with schoolchildren – and he was given an Equity card. Acting, I suggest, doesn't seem an obvious choice for someone who has difficulty in displaying his emotions.

'I cannot show my feelings unless I'm acting,' he replies. 'I was fine working with the kids in Nottingham because it was a lot of improvisation. Then I moved to work for the first time on the real stage at the Contact Theatre in Manchester and I was working with people who'd done a lot more and who had the techniques. They were twenty-five and I was twenty-nine, they could do it better than I could and I couldn't suss out why because I had the talent but I couldn't put it over. I discovered it was a matter of confidence. It took me a long time to work through.

'It was just like learning to teach. I mean in the first two years at school

I probably destroyed more kids' lives by inefficiency and inability. Acting was the same thing of getting over feeling self-conscious, being watched. Suddenly, one day, you feel, I'm being watched, it doesn't matter, I know what I'm doing. I suppose it's the obvious outlet for someone like me – you can be so many people other than yourself.'

Andy Rashleigh's father came to London from the West Country in 1938. The family lived first in a two-room flat in Forest Gate with a Miss Rush residing upstairs. In 1956, they bought a £2,000 house in Upminster; the mortgage was finally paid off ten years ago. Andy's mum was an East Ender born in Forest Gate. Once Andy left home for college, she had a job in a playgroup until her death two years ago.

Andy's father worked in Customs and Excise for 40 years. His sister, Viv, is four years older. She went to art college, then teacher training college (as Andy did) and eventually married and became a Deputy Headmistress. She is now running a gym club – also a switch in careers.

At home, Viv was the ginger-haired tomboy, he says. 'It was her rather than me who beat up people at school. It was acceptable because she was "arty". She wasn't as academically bright as I was. Her bedroom was just an artist's smelly old bedroom and I think I was the one who was supposed to be the academic and go to university and become a bank manager. Viv and my mum didn't get on, they were too much alike, I was more passive.'

He and Viv never discussed her relationship with their mother, he says. What they did talk about when she was in her teens was sex. 'She was obsessed by it,' he says, laughing. 'She used to tell me all about it when I was too young, ten or eleven.

'My parents made sure both Viv and I read, that was important to them. We read ever so much, I still do to an extraordinary extent. Every Friday night, dad would take Viv and myself down to the library and we would change our books. He'd take us for walks at weekends out on the edge of the Green Belt. He'd come from the country so he knew the names of all the birds, trees, flowers. He *did* talk, I mean he was great. But he was always pushing us on an intellectual level which Viv didn't respond to. She became an artist.

'I responded to it because I wanted to be an image of my dad. But I'm not an intellectual, I'm not an academic at all. I'm sure that's an easy mistake for him to make, a mistake I'm sure I'd make with my kids. Whereas mum pushed us more to be ourselves, or on how to behave. I think my fear of my dad was more to do with me than him. I had security but I had a miserable adolescence.

'I didn't rebel as all my mates might have done. I used to go up to my room, I'd spend twenty minutes on homework doing it easily and being bored with it and two hours on my guitar or reading or talking to myself or putting on funny voices.

'I think it had a lot to do with conditioning. I would just withdraw. Until I was about eleven I was fairly scrawny but tall for my age. I went fat at about twelve but I was all right at school because I didn't waddle and I cracked jokes. At fourteen, I shot up to six foot and became gangly. The school uniform said eighteen-inch trouser bottoms and I had them when everyone else had drainpipes. I had toecaps on my shoes because they said you must and the lads from Aveley and Grays would come in with chisel toes and cuban heels . . .

'They had coloured socks, I had grey uniform socks because my parents wanted to please, it was part of escaping from their lower-middle-class roots, I suppose. At school, I wasn't a loner,' he adds. 'I had lots of different groups of people who I was friends with and some of them I still am. I moved about, I never got fully involved with one group of people to the extent that I was part of a gang or group.

'I was accepted by all groups whether they were the ones who wore glasses and who were interested in model railways or the lads playing soccer for the school. They all accepted me. And I made a lot of jokes.'

He thinks now, he offers, that he was for a time 'too close' to his mother. 'I think I needed her love and affection, not to an unhealthy extent, but I found it very difficult to get away from. I think that's messed up my relationships with women since. It's as simple as that.

'It was her fussiness. I think it came from a form of pride in me, a lower-middle-class pride. She was brought up with this strong free-church, "we're poor but we're honest" ethic. We don't get drunk, we've got clean knickers . . . the whole ethic. And it was me living up to that. "This is my son, look at him, clean white shirt, crisp white shirt, behaving well, saying please and thank you . . ."'

It seems, I suggest, like total control. 'It is, it is needing to do that for society's sake. That's what it was like. "Andrew's not going to do badly, he's going to do well," and not realising that I *needed* to behave badly.

Compliancy is often expected in a girl, I say, in a boy it must have caused some unexpected problems. He offers an example: 'For instance, when you're fifteen or sixteen if you're like my sister, you get asked out by boys. If you're like me at fifteen, you don't get asked out by anyone. *You* have to do it. And I didn't have the confidence. Until I got to college, it was all very tentative.

'I was terrified. I was absolutely obsessed by it but I just clammed up. I could walk down the road with a girl from the Church Youth Club and not say a word. I didn't know what to say.' What consequences does he feel his constant childhood attempts to please have had on his adult relationships? 'I think every one of my relationships has followed a pattern of dishonesty. I can be very charming, thoughtful, interested, bored by somebody but get through all the rituals and then I cop out. I switch off.

'The need to please has become a game of winning to me; the need to win. It's saying, "I want to score" or more usually it's not as banal as that, it's, "I want to be loved by this person." You make them love you and when they've done that, you switch off. You don't actually abuse them but you take advantage of it. Knowing my mother loved me, I abused it to an extent, I would clam up and switch off.

'I could eat my tea and watch the telly for the whole evening and not say a word. It is and was depressing, how easy it is. I hate myself for it. I don't know what it is, I recognise it in myself now. I've had four what I'd call serious relationships. In each one there's been a conquering. It hasn't happened with Maggie, it's more equal, but the other times, the woman's ended up loving me and when that's happened, I've become nit-picking and drifted away and lost interest.

'It's the bolshiness of being man and master,' he volunteers. 'It's a strain in my mother's sisters, the grain of stubbornness. There was a time when I'd walk out in the middle of a meal. I'd not explain, not lose my temper, just go to the pub, talk about football. It's a cop-out. It's not confronting, Why am I miserable? Why am I doing what I'm doing? I've done the cop-out so many times now.

'I just wish I'd had a normal series of boy/girl disasters in my teens. I never had all that bopping in the disco, necking, seeing her again. I think I was solitary at that stage. Now a great part of me says, I'm not going to admit that I need Maggie, that I want to be here, that I want to be with her. I'm not going to admit it to anyone because that weakens me.'

How does he resolve the dilemma that he wants women to show affection, yet once they do, he starts the process of withdrawal? 'I haven't resolved it yet. It's selfish, irresistibly selfish. Maggie and I had a week on the coast together when I was doing a bit of filming. I coped with that and I coped with a month in Mexico, I was amazed that I did.

'I say coped because I'm aware I need time on my own. I've got a pigheaded desire for my own privacy. It's an obtuseness, there's an area of me I don't want anyone else to have. There could be thousands of reasons for it, I don't know why it is. I just know there's a part of me that I want to keep safe.'

At time when Andy's father was on the point of retiring, Andy's mother was diagnosed as having cancer of the stomach. 'She kept having these vague sort of recoveries. She used to get fluid or something on the stomach and she'd have it drained off and be fine for a couple of weeks. Then gradually . . .

'Until the last month, I suppose, I wouldn't admit it. I felt there was still a chance. You hear about people pulling through. It was at that awkward time when Bob Champion won the National, "Bob Champion Conquers Cancer". So the implication was always that my mother wasn't strong enough to fight it. I resented that because she did, she fought it incredibly.

'She was a very sincere woman, utterly uncompromising about certain things. The way she fought cancer was really extraordinary. Her strength came through deep religious conviction and that sort of working-class gutsiness and dignity. I mean none of the three I think our generation's got. I certainly haven't anyway. I think some of it came out of seeing a lot of her friends being killed in the War, most of the lads she was at school with didn't come back.

'That's not happened to me or my generation in this country. I remember an American I met in Jamaica said a friend of his had been killed in 'Nam and I thought, God, they're our age, how bizarre.' Does he think a sense of loss is necessary to underline values, I ask?

'I think it must be, yes. If you accept things and suddenly something is cut away from you, you *must* reconsider. I don't mean it justifies war. I hate all that nostalgia about how we were all much better in the war . . . But when I consider how my mum died and the trauma, it's the only loss I've ever had.

'She died gradually. I remember the last Christmas and all that. We never talked about it. She said, "Look after your dad," or something like that but we never talked about it . . . My dad didn't tell my sister, this is the odd thing. He is an old-fashioned countryman, he comes from the West Country where the men, in his day, used to go to funerals and the women didn't. He felt it was something Viv as a woman shouldn't know I suppose.

'It took about a year to cope with it and throughout it all my dad was brilliant, wonderful. I remember two or three weeks before she died, I arrived at dad's place one morning. I was in a state, he came to the door and I just got so worked up, I burst into tears and he did as well.

'It really is one of those moments when you think, this is the first time we've admitted to each other that we're upset. On the day she died it was the first night of a play I was in in Manchester. I'd seen her on the Sunday and said, "Goodbye," and she'd said, "God bless you," twice.

'I'd walked past her in the ward. She was like an old lady. I'd seen her the week before and I thought, this can't be my mum. But it was.

'My dad and I have never talked about it. We never will. Perhaps not until he or I is dying or something. We still fence a lot. He's not a nasty, drinking, swearing, let's talk about football kind of man. He's a nice man. He's charming, he's a lovely bloke. He gets on well with Maggie, he's informed about things, but there's a barrier about feelings.

'I felt angry and resentful that my mum should die. I don't think I've got over it yet.' I ask if he ever discussed his own view of his childhood at all with his parents. 'I could have done with my mother if she'd lived, I think, but not with my dad. It's too late. Or perhaps I will one day.' Does he resent his upbringing – how does he cope with it now?

'I don't know, I can't change it. I wish it hadn't happened. In some ways, I'm very lucky in the parents I had, but they've given me problems in other ways. I don't resent it. If it hadn't been those problems it would have been others. Part of the difficulty I think was that we grew up in the fifties, it was a peculiar time. That and the transfer to the sixties. I just wish I'd made the transfer more easily.'

In 1973, when Andy Rashleigh left Britain for Jamaica, he knew women who were radical and/or left-wing and/or in the Labour Party. When he returned in 1977 he came across the same or similar women, but this time they also called themselves feminists.

'I felt it was a threat then,' he says. 'It manifested itself in the crass way that it did, burning bras and all that. You know, "We're not watching this programme, it's a nasty sexist programme." That sort of thing. It was fairly simplistic. I understood it but I still had much more interest in racism.

'I sussed fairly early how to play the game. I'd lived on my own for so long, I could cook, I could wash, I was seen as a liberated man. I didn't realise I *was*, but at the time I had a girlfriend who was an arch-feminist. On the night she first grabbed me I knew I was all right.

'I had a friend who is very similar to me but he wasn't considered all right. Mark said things and did things in a slightly different way. It's a matter of being sensible about vocabulary. Being acceptable to feminists was about social dishonesty, something I've learnt all my life.

'For instance, my natural reaction might be, "Cor, Les Dawson, he's great." But I wouldn't say it, and if people switched him off on the telly, I'd say fair enough, even though privately I *would* want to watch him and laugh at the jokes however sexist. That's social dishonesty.'

How did he see women – as natural homemakers in the traditional sense or as something else? 'I don't know really,' he replies. 'I find women interesting. Maggie is older than me but I've worked with a lot of women who are in their twenties and it's a totally different ball game.

'It's as if there's a rejection of things from the sixties. All those things like love, peace, anti-racism, feminism. All those things our generation has developed are rejected and yet encapsulated at the same time. As if women in their twenties have got this on board already: "OK, I don't need to talk about feminism, I know, I'm me." They've arrived already and often start on better terms than blokes of their own age . . .

'I think now I just accept feminism as a way of life. The thing is, it's assumed it makes you want to stay more at home and get involved with children and that side of things. That hasn't happened for me. I think I can express my emotions more easily but that may be a matter of just getting older, less vulnerable.

'I'm sure I've changed. At eighteen, my attitude to girls was fairly traditional boys' grammar school. Since then it's evolved, I'm now acceptable in polite society. I seem acceptable to feminists although I can't actually say what I've done or how I've done it.'

His natural bolshiness, he says, means that he has no desire to talk to separatists – some of whom figure amongst Maggie's friends. 'If they don't want to talk to me, I don't want to talk to them. I found it difficult at first with Maggie. Maggie was a card-carrying feminist, if you know what I mean. She would sit with all her friends and they'd talk in a macho way about willies and sex and lump all men into the same group.

'I mean I don't choose to join rugby clubs and mix with men who say, "Who did you have it off with last night?" So I resented getting all the blame. I felt, why are you doing this? Now I understand, it's a stage some have to go through.

'I dislike the fact that with separatists I'm an earpiece for their resentment about people I'm not. They should be lecturing the bloke in the corner of the pub not me. Fine, I'll listen because I'm a good *Guardian* reader, just a nice, fairly liberal man, but I reach a point sometimes when I don't want to know.

'The idea that because it's a male-dominated world and it's a shitty world therefore all men are shits is nonsense. I think it's because people who seize power and control power happen to be of a certain type, if women are given a chance to get there, then the same thing tends to happen. Although I agree certain feminine values are better than certain masculine values.'

Does he still consider Maggie a card-carrying feminist? 'Yes, but she's not so stupid to be that dogmatic. I mean she was defensive with me to start with, quite rightly. I was defensive with her but now the fencing is over.'

Have the women with whom he has had relationships had qualities he wishes he had? 'Absolutely yes,' he replies. 'They've all been independent, together women which I find very attractive. At the same time it terrifies me, which is where the jealousy comes in. Someone who is hanging around and doesn't do anything is awful. But if you *do* have someone who's independent you've got to share them with their other life.

'I can be very, very jealous, aggressive, and I bottle it all up. It's not just to do with women, it's to do with being a success, ambition, being the centre of attraction, desiring attention from either my mother or father or girlfriend and needing to be pampered, needing to be told you're very good all the time.

'It's something theoretically I should have got over. I'm sure it's to do with missing out on that period of adolescence, not having the attention that I wanted as a kid, having the wrong sort of attention. I want to have everything all the time. I can't admit there's anyone else important in the world.

'If we're watching television and someone says, "Oh, he's a good actor," I say he's not. Or, "He's a good footballer," well, I can do that. None of my girlfriends have been like it, they've all been great.

'I do feel that rage of jealousy. It makes me wonder if it isn't a male thing which can lead some to the capacity of rape. It's a whole area I don't know. But realising that I *am* stronger than you and stronger than Maggie physically and knowing there is an aggressive streak in me that I can sublimate quite easily, it adds up. I couldn't rape someone but I do wonder if that possessiveness and rage aren't some of the ingredients?

'I've got no self-esteem at all,' he offers. 'I know that. I think I'm a shit. An absolute prize shit,' he emphasises amiably. 'I know enough about my past to know that I am – or can be.

'My only self-esteem is that I know I'm very bright, very quick and very talented, very sharp. And, apart from the talented thing, I have no respect for being sharp or quick or sarky. I don't respect the things that I am good at – apart from the fact that I can act and I can write a bit.

'I have ambition in that I want to be the best in acting – absolutely. I used to think in the theatre it meant being respected by your peers. It's that, but it's also being a success in a commercial sense. I need to be reassured that I am very good all the time but I don't know that I *am* very good. I've also been told that I'm very bad. I'm very insecure about it.

'My ambition doesn't come out as vaulting ambition,' he explains. 'It emerges as working hard so that sometimes there's no energy left for private life. I suppose with Maggie it's happened but she's very understanding. I'm not one of those people though who comes out of rehearsal and spends the whole evening talking about it. I rehearse for three hours and that's it.'

'It just so happens,' he says, returning to the subject of feminism, 'that the only seemingly intelligent, interesting women I meet happen to be feminists. I don't think that's chance. I don't know many women who aren't feminists but those I do know are still soppy, giggling, pouting women and I'm not interested. They're not interested in me either because they're interested in macho men who will fill them up with drink, tell a few jokes and have a good time.

'I think one massive difference between women and me that I've noticed is that women are far more attuned to bodily functions,' he says with a smile. 'Things like shitting. It seems to be something women are quite happy to talk about; constipation. I'm not, I'm a bit restrained about it.

I don't know whether it's to do with them having periods . . . whether it's some sort of awareness of bodily functions which boys don't get, apart from wet dreams at thirteen or whatever. We don't have to go through that sudden reassessment and talk to our Dads about it. I wish I could be that open. I'd hope I'd be more open with my kids if I had any.'

In the house, he says, domestic duties are evenly divided between himself and Maggie. She has been out of work more frequently than he has in the past year so he has more money. 'It's difficult because I don't want the role of provider and she doesn't want me to have that role either. She wants to pay her way, which I'm in favour of absolutely.

'At Christmas, we spent a week together and set a limit of £50 each. I spent more than that, she knew it but we accepted it because I was earning. But if possible, she pays when she can.' How would it be if the financial position was reversed?

'It never has been. I'd find it really difficult. I'd resent it. It's the lower-middle-class puritan ethic. I'd resent getting money from a woman. We're not supposed to do that, we're supposed to provide for ourselves. It's everything I was brought up to believe in.'

I suggest that he seems to find much of his identity in work. How would he feel if, for some reason, he became exclusively involved in domestic life?

'I'd find it very difficult to see what I was achieving. At school I was defined by how well I did in class. In teaching, it was how good I was as a teacher. Success is important, it's absolutely ingrained. If I was in this house and I had certain mundane tasks to complete each day like cleaning and cooking, I couldn't see what I had achieved. It's got to be something like four pages of typed script or learning a part in a play.

'I don't know how Maggie copes when she's out of work. I'd get out if I spent too much time without jobs. I'm employable but if I thought that was the only reason I was given jobs, I wouldn't do it.'

Does Maggie draw on him for confidence, I ask? 'Yes, I mean I suppose she does, not directly. We get on very well together.' Why does he think she wants to be with him? He laughs and says with irony, 'I don't know, I'm quite a jolly person to be around, quite amusing. I can do the *Guardian* crossword, sometimes I tell her jokes that she laughs at. I've read lots of books, I cook quite well. I think I'm in love, I don't know.

'I'm very happy. No, happy's the wrong word. I refuse to be happy,' he smiles. 'I'm very content. I mean, it's fine. It's as stable as anything

I've ever known. It took a long time for both of us because we're both fairly prickly. I don't find it easy to commit myself emotionally. I've said, "I love you," but it doesn't take much does it?' I reply that it does take quite a lot for some people. 'It does, yes, that's true. Yes, it took a long time for both of us.'

Maggie had been living with another man for twelve years when she met Andy – she left her partner for him. Would Maggie like children and marriage? 'I don't know. She never did before, certainly not with the bloke she was living with. She has since said she wants to have a kid with me, the first time she has ever felt that. It flatters and frightens me. But on the other hand, for somebody to change their style of life for me . . .

'I love kids, I've always wanted kids, but kids with marriage? I hope I'd have children eventually. In a way I wouldn't feel really fulfilled if I didn't. I have that drive.'

How would he respond, I ask, if Maggie announced she was pregnant so it became a *fait accompli*? 'My whole life has been governed by other people's decisions,' he replies with a broad smile, now dealing in the familiar. 'It was Maggie who chatted me up. Maggie made the decision to leave her bloke and so did the girlfriend I had before her. I never know when someone's making a pass at me, unless they take the decision to do something about it in practical terms. I can't think when I've been the instigator. I must have sometime, mustn't I?' I ask if he dislikes being in that position. 'It just seems that's the way it is.

'I'm sure I'd be very jealous of Maggie having a baby,' he says. 'I'd be jealous of her attention being divided. I would have to channel myself consciously into giving attention to the baby as well so that I didn't feel excluded. I'm sure I *would* consciously make an effort.'

Would he be prepared to do less work outside the home so he could spend more time with the child? 'It depends,' he replies. 'Not at the moment. I can't afford to at the moment because my career's at the stage where so many things could happen and I want them to happen.

'If we had a baby and Maggie had the work so she worked for a year and I was the house husband or whatever you call it, then I'd accept that. But I don't think that *would* happen, because for now I'm more marketable. Maggie is in her mid-thirties, five foot tall, and it's difficult for women in that group to get good parts.

'If she was at home too, then I'd work to earn money to keep us both because I'd feel she was working with the baby as hard as I am outside the house. I feel I've already missed out on what most of my thirty-five-year-old male friends have got – and that *is* kids.

'If I have them now, I'm going to be fifty-five when they're twenty, whereas now when I visit friends, there are all these five- and seven-year-olds rushing about. In the past, I suppose I wanted kids without the woman but I've seen how difficult it is for single parents.

'If I did have children,' he says, 'I'd try to be emotionally honest with them. I wouldn't worry about losing face in front of them because it was a shock to me to realise my father wasn't everything.

'I'm reading *Mosquito Coast* at the moment, which is about this extraordinary strong father ... so many books are about the strong father who suddenly shows himself either to be having an affair or to be a weak man. I would genuinely try not to be the Big Father.

'I'd be appalling with a daughter,' he adds a shade ruefully. 'I'd be so protective. I'd be awful. I wouldn't let anyone near her. I'd be soppy. The poor lads who came round as boyfriends would suffer.' Those traditional feelings are still there then, I say. 'I don't know, I'm sure they would be. If I had a boy, part of me reacts against making him do the cooking or having dolls. I'm sure I would influence him more in a manly direction than in a girly direction. I don't know how I'd do that but it would happen, I'm sure.' Does he think the price to be paid for that is a bit high – given his own experience of training in 'manliness'?

'I'd react against what my father did and how my father behaved. But on the other hand, I wouldn't want my son to be a sissy. I'd be genuinely worried. Partly because if he was going to be a homosexual, I mean what a hell of a life. But there's also all this cheap Freudian stuff, that feeling of analysis that something's wrong with the father if that happens to the son.'

Apart from a few rejected approaches, he himself has never had a homosexual experience, he says. 'Too burly, I suppose,' he smiles, 'I was never fanciable to other men ... it doesn't appeal at all.'

His closest male friend is a teacher training to be a psychiatrist. He is thirty-seven, twice married, with a son of twelve and now living with a twenty-two-year-old woman. 'He's a bit like my dad, he's very much like my dad, very serious at times, wears a sober suit, unlike me.' They met when they were both teaching in Ilford and had nothing outwardly in common. Andy taught drama, he taught maths.

They began to talk in the staffroom, then instituted the 'Thursday

Club', a meeting in the pub where 'we got pissed for six hours and went into school the next day with Paracetemols rattling around our heads. We'd invite others to attend. It was wonderful. We got to know each other, became mates but always when we met, then and now, there is utter antagonism from the first moment, we parry and play around. But on the other hand, I think we trust each other. And get on very well.

'We *are* very different, he needs the old roles, men are the hunters and all that. Maggie finds him impossible. He's belligerent. When he gets drunk, he's impossible. There have been times when I haven't wanted to be with him when he's pompous and arrogant. But I'm a soft touch as far as he's concerned because I'm happy to pick his brains about psychoanalysis. I'm fascinated by everything he knows. I could talk to him about anything.

'He has a capacity to destroy,' Andy adds. 'He's not actually destroyed relationships of mine but he hasn't been much help. He trained in the priesthood in Canada for three months and he feels because he's learning about psychoanalysis that he understands everyone.

'I cooked a meal at his place once when I was staying with him to introduce him to Maggie, she was still living with the other bloke. We had a few glasses of wine then he started to go on about religion, how wonderful it was . . . and he didn't know what women were doing here. Maggie can be sharp and she went into attack and they started going at each other. I just erupted, I shouted and bellowed and shut them both up. I've never seen two such surprised people, they hadn't seen me do it before.

'It was the tension of the meeting. I wanted their mutual approval and I knew they'd be as bad as each other.' Why, I ask, does his friend feel a need to intervene in his relationships? 'Because he's an interfering old fart,' Andy Rashleigh offers and laughs. 'I don't know why. But he's one of the few people I can be rude to and have arguments with and know this isn't going to affect us because we've known each other for years and years.' So the need to please isn't present, at least in this relationship? 'Yes, perhaps that's why it's so durable,' he says and smiles wrily.

James Righter   *Tyneside*

'How are you doing, James?' The man stands at the bar. The decor consists of the colours of a ripe guava; pink, maroon, 'shades of fuschia' might be the posh description. At the man's elbow, the keys of a white baby grand piano bump up and down, untouched by human hand. It could be playing our song or somebody else's, the tinkling acrobatics make it hard to tell. The logo of a willowy palm tree make it easy to guess the club's name.

'Palms' has been open for three years. It is housed in a converted warehouse in an area of blight; devastated housing estates, the betting shops and drinking joints easily outnumbering the job vacancies. At night, the neon sign on the club's roof, a palm tree like an exclamation mark, glows like a live coal in a dead fire.

'Palms' had a difficult first year; now, at weekends especially, it is doing all right. Its customers are a mixture; the out-for-a-good-time once-a-week crowd, the young and in work, the rich of the 1980's – the software millionaires, the owners of fast-food takeaways, the traders in luxury goods. They want California with a northern clip. At Palms, they get it.

The style of Palms is reconstructed art nouveau. Tiffany lamps are in abundance, along with angular furniture, lead glass. In the foyer, a display of photographs show contestants in a recent Miss Wet T-Shirt competition. The winner, her T-shirt about as concealing as cling film, seems gripped by acute intestinal pains; she pouts, leans forward, clutches her crutch or rather the material which covers her crutch.

In a second room, the disco floor is small but extravagantly illuminated by a light show. At the rear, raised slightly to allow a view of the dance floor, is a small restaurant. The menu offers basic steak and scampi, plus food for those who collect meals like hunting trophies; an experience probably never to be repeated but discussed often. Examples: mushrooms wrapped in spinach, deep fried in breadcrumbs and served in a honey and chili sauce, or duck pot-roasted in lemon and ginger sauce.

'How are you doing, James?' the man says again. James, reflected in a dozen mirrors, is slim, tanned; he wears pale blue jeans, shirt and an expensive white jumper. His jewellery consists of a gold chain, gold bracelet and a gold ring plus a Cartier watch. His hair is slightly long, slightly receding but cleverly cut and curled. He is good-looking, but even if he wasn't the aura of Los Angeles chic would make him seem so to some.

James and his partner John Steel, also thirty-five, and a third sleeping partner, a millionaire, run the club together. It cost twice as much as they intended, £300,000 and every detail is their own. They will also shortly open a bistro which they plan to call 'The Office'. 'Where do you think you've been, coming home at this time of night?' 'At The Office, dear.' A good gimmick, James says.

James is the general organiser, frontman, publicist. John deals with the details. The two have been in business together since 1976. They met when they both worked for the owner of a chain of boutiques. James didn't like John's influence. James put a pair of slacks in John's car and denounced John in front of the boss for theft. Somehow, they survived, became friends.

James says John doesn't trust anyone. Particularly when they're being nice to him. He wants to find out first *why* they are being nice. James, on the other hand, gives them the benefit of the doubt, he wants to be liked. His job is to smile, keep everyone happy, make them feel wanted, special, a regular even if you don't see them from one Bank Holiday to the next.

That's why when James gets asked, 'How are you?' for the ninth time in a night, he smiles and cracks a joke and says, 'Fine, fine'. But sometimes he thinks, Funny you should ask that because what I'd love to say is that my wife's gone off with the milkman, my son's been expelled from school, my car's in several pieces on the motorway and I've just been told I've terminal cancer. And if I did that, you'd still say 'Oh good', as if I'd just given you something pleasant. So, instead, no matter how he feels, James says, 'Nice to see you, I'm well, should be a good night tonight . . .'

When it *is* a good night, he enjoys it. He is the star performer; the centre of attraction. He can watch others hustle and know that he stands a better chance of pulling almost any woman he wants – because he is the boss. On a bad night, like tonight, a Wednesday, early evening, in the slump season between Christmas and Easter, he says you wonder what the bloody hell you're doing there. How many more years do you go through with the same old stuff? But you act two-faced. And gradually, you forget where the acting begins and ends; the acting begins to take over your whole personality.

James says, at times, you don't know what you do really feel any more, or even if you *can* feel. James had a two-year affair once with a divorcee with a small daughter. Jean, he really liked, perhaps even loved. But her daughter was handicapped and when it came to it and Jean wanted to know where the relationship was going, James ended it. He couldn't accept that somebody might think he had a handicapped child.

On the night the relationship ended, he stayed at home. Rare that, for him. He didn't drink, he just stayed at home. In a funny way, he felt quite pleased that it did hurt so much. For the first time in his life, he could really *feel* something.

He often says he is like a pack of butter, taken from the fridge; leave it for a while and it goes soft on top but underneath it's still very, very hard.

Quite often, these days, James in a certain mood will say he doesn't much like himself. He is single – or rather separated – and wants to be in love. But he sees women as challenges. You coax them, woo them then and once they offer commitment, you've won. You chalk it up in a book somewhere and move on.

James says he wants to be in love because he is scared of growing old. He looks in the mirror and he sees the lines, the receding hairline, he won't have such a wide choice once the looks go. James also desperately wants a son. Six years ago, two weeks after he married Lucy, John married Stephanie. John didn't want to be left alone now his mate had gone and done it. James and Lucy split up; John and Steph have a son, Ben, a four-year-old.

James would love a son; a daughter wouldn't be the same. He once even thought of buying a son, he knows himself though. Once he wanted a dog almost as badly. He got the dog, the dog ran wild, the novelty wore off, the dog went. Perhaps a son would be a short-lived novelty too?

James has had his fortune read and the man got a lot of it right. He said most of James, like an iceberg, was under the surface. 'You become another you,' the fortune teller told James, 'you hate this part of you and you're frightened of it.' James knows he can turn into an evil, conniving, nasty, dubious animal at times – women tend to be the main victims because when he is not working, his social life and the social life of his friends is focused on women; how many you can meet and take to bed.

In James's view, sexual intercourse, like social intercourse, has a certain etiquette. His ego demands that he should not have to coerce or use force on a woman, she must fancy him even when she is sober. He hates to see a former bed partner with another man. Although he rates himself as a poor lover – maybe five out of ten – his reaction is, 'After someone as fabulous as me, how can she go with another man?'

James reckons he is a poor lover because he is lazy in bed. At one time, he didn't bother too much about whether a woman came, now he tries harder. He has to because women talk more than before and he doesn't want it getting around that he is a poor lay. Women tend to say, 'I love you,' in bed and James likes to believe that, for that moment in time, they really do. He used to say, 'I love you too,' now his conscience jerks him back.

James has never been with a prostitute, he could never pay for a service. He feels if anyone should be paid, it should be him. The oldest woman he's screwed was sixty-two. She looked all right on the dance-floor at the club; blonde, shapely, the lights did her a favour. She was American in a low-cut sequinned dress. John had a girl too and that night he had said, 'Come on, let's go for a bang,' so they took the two women home.

It was in the bedroom that the woman asked James, 'Hey buddy, where shall I put my wig?' And underneath she had the tight curly hair of a sixty-two-year-old, James says. John shouted, 'Ask her if she wants a glass for her teeth.' It was too late to back out. James decided in for a penny, in for a pound. It didn't make that much difference in the end anyway, so he went ahead. He felt too tacky to drive her to her hotel in the morning, so he pretended to be asleep. Shows he doesn't have much discrimination, he says. Men can have sex without a mental involvement, women can't, he reckons.

Occasionally, he meets someone and the conversation is really good. Then he is too worried to get into a sexual involvement in case the friendship gets spoiled. Probably he's frightened to fall in love in case he gets hurt, he says. Image, cool, being seen to be one of the boys is important.

The boys had a say in the demolition of his marriage. 'Staying in again, tonight?' they'd say. 'Under the thumb?' And he cared what they thought. Instead of a cosy night at home, he'd go out. Then he'd wonder, 'What the hell am I doing here?' But the pressure worked. If he stayed at home, he'd then wonder what he was missing by not going out.

James and Lucy met in Marbella in 1972. James and John usually did Ibiza but this time it was Marbella and they felt out of their depth. They could be flash but these types were flashier – and much richer. Lucy was a model, doing well enough to travel the world, buy herself a mink. James liked her because he could talk to her and he could make love to her.

They lived together for three years and then married. They fought often in the time they lived together. They would argue, Lucy would move out, and two days later she would phone and ask to come back. On one occasion, she moved out but didn't call at all. A girlfriend had advised her that that was not the way to get her man.

James called her instead and asked her to marry him. He married for the wrong reasons, he says. He didn't love her, it was just something he thought he couldn't have. The two decided Lucy would be a 'proper' wife and give up work. James might not have loved her but he believes in the sacredness of marriage. He owned a club thirty miles away then, he didn't give up night work but he *did* come straight home once the club closed. At least for the first six months.

Then, Lucy started to ask questions and he grew resentful. And he *did* begin to play around and somehow she always found out. Then his mates started to put the pressure on, they really did. Maybe they resented the fact he had somebody, he says now, looking back. But at the time he listened to them.

James didn't feel Lucy should gallivant around but it was OK for him. He's seen in clubs what married women get up to, doing what he does. He can't help himself, he says, he hangs on to the idea that a woman who sleeps around is a scrubber whereas a man is a jack the lad.

One time when he and Lucy were apart, he found out she'd had an affair. After that, it was all over. She was soiled as far as James was concerned. He knows it's a double standard but when *he* was screwing around, his emotions hadn't been involved; when Lucy did the same, she *must* have been emotionally involved because that's what he believes about women.

A year after they married, they separated. Now James says the truth is that he's nervous of women. He can switch on and have a conversation, but it's got to be a conversation which is part of the act. He has to be in control. If he isn't in control, he might blush, be embarrassed, make a fool of himself.

He had affairs when he was with Lucy because he was still in search of perfection; he was – and is – still looking for love. But in that, he's built his own trap; the kind of women he feels comfortable with are those he can dominate, the kind he wouldn't want to love. If he ever did settle down, he'd be wary. Once he told Lucy: 'OK, we'll stay in and do what you want to do.' He's sure she saw that as a victory, a weakness on his part. It's a game after all, isn't it?

James says he really hates to be hurt. Women he's had a few times whom he knew he could get close to, he's treated very badly indeed, walked all over them, he doesn't know why. He's not even sure now, he knows the difference between love, lust and infatuation. At thirty-five, he says, that's sad, isn't it?

He has three girlfriends at the moment. The relationships will end not when he ceases to like them but because he will get bored. He can't help himself, he always thinks there is something better somewhere else. As he gets older, he's beginning to realise there isn't, of course. A good relationship isn't something you 'find', it's something you make. He knows that, but he's set in his old ways. And besides, in the club, he's hardly likely to meet the kind of woman who can give him more, is he?

Everyone tells James he is good at helping with problems. He likes people to bring him their worries, he likes to feel they're dependent. He wouldn't ask anyone for help himself. Others couldn't advise him, how could they possibly know what is good for him? That's arrogance, he supposes. Besides, there's so much of himself he doesn't want to reveal. If he did, he's terrified another person might laugh at what really exists in his mind and his emotions; behind the twenty-four-hour act.

Men are the natural head of the household, James believes. If he takes a woman out, he insists on paying. After a time, he might allow her to pay once or twice but only because *he* is allowing her to do something for herself.

Pride matters a lot; pride he translates as what others think about what he does. He goes for models a lot because other men find them attractive. He thinks women are cleverer than men, more mature. In his opinion, a clever woman plays the game: you ask her where she wants to go and she says, 'Anywhere you like darling, but there's a fabulous film just started at the Odeon.' A clever woman does not say, 'I want to go to the

Odeon.' Because then the man draws back and says, 'Who's the boss of the family?'

A clever woman is far, far superior to a man, James insists, because she can get more of a man than anybody. Woman's best asset is her ability to manipulate. Ironically, that's why he doesn't trust them. Still, he wishes now he could take a settling-down pill. But maybe after eighteen years of living the high life, he says, it's already too late? Perhaps he doesn't have the capacity, the courage, to risk getting hurt?

It is eight thirty p.m. James is in his office. It is as stark as the club upstairs is lush. He asks Sal, a secretary, to buy a nice birthday card for a bird. He orders a bitter lemon and the barman brings it mixed with vodka. 'Sorry, I thought you wanted the regular.' James doesn't drink much he says but he does drink steadily.

He leaves the club and drives his sports car to his home four miles away; the day's routine is half over. James usually gets into the club at one p.m., he leaves again at around eight, goes home for a couple of hours and returns at eleven. Six hours later, at five a.m., he is back home and sleeps at around seven. The house is detached, mock Tudor with a gravel drive. The sitting room is like something out of the Good Life; red velvet curtains, chintz three-piece suite, a few antiques, large televison set in a wooden cabinet. Nick is watching television dressed in a short towelling dressing gown.

James says he cannot bear to be alone so he has three lodgers, each pays £30. Nick is twenty-four and is the manager of an upmarket men's clothes shop; Giorgio Armani and all that. He works nine to five; goes out to the club from ten p.m. to four. Sometimes he just has time to come home and shower.

Also resident in the house is Sasha, twenty-six, the female disc jockey at 'Palms', and Robert, a hairdresser who has been James's lodger and friend for five years.

James says Robert is just like a woman, he does the cooking, cleaning, keeps things in order. He looks and acts gay but he isn't. Robert, when he appears, is small, carefully groomed. He has an obvious influence on James. Robert says you grow cynical when you see women as they are reflected in a hairdresser's mirror all day. It's true what they say about the sex life of stylists.

Once he had a woman who pulled down the zip of his flies while he was trying to cut her hair. She didn't have the nerve to go further.

He'll often get a phone call from a married client, asking him over after the salon closes. He goes and they have a glass of wine, make love and that's it. 'Bored women,' he says dismissively. Robert doesn't seem to warm to women, yet like James, perhaps even more so, he spends almost every night in the company of one, usually a different one. 'It's the challenge.'

Women he rates as sources of physical satisfaction rather than as people with personalities. Later, at 'Palms', he attempts to demonstrate how easy it is to pull a girl. All they want is a bit of chat, he says. He can screw two women in an evening; that's not that exceptional. He hasn't seen his own family for five years. Why should he pretend he has anything in common with them when he doesn't? Robert's cynicism seems second nature, intentionally offensive; James's cynicism is more acquired, a shade defensive. They both express their dislike of feminists; unattractive women who don't know what they really want.

At the house, James's bathroom is in a converted bedroom. The bath, altar-like, is up three stairs. Deep pile carpet virtually comes up to the water's edge. In one corner, there is a portable TV and a telephone and a stereo system.

The bedroom, as might be expected of a man who devotes so much time to one hobby, is fully equipped. The bed again is on a raised platform with carpet to the edge of the bed like encroaching moss. A control system operates the curtains, the lighting, the television set and video. A gold-plated nude holds up a ball of light on either side of the bed. James knows it is so much over the top he laughs at the joke against himself; still, it impresses some. He changes into soft grey-leather trousers, a white silk shirt, three top buttons undone; white casual shoes. He will eat at the club; lobster soup, steak, vodka – he doesn't go for wine much.

James's mother, Sarah, was eight months pregnant when James's father was killed in a riding accident. She was quite debby, a model; he was the son of landed gentry who bred bloodhounds and had never worked in his life. James doesn't believe they were married.

During James's first two or three years, his grandmother began to die of cancer, so while Sarah cared for her she sent her son James to live with an aunt. The aunt was cruel, she hated youth and she hated men even more, James says.

He remembers once, because he disliked eggs, she gave him a cold boiled egg and when he refused to eat it, she beat him with a wooden spoon. Her husband had left her, so that's why she was so vengeful, James reckons.

The aunt sent him to a convent as a boarder at four. Sarah would telephone her son, but he was too frightened to say anything except that he was all right. James likes to think that his mother was too preoccupied with his grandmother to come and visit, but that she really cared.

Eventually, in school, James was injected with a blunt needle and became ill. Sarah arrived and the truth came out. Sarah and the aunt had a terrible fight from which Sarah appeared covered in blood; the aunt had attacked her with a soda syphon. James was rescued.

On James's sixth birthday, when Sarah was twenty-nine, she married. Her husband, Peter, was a racing driver. James says he took to him instantly and still feels he is a good father. Eight years later, Elizabeth, a daughter and a sister for James, was born. Later, James paid for Elizabeth to go to finishing school and paid for the rent on a London flat.

He adores Elizabeth, he says. She is the only woman he feels he can trust. She is now in her twenties and goes for older men. James may be out with a nineteen-year-old but if his sister comes in late after a similar exercise with a man, his reaction is anger. He mocks himself.

Up to about three years ago, he says, his little sister was a virgin to him. Never mind the reality. The thought of any man touching her made him fume.

He wouldn't like to marry a woman like Elizabeth, he and she are too similar. But he thinks she is the only woman he will look after all his life because she is the only woman who will depend upon him and won't be false to him in any way.

James was set to to go Harrow like his father and grandfather before him but he asked to go to a minor public school in the north and Sarah and Peter agreed. Peter has always been a wheeler-dealer. He is always on the verge of making big money and always surviving very well or only barely.

Homosexuality was very common at school, James says. He had a minor affair himself. He arrived at the school a term later than anyone else, which caused enormous hassles until a senior grew interested. This gave James a certain status, but then the senior tried to kiss him; James, who hadn't even kissed a girl yet, thought he was being friendly like his mother. Until it suddenly clicked.

James whacked him one and fled, crying. He became a hero because he'd hit a senior and suddenly, to bolster this image, he had to invent a love life for himself which involved dozens of girlfriends. In reality he knew none until he was seventeen. He was so shy, he sent off £5 and received ten booklets in a plain brown paper envelope on how to overcome his handicap. The advice was simple: whatever you're frightened of doing, put yourself into a situation where you've got to do it. So James became a shy extrovert; a disc jockey.

James says he feels he may have disappointed his mother. She is a very strong person with no idea about the value of money. She also speaks her mind. When James was around seventeen, her husband Pete's latest business deal failed badly. Sarah told him so, so Peter went off and found himself a young dolly bird.

Up until then, James thinks, they had been happily married, at least from what he saw of it all in the school holidays. But the problem was money. Then he remembers them arguing all the time. On one occasion, the racket was so loud, he left his bedroom and went into the bathroom where they were both shouting. It is, he says, the only time he has ever hit a woman.

James believed the fighting wasn't his stepfather's fault and suddenly something just snapped. He'll never forget it, he says. He picked his mother up and shook her so much his stepfather swung round to protect her. James picked him up in turn, all fifteen stone, and put him fully clothed into the bath of water. Then he walked out and didn't come back for three hours.

He says what made him angry was that they were so selfish, thinking only of themselves, not of him. But perhaps that's selfish of him? Now everyone gets on well again. James's mother thinks no one is good enough for her son. James says she loves him because she's got to, but he's not turned out the way she would have wanted.

At seventeen he was an articled clerk. He had ambitions to be the youngest accountant ever. He was earning £5 a week as an accountant and £250 as a disc jockey, receiving a commission on each person he attracted into the club. He failed a set of accountancy exams and club work took over. Two clubs later, he and John opened 'Palms'.

James says he is at a time in his life when he's not very sure what he wants from the future. He enjoys money but the making of it isn't sufficient motivation – and on those nights when he gets down, he wonders what it's all for.

At eleven p.m. at 'Palms', a beauty competition is taking place; the contestants outnumber the audience. The women look similar; white swimsuits, wobbly buttocks and breasts; skin tinged to a yellowish tan either by the lights or a sunbed; blonde hair; blusher like a giant's fingerprint on each cheek. Robert expresses contempt; not much in the club tonight, he says.

One of James's girlfriends turns up. She wears a fringed leather outfit; blonde hair; heavily made-up eyes; she is sulky because she feels she is not receiving enough attention. At the table, James suddenly finds two arms entwined around him. They belong to a woman dressed richly in pseudo-poverty; 'torn' chamois leather and an oatmeal jumper, artificially laced with holes. She is in her late twenties, drunk and totally happy. Her breath, warm like a radiator, is perfumed with Paco Rabanne, alcohol, the sweet smell of lipstick, thickly applied. 'I'd like you to have a little drink of this, love,' she says, giggling; she makes it sound like a transaction of ultimate intimacy.

The drink is a Kew Garden of a cocktail, a 'Palms' special, Rainbow liquid, in a fishbowl on a stem, decorated with the regulation cherries, parasol, greenery and citrus fruit. 'You take it,' she says, 'I'm as pissed as a newt.' James smiles, he moves neither away nor towards her so he appears paralysed in a state of amiability. 'Are you having a good time?' he asks.

She is a regular, a really nice woman, James says later. Her cohabitee is a self-made millionaire. James says that the millionaire had nothing when the two met. 'Live with me,' he told the woman, 'and I'll be rich in six months.' She did and he was, James says. It is impossible to tell whether there is envy or satisfaction in his voice.

At the bar, a man speaks to James as he passes. 'How are you doing, James?' 'Fine,' James replies. 'Fine thanks.' And no one knows what he's thinking.

Ken Smith *Sussex*

Louise, aged four, waits patiently a few doors down in the cul-de-sac of semi-detached houses for Ken Smith to give her a lift to ballet classes. He leaves home at three fifteen, picks up Louise and drives the camper van, elderly but with a respectable shabbiness, to the primary school where he will also pick up his sons, Ben and John. Like marker flags, a string of women, some with shopping bags and pushchairs, some more glamorous in fake fur and ski-pants, line the route.

Outside the gates, it is icy. Ken and one other man wait among the women. A neighbour chats about a birthday party. Then the children emerge. John, six, and five-year-old Ben, dressed in school uniform, spot their father and swoop. At first glance, they seem all giggles, fringes and freckles; each vies with the other to give the news. And then it's time for home; Ken's fourth trip of the day.

In the back garden, three chickens hover anxiously around the door. The television goes on in the sitting-room, Ken prepares baked beans on toast for the children. John is due to leave for a swimming lesson at five thirty. From time to time over the next hour, Ken tries to coax him into changing out of his uniform. Eventually, John gives in and changes.

Ken says that he is very lax about discipline. Bedtime is flexible and when the two *do* go to bed, they tend to watch the portable telly in his bedroom.

'I try to teach the children respect,' he explains, 'I don't want them to tip an ashtray up in somebody's house. I try to teach them by explanation. I remember at home, it was "Why shouldn't I do that, Mum?" "Because I told you, son." And that was enough of a reason. But I don't think it is . . .

'I feel they get enough discipline at school, the school will shape them. I know I pass the buck. But I think it's healthy that they get a balance at home.

'I try to give them all the encouragement when they do something right rather than discipline them when they do something wrong. If I say, "Look, you've really upset me doing that," that'll go deep with them. Ben was ill last week and John was very caring. I was very proud of him and I went out and bought him a nice toy because of it and told him so.'

Ken smiles a little cautiously as if unsure how his theories will be accepted. 'For instance if I say to Ben, "Put your coat on," and he replies, "I don't want to wear my coat," I say OK. If his mum were here she'd tell him, "You've got to wear your coat, it's cold outside," but I reckon if you give them the freedom they'll find out for themselves.'

Ken and I sit in the kitchen and talk; from time to time the two boys visit from the sitting-room. A golliwog, Pedro the toy dog and two baby mice are introduced. Ben is enthusiastic about his tap-dancing lessons. Only once does their exuberance entirely shower our conversation, like a Roman Candle. Ken quickly checks them and they take it in good humour.

Ken Smith looks a gentle man, he wears jeans and a jumper and seems much younger than his age. Three years ago, he gave up his work as a mechanic to look after the two boys while his wife, Sally, resumed her career as a nurse. The boys were three and almost two. Two years ago, Sally left home. Now, the boys spend two nights with her and the rest of the time with Ken.

Ken gave up work because he dislikes the idea of latchkey children but, more positively, he enjoys being 'a houseperson'. 'That's what I put on forms and so on,' he says. 'I don't feel a lesser person because of it. I don't need a job for status. I don't feel trapped. Perhaps because unlike some women, it's something I've chosen to do. Still when men ask me what I do, they look at me sideways. They can't begin to grasp it.'

I ask if he doesn't feel a loss of status, not having a 'proper' job – at least not by society's present standards. 'No,' he replies instantly, 'I think a woman's life can be much more interesting than a man's – at least some women's lives. A man leaves school, gets stuck in a career and that's his lot until he's sixty-five and then he's pensioned off. At least a woman has got much more diversity if she wants.'

He has been surprised by some of the reactions of his male friends – most of whom are fairly conventional, he says. 'They're stuck in a job, they've been promoted, they've got quite a decent job, they look at me and they see the freedom I've got, a fair life wheeling and dealing and my relationship with Ben and John – they say they hardly know their children. They all say, "I wish I could have a go at it. I wish I could be made redundant tomorrow," but they're just not prepared to take the step themselves.'

He was luckier than some, he reckons. He decided early on in life that he wanted neither promotion nor 'success'. He wanted to travel and meet people and 'be free'.

He doesn't enjoy the company of groups of men but even those friends he *does* see talk with a lot of bravado, he says: 'They say things they don't really mean. Sexist, racist remarks that I know they're winding me up because of my politics, because of what I feel, but I know in their heart of hearts they don't believe it themselves so . . .'

But they live it, don't they? I ask.

'Often they have to. It's the status quo. A lot of women resent it if you go in the kitchen, that is their domain and they need it. That's fine if that's what the man wants and that's what the woman wants. But then, as I say, they're bringing up children, passing on their values and standards to the children and so it continues, that's how it goes on. That's why you get a hierarchical society.

'Women have influence over the status quo as mothers, teachers . . . they could make the changes but they're reinforcing it, aren't they? They're bringing up their daughters to help in the home and she's bought an iron and the boys plays football. And, just like his dad, he never so much as makes a cup of tea. So of course it's going to carry on.

'That's the norm for the son, he's getting conditioned, he'll be expected to achieve, I think he'll lose out a lot.'

Ken tries to encourage Ben and John into his way of thought but says, a shade ruefully, they've got minds of their own. John for instance wants to learn judo. 'I'm a bit of a pacifist so that's out of order in my book. But it's John's decision. You can't push kids the way *you* want.'

Ken Smith was born in a small town in Sussex. His father is a printer, a 'conservative' man who found it hard to show his feelings. 'He couldn't hug us, he couldn't sit us on his knee and give us love.' He was always cautious, 'planning ahead for a rainy day'. Ken's older sister is also cautious, Ken says. His mother is now a hospital receptionist. In his childhood, she didn't work, She is 'easy-going, extrovert, happy-go-lucky', very affectionate. Ken says he takes after her more. He likes to take risks, show a lot of affection.

On the news that Ken was going to become a houseperson, his dad's reaction was, 'How's he going to cope?' His mother instantly said, 'He'll cope, he'll get by.' Both now express pride in what he does.

Ten years ago, Ken's dad had a nervous breakdown. 'It changed his life, he's so much better for it. He's easier-going, more contented. Ever since I left home, though, we've got on famously. I have got a lot in common with him and I can see virtues and strengths in him that I couldn't see when I was living there.'

Looking back on his childhood now, Ken says it was 'idyllic': 'Very sheltered. Lots of picnics, days out, summers on my grandparents' farm. It was a conventional home, my mum did everything. My mum was the mainstay. They were very contented in their marriage.'

Ken Smith went to Secondary Modern, failed his GCEs and began a five year-apprenticeship as a mechanic. He felt no pressure from his parents to 'succeed'. At twenty-one, he blew the savings he had reserved for a Lotus Super Seven on a trip to Spain and Istanbul. He had seen men working around him who had been on the same piece of machinery for forty years: 'They had become so blinkered, I decided I wanted my freedom more.'

On his return, aged twenty-two, he married Sally, then aged twenty. They had met on a blind date and knew each other in all for about six months. He hadn't thought about marriage but she was 'quite a strong' Catholic and so were her family. 'When we said we were going to live together, her mother came the old "She'll be no daughter of mine . . ." After that I said, "All right, we'll get married" and we did.'

From the outset, Sally had all the ambition, Ken says, more in admiration than rancour. 'I was a bit too easy-going for her liking. I'd rest on my laurels.' She became an SRN, then the youngest ward sister, then she taught nursing and now she is studying for a degree. 'I was always "live for today", she always wanted to climb the ladder.'

At one stage, Ken was offered the job of foreman. Sally said, 'You've got to take it, it's promotion.' He says he didn't really want to but he did – and resigned and reverted to his former position six months later. 'I wasn't enjoying it, I was getting stick from the management and stick from the workers. Sally couldn't fathom it.

'I just took it that she had a basic drive that I lacked and I admired that drive. Opposites tend to attract and we were attracted to each other.

Gradually, in the late seventies, Sally grew more interested in feminism. Ken says he supported her. 'When she was a Catholic and I was an atheist,

we had conflict but I agreed with feminism, I still do.' Housework and
money had always been shared equally anyway.

They had worked together on the house – then almost derelict – when
they first moved in. 'We worked together very well. She helped me with
the roofing and things and I always encouraged that. I've always believed
that if a woman's a good mechanic let her get under the bonnet and I'll
cook the soup . . .'

He says he doesn't know what influenced him in that attitude – it
wasn't an example set at home. If he eats at his parents' house, he never
washes up, for instance. 'It's sort of expected of me *not* to help there.
What changed me, I think, was that I had to look after myself for a spell.
All men should do that. So many men are looked after by their mothers
at home, then they leave and they're mothered by their wives. It's wrong.
It's not their fault but they're blind to it often. They think shirts iron
themselves!'

A year after Ben was born, Sally said she was desperate to go back to
work. Ken volunteered to give up his job and look after the children
full-time. According to Ken, the couple never had any difficulties over
money or who should be the breadwinner. After Sally finally left, she
continued to pay £25 a week maintenance 'because she felt that was her
duty'.

Ken found his first problem as houseperson was fatigue. Ben was at
home, John in a nursery.

'I had to get used to the workload spreading over a long period. If
you're a man, you go to work in the morning and finish at five and that's
your lot. You come home, put your feet up, do a bit of decorating . . .

'Once I took over the boys, from the minute I woke, it was getting
breakfast, getting them dressed, cleaning teeth, combing hair, coats on,
nursery . . . it's never hard but it *is* continuous . . .'

He avoided the monotony by doing a nursery diploma on day release
at college. A group of women who ran John's nursery needed help with
ten children. 'It was absolutely exhausting, I take my hat off to those
women, day in, day out . . .' Now, he is involved in summer playschemes.
He likes working with women, he says.

'I went to a boys-only school and when I became a mechanic again it
was solely men. But I enjoy men too, they're a lot more mellow than
women, aren't they? I find that some women can be very reactionary.
They've got their views and that's it. Maybe I'm wrong.'

A few women felt threatened by him, he says, and they then just cut him off. Some, even after three years, see him as a novelty. A few patronise him because he is a *man* doing what they do all day anyway, an attitude he finds perplexing. 'Just because I'm a man – I'm "exceptional". Why should it be so?' A number of the women are upper-middle-class, women whose careers have been frustrated by motherhood and whose husbands believe they should now stay at home. 'I think it's terribly sad.'

'I went to one woman's house and she told me she'd been waiting three months for her husband to build a cement base for her rotary dryer. I said, "Well, you're at home all day, you've nothing to do, why don't you buy a bag of cement and sand and mix it up." And she laughed. She couldn't begin to understand that a woman might be able to do that. That kind of attitude is sad too.'

He says he now knows two sets of women – both only in small numbers. The feminists are very supportive of each other. The second group are the housewives and mothers who live in his neighbourhood. And they are not supportive of each other at all. 'Not at all, almost as if it's part of the big con for women – divide and rule. They're kept in their own little isolated groups. They've got this funny set of values that I can't begin to understand. Their idea of promotion is a tumble dryer.'

What is it that makes them like that, I ask.

'Conditioning, isn't it? I mean like the house we're going to tonight – she would never dream of painting. She says, "Oh, Harold's been working all week. He goes to work at seven in the morning, gets home at seven at night and this weekend he's got to paint the house and he won't see anything of the children." I said, "Well why don't you paint it for him," you know, "because you've got a lot of free time and the kids are at nursery and that." "Oh, I couldn't do that." '

In his opinion, this kind of woman looks on feminism more as a passing vogue, a trend, something too radical for them. 'They feel that because they want to wear make-up and a dress, it almost excludes them. It *isn't* a trendy movement, but in their eyes it is . . .'

A year before she left, Sally told Ken she thought she might have lesbian tendencies. He suggested she go out to gay clubs, have some lesbian relationships to see if that was *really* what she wanted. Sally continued to live at home during the experiment and therefore Ken came into contact with separatists.

Men didn't exist, as far as they were concerned, he says, but he can understand their point of view. 'They've always got bad stories about men, usually their fathers . . . I don't take it personally. I think separatism is right for some women but I'm glad that the majority of women don't feel that way . . .'

Separatism at one stage too had an effect on his relationship with Sally. He read a lot, particularly *Spare Rib*, the monthly magazine, but still he was hurt.

'I could agree that men had taken a hierarchical role and I felt it was time to redress the balance. I was only too pleased, especially because I was keen to look after the children and I didn't consider that a lesser role at all. I think that's one thing where the feminist movement goes wrong, it almost pities housewives, doesn't it?

'I encouraged her. I thought, That's great, but still I was a man and there-fore, in some respects, the enemy. That saddened me because I thought our relationship was stronger than that. We'd had five happy years, I'd be-lieved. I felt obviously I'd been unfair in her eyes. Unjust . . . I felt I'd failed.'

Had he been unjust just by being a man?

'Well, I can't – that's the only reason I can find for the fact that she'd leave me,' he says. 'It was a shock when she decided to give it up. I felt our relationship was strong enough. It would be all right and she was giving up a helluva lot: the house, a nice lifestyle, freedom to go back to work, no hassle from me. She gave it all up to live in a squat in Harrow, that shook me.'

Ken says he doesn't regret the choice Sally exercised. 'I was very influenced by the hippy thing in the sixties. You know, the freedom to search and find what you need for yourself; self-determination. I had to give Sally her chance to find out because not only were be both unhappy, my principles were at stake. You know it was hard for me, it had called my bluff, what I'd always preached . . . freedom to search and find and there it was staring at me in the face.' He speaks without bitterness, only, perhaps, some sorrow. Did he love her very much?

'Funnily enough I still do. She's the mother of my children, she gave me those and that's reason enough.'

I ask, as gently as I can, if it had been easier or more difficult that she had left for other women rather than another man. Ken thinks for a time. 'It was easier,' he finally says, 'I would have found it hurtful if it was a man because there's a comparison. Whereas with another woman, there's a different kind of comparison. I think it *was* easier.'

He says that Sally seems happier now. Reconciling Catholicism and her change of attitudes was traumatic for her but she is even more ambitious and she has found an identity. She has a stable relationship with the woman she lives with, whom Ken likes very much. 'I've liked all Sally's girlfriends,' he says. She is buying a flat close by.

The children seem to have accepted the situation. 'It's very difficult. They're too young to sit down and spell it out . . . but they seem happy enough and there's no animosity between the three of us.'

Ken feels he was more keen to have children than Sally. He was teased at work because he suffered so many sympathetic pains during her pregnancies. He was at both births and took an equal share in caring. He didn't envy Sally's ability to have the children but he did want the involvement.

'I believe if there's a maternal instinct, there's a paternal one too. It's just because society says, "You should act this way," that the father doesn't stay at home and change the nappies. If laws were changed so that fathers got more leave to stay at home, I'm sure they'd get more involved. It would evolve that way . . .

'I mean even when I was working after they were born I had this job as a mobile mechanic, driving this Transit van, and I had a babyseat put there from the minute they were born and from the minute they were three months old they used to come out for drives with me. And I'd have given up the job then if the boss had said, "You're not to take the children out with you." It's part of – it's a very important slice of my life.'

On the separation, Sally had asked about the children. Ken says immediately, 'I was quite hard on her about that. I mean I was easy-going, I gave her a year's grace and she decided what she wanted in life and she tentatively said, "What about the children?" And I said, "If you try and take the children I'll throw everything at you in Court," and I would have done. They're the world to me. They mean a lot to her, don't get me wrong, she's a very loving mother and she worries herself to sleep about them, I'm sure. But I felt that I was a more stable person at that time.'

Now Sally is settled again, Ken says he worries that she might try for custody. That, he says, would 'break' him. I ask a question which would rarely if ever be put to a woman who is a single parent. Does Ken fear that he might be depending too much on his relationship with his children?

'You mean do I rely on them too much? Yes I can understand that,' he says. 'Yeah, I can understand that but I mean if my situation was the same in ten years' time then it would be a worry. I don't own them, they're not part of me, they're only passing through so to speak. But I'm not sure. I don't make terrible demands on them. I don't expect them to live a life that I would have wished to achieve. I think it's in balance.'

He says he feels satisfied with his life but he regrets that he hasn't had a relationship since his wife left. At times he feels 'isolated': 'I know what women mean about their confidence going. It's happening to me . . . you get so used to not meeting people, you don't know what to do when you do . . .'

He keeps the family on £44 a week (Sally no longer contributes as she is a student) and he goes out occasionally, often with old school friends.

Ken says he would like a relationship now but not if it threatened the boys. He misses not so much the sexual side but the intimacy, having someone to confide in.

At the time that Sally left, he would have liked to have been able to talk to someone or even cry, but he couldn't. 'I've got a best friend but men don't talk about personal things, do they? It's the way we're brought up. When Sally left, it was a very self-doubting time, I went through a lot of different emotions. And just when you think you're over it, it all comes flooding back. Even now, you know . . .'

Sally remains his best friend – and when she calls in at five, to the unzipped joy of the boys, the closeness of the family is still plain to see. Everyone hugs everyone else, Sally smiles a great deal but the boys outdo her.

Ken Smith obviously has a large investment in feminism because it has provided him with a slip-road away from the usual masculine path. He says he hopes men and women will continue to evolve but he worries that there is a very right-wing climate about – and women *do* seem divided into different camps. I ask him what he thinks will make a traditional man give up his present position – food cooked, shirts ironed, home clean – for the kind of life which he is bound to find quite painful to adjust to, if he wants to adjust at all?

'I agree on paper it doesn't look like anything, does it?' Ken replies. 'It's like giving up a materialist state for a spiritual state isn't it? There's no logical reason why they should give it up except that they're missing out in so many ways. All I know is that I did what was right for me.'

Ken says he knows no other man living in similar circumstances – and then he has to break off to ask John if he thinks it is a good idea to play football indoors. 'Yes,' says John with a grin. Ken smiles. 'You would.'

'I liked a mixed balance in society,' Ken picks up again. 'I don't like conditioning. Conditioning for conditioning's sake. It's just not on. I mean my father, that's something he instilled in me, he always used to say, "Now whatever you do son, use your loaf." That was his favourite saying, think about things, you know and I think in a way I did. I was a bit slow, you know, and I didn't achieve at school, but I used to try and observe what was going on around me.'

Does he feel he's achieved what he wanted?

'Yeah, very much so. I'm doing very nicely I think, for myself. I certainly feel much happier in myself with my lifestyle. I feel I'm doing a much more worthwhile job. Bringing up my children is something I really enjoy doing – I really look forward to the summers, for instance, when Ben and John and I go out to the parks. I feel very lucky then.'

I ask if he thinks he could ever now have a relationship with a traditional woman. He laughs at first, then says, 'No, I don't think so. I like a lot of freedom, she might expect me to work nine to five, I like the easy way of life, I'm afraid.' Then he pauses and smiles again as Ben and John try to explain how they once accidentally broke a pane of glass because Ben did a rugby tackle.

'Love's a funny thing though, isn't it? It changes you. The most unexpected things come out in you.'

Richard Ware *Stoke-on-Trent*

Richard Ware was runner up in the 1982 Salesman of the Year award given by the Institute of Directors and British Airways. He was pushed into second place by a man who sold musical instruments to the Pakistani army.

Richard Ware heads two of a dozen UK divisions of Josiah Wedgwood & Sons called Wedgwood Hotelware and Midwinter. He took both over in his twenties, overhauled them drastically and pulled them into profit. The citation for the Saleman of the Year award tell you that in 1982 Mr Ware travelled 123,000 miles by air, 21,000 miles by road, visited twenty-four countries and *personally* increased export sales for Midwinter by 69 per cent and Hotelware by 41 per cent; obviously no ordinary travelling salesman.

Top Table News, hotelware's in-house magazine, devotes its June 1983 middle-page spread almost entirely to Richard Ware. Rather like a family album, it shows photographs of Richard Ware outside the Café D'Amigo, Hong Kong; Richard outside Raffles Hotel, Singapore; Richard outside the Restaurant Piaget, Tokyo, and more. Now this may demonstrate that Richard likes his (good) food – which he does; more to the point, it underlines that he is a man of ideas. Each year, on his instigation, Hotelware gives awards to the fifty top restaurants in the world, hence Richard's appearance at the presentation. They all, of course, buy Hotelware china.

A cutting from the Stoke *Evening Sentinel* was the cause of our meeting. 'Perils of a Top Pottery Salesman' read the headline.

It showed a passport photo; square face, slightly receding hairline. The article explained that Richard had arrived at Manila airport hours after Benito Aquino had been shot. Under prompting, our china sharpshooter had gone on to reveal that in the course of his journeying, he had passed through an attempted coup in Thailand, been threatened by a policeman with a gun in the Middle East and had been forced to make an emergency landing in Kuala Lumpur after his plane had had a burst tyre.

All this and work too seems a lot to suffer for the price of a plate. But there is obviously much more involved, not least money. Hotelware, as the name implies, provides china to hotels, restaurants, airlines. One airline may place an order for a third of a million pieces of china; one hotel, such as the Plaza of the Americas in Dallas, Texas, could easily spend £¼m.

Richard Ware believes in 'being British and being best'. He is also against being deskbound. He lives in Stoke-on-Trent, where he has two offices; he has the use of a third in London. He spends on average two hours a day at his desk. He recently won an order from an Australian airline by judging what the airline might need, offering samples and cutting his Japanese competitor's delivery date by three days.

'There is nothing worse than asking a customer, "What do you want?",' he tells an interviewer in an article entitled 'Selling and Winning' in *Management Review and Digest*. 'You need to establish beforehand what you believe the customer might *need* . . . We train our salesmen to arrive with as much information as possible . . .' He attributes his 'spectacular growth' to 'Motivation and communication . . . concentrate on the motivation of your own people, let them know there is a goal . . .'

The interviewer, referring to the Salesman award, asks him about plans for the year ahead. 'Let me just say,' comes back the reply in the best, if unintended, tycoon tradition, 'personally, I don't like coming second in anything.' It tells you something of Richard Ware's technique – but what about the man?

I was interested because he seems to belong to a group which is hard to find among women, a group represented by a man who is ambitious, successful, usually a workaholic. He is often a shade peremptory, sometimes unconsciously so. He asks, in the expectation that the service he is about to be given will not be quite right – or very badly wrong, unless he does it himself. To use the old cliché, he doesn't suffer fools gladly, or even those who demonstrate a temporary state of stupidity. Euphemistically, it is known as 'keeping people on their toes'.

In the case where this is executed with a degree of charm and due reward for effort, the businessman is often regarded as 'exciting to work for', 'a catalyst'. In the instances where the man becomes tyrannical it seems he is still often shown loyalty, for some strange masochistic reason.

Businesswomen exist with a similar style perhaps, but significantly they don't often also manage to have a partner and family at home, the product of one marriage. It may be that as more women do enter management, the manner of doing business may change, but in the meantime I wanted to discover from one man what satisfactions his work gave him; how his private life fitted in; what he had forfeited, if anything, to become 'successful'; whether he thought the position he had attained was possible only for a man and how he felt about women as colleagues and as partners. I also wanted to discover, if possible, whether a man in his type of job showed allegedly 'masculine qualities', such as aggression, confidence, a willingness to accept criticism, which women normally are supposed not to possess.

It is November and the senior management of Midwinter are holding their regular monthly meeting. There has been a 'bit of a flare-up' before I arrive but now harmony is restored. Driving from the station to Midwinter's headquarters is like wandering through a china showroom built of redbrick. Every other building provides the frame for a well-known name: Minton, Royal Doulton, Coalport and Crown, Spode.

The headquarters are homely rather than high tech. Displays of china are dotted around in glass cabinets; rooms are haphazard in shape and size; the secretaries are friendly and call you 'love' and refer to the boss as 'Richard'. The impression this is a cottage industry is soon corrected, however.

The boardroom is upstairs. In each corner there are displays of Midwinter's ranges, pretty, delicate china. Around a square table sit Eve Midwinter, the designer; Norman 'Norm the Storm' Tempest, the Sales Director; Paul, the company secretary, equipped with a packet of Silk Cut and a pocket calculator; the technical manager, the production director, both male, and Richard Ware. He is by far the most flamboyant.

He is over six foot, well built, careful about his clothes. Today, he wears a double-breasted brown suit with a thin stripe; a brown hanky which matches his tie, a brown-and-white shirt, brown shoes and socks.

Apart from Richard Ware, those at the meeting did not know I was coming; they continue the meeting as normally as possible considering a stranger is present.

The discussion is about production of new lines; the advantages and disadvantages of a package as opposed to china being sold as loose stock; the new patterns to be launched at Wedgwood '84; the amount of discount necessary to give a line a boost in the USA.

Midwinter sells middle-market china; the type which seems particularly suitable for wedding presents (and which, if you don't marry, you often somehow never acquire); 'cookware' or oven-to-table china in rustic harvest motifs; tea and dinner sets with escapist names such as Celebration, Calypso and Confetti.

The men and its designer, Eve Midwinter, now drink coffee out of Confetti; it is delicate white china with a spray of flecks in multicolours. One man proudly shows me the 'beverage dispenser' (tea or coffee pot in laypersons's terms) moulded handsomely on Japanese lines and a good seller.

The meeting seems open and straightforward. To an outsider there are no obvious yes-men or women; no creeping to the boss. Indeed, Stoke style seems rather the reverse; autonomy at any cost. Richard Ware dominates physically and mentally.

He sets the pace at very fast, asks basic questions and is curt if the answer is unsatisfactory. 'When you do accounts why isn't there a way you can show the discount we've offered?' At one point the meeting continues while he takes a telephone call from his secretary, arranging a dinner for Lord Harewood at the Box Tree Cottage restaurant at Ilkley on a forthcoming Saturday night; a mixture of business and pleasure.

The impression is that he asks a lot, he expects satisfaction; he could intimidate the weak but provides a challenge to anyone half as strong. He is firmly Number One and enjoys it; the atmosphere is cordial.

Later, he demonstrates his forcefulness again. A buyer has come from Boots the chemist. It is a contract worth £100,000 which Midwinter has been trying to secure for a year. These are the final discussions on the best patterns; the best shape for plates; the wording on the china. 'If you put "oven-to-tableware" on the china can you guarantee it won't crack in intense heat?' the buyer asks. The matter is discussed.

The buyer is female, in her late twenties. She wears business clothes, neat and grey. If Richard Ware looks authoritative, she appears much less well defined until she speaks. She knows her job; the men do not patronise nor flannel.

Lunch is eaten as they talk; bridge rolls, slices of pork pie, German wine. The buyer says decisively that the final word lies with London but she favours what has been decided today. Richard Ware makes his apologies and leaves at two p.m.; he lives life by a tight schedule.

Later he says that if a person can do a job, the sex of the person is irrelevant. His Sales Manager is a woman, 'bloody good at her job'. Two Sales Reps are women. However, if a man and a woman with an equal set of qualifications applied for the same job, he would opt for the man, he says. 'Women do tend to go off and have children; even when they say they won't, they eventually do – and that messes up the system.'

Richard Ware's main office is in the Hotelware factory; it is small and unostentatious except for the odd flashes of indulgence. On the desk are hand-rolled cigars in a box on which his name is engraved, and a Wedgwood smoking set, but no photographs of the family. Those, he says, he keeps in his wallet. On walls and surfaces are samples of china and photographs of events; a plate made for Sir Freddie Laker; a snap of a grand Dinner of Dinners. 'It cost £1,000 to organise,' Richard Ware smiles. 'The chairman might have objected but it got his picture on the front page of the *Daily Telegraph*.'

Wherever he moves, calls or people arrive waiting for orders like a stream of runners. On one occasion, he says, he had to have lunch in London and dinner in New York. He did it by driving to Heathrow on a motorbike. The constant demand for his attention happens again in the office above the Wedgwood Showroom in Wigmore Street, London. Coffee is brought in more exquisite china; arrangements are made this time to take a client to lunch at Scott's (if a restaurant doesn't buy Hotelware, Richard Ware doesn't buy their meals); a couple of memos are dictated. Richard Ware doesn't look at his watch, he is extremely pleasant, but you feel that he is automatically counting the minutes as they tick by.

He gives the impression that he is a man of instinct who doesn't have the time and/or the inclination to analyse emotions. He may also lack the need; home and work appear to be in harmony enough to suit his needs. Fairly frequently, I ask a question to which I expect a reply in terms of his personal life and he answers instead in the context of work (a response given by a number of the men I interviewed). This may be less an indication of the priorities in his life more a matter of being unused to someone expressing curiosity in what happens in his private life.

He joined Wedgwood in 1966 at the age of eighteen and has moved to a new job almost every two years. He would like a new challenge now, he says. If a good offer doesn't materialise by the time he is thirty-eight or so, he could well move on. As it is, work gives him total satisfaction. He enjoys getting results. He still has a lot to learn in ways of handling people he says, but he tries.

'My chairman has taken me on one side before now and said, "You're doing very well, son, but stop antagonising Joe Bloggs".' He adds that he likes criticism. 'As long as it is meant to be a constructive appraisal of a particular situation. I just blow a fuse about political criticism, somebody trying to get one back on you.

'About every year or so, I always like to ask one of my superiors what I've done wrong in the previous year. I don't want praise for what I've done right. I really want to hear the half a dozen things I haven't done well enough.'

I ask if he has a mentor in work. He replies that while there are suitable people on the board they are very busy people, 'you have to catch them at the right time', so he operates as a loner.

Did he plan his career from the outset (advice frequently given to women) and if not, at what point did he know that he was going to go far? 'I think it only became clear when I suddenly had somebody older than me taking instructions,' he says. 'I think I was about twenty-one or twenty-two and I had two reps working for me, both older. If I look back, it's about that period that I thought, Well, maybe I've got something they haven't. I didn't know what it was, but . . .'

He doesn't have a blueprint as such, he says, 'because as soon as you do that then you're going to be unhappy when it doesn't happen. I've set certain goals over the last ten or fifteen years. Three years before I became managing director I said within five years I'd like to have that job and I got it within three. You set yourself targets but I'm not suddenly going to get despondent if it doesn't happen.'

I tell him that I feel people around him aren't so much on edge or frightened in his presence but they're certainly alert. 'That's probably a fair way of putting it,' he replies. 'At Midwinter we had a bit of a session before you arrived. I'd rather have somebody make their opinion known, say what they want to say and get on with it. You see so many people who become indecisive, then worry about it and take it home. What's the use?

'If you've only so many hours in the day and you want to spend the evening with your family, what's the use of spending the whole time asking yourself if you made the right decision at the meeting at ten a.m.? You won't solve anything. If you genuinely feel you've made a mistake then the thing to do is reconsider the next morning.

'I firmly believe that *a* decision is better than *no* decision as long as you make more than fifty-one per cent right decisions. I can't stand somebody saying, "Let me think about it and I'll give you a ring tomorrow."'

His day begins at six fifteen, he gets into the office early and makes a list which he works through. His trips abroad are frequent and usually last three weeks. 'I work in the evening in the sense that, say, I've been away for a few weeks, then there's usually about forty or fifty trade magazines I want to go through. I can watch telly and do that at the same time. It's not a matter of sitting at home the whole evening locked in a small office.'

I ask if it's a myth that you have to work sixteen hours a day, seven days a week in order to be successful. 'I do work longer hours than perhaps I need to do,' he says. 'But I don't find work tiring. I only get tired if I'm stuck in the office all day pushing paper around. If you don't worry, then you've taken away half the anxiety of it, which makes you tired.'

Did he train himself not to worry or is he naturally relaxed? 'I wouldn't say relaxed. I tend to go up and down like a yoyo. I'll shout at somebody without meaning any malice one minute and be quietly talking to another person the next.'

He adds that he wouldn't like to retire early, he likes his job too much and he doesn't really feel that the kind of hours he works causes him to miss out on much. 'There are always things that you want to do that you don't get time for. I mean I've been promising to redo the dining-room for months and I finally got pinned down on Sunday. It's my job to hump all the furniture out and wash the walls down.'

On a week's holiday in Spain he and his family stayed at a Marina with expensive yachts in the harbour. 'All those people had obviously made themselves a fortune. But I can't really see that I'd permanently want to sit on a yacht with my Campari and soda. It's very nice for one or two weeks but I can't see that's how I'd want to spend ten years or more.'

I ask him if he could contemplate the idea of role reversal; he at home while his wife worked. Could he visualise that? 'No,' he answers briefly and smiles. Did he feel he would have enough resources to enjoy life without work? 'No.' I ask if he thinks it possible for a woman to come as far as he has and have a family life similar to his.

'I don't think it is,' he answers after some thought. 'The kids would have to come in between somewhere. My wife would like to go out to work but she feels the children should come first. If she could find a job that was term time, ten till three and mentally stimulating, then she would like to do that.'

Does she ever feel resentful? 'I suppose on occasions if she's not feeling on top form perhaps slightly, yes. She's slightly resentful of the area we're living in because she knows if we lived in London, she could get a job with her old boss straight away on the hours and terms she wants. So she is resentful of that fact.'

Was there anything he felt he could do about it? 'I don't see that there is. In the end, it's a matter of what's the worst of two evils. Yes, I can go and find another job in London but there's no guarantee that Jenny would be happy.'

Could he conceive of a time when a man stays home to mind the children while the wife works? 'All that would probably do is upset two careers instead of one,' he says. 'If a husband and a wife have brought children into the world is it really right that they should give the responsibility of bringing them up to somebody else? I think it's awful to send a child to boarding school. Somebody, in my opinion, has to look after the baby and that should be one of the parents and it tends to be the woman.'

I ask if he has ever worked under a woman. 'No,' is his answer, 'but I don't see that it's relevant. I think if somebody is good at their job that's what matters. Normally, women that get into good positions have to be better than a man anyway. I respect women that have got themselves into good positions.'

Richard Ware is reluctant to discuss the salary and perks which go with his job. A guide comes from the Institute of Directors, which recently published a survey of directors' salaries. They average out at £30,000 a year including perks such as private health schemes and a company car; expense accounts and time spent travelling on the company's money.

Richard Ware has a detached house outside Stoke, built in 1820, which stands in half an acre of land. He paid £35,000 for it, but it has now more than doubled in value. His two children, Katy and Gareth, both go to private schools in Newcastle-under-Lyme; Jenny Ware has to drive over thirty miles a day to ferry them to and fro.

'We sent our children to private school only because the local schools are so "ee by gum lass".' Stoke is much more class-conscious than London, he explains. 'Some of the parents are pleasant enough, but some make a point that they are seen arriving in their Mercedes. You're told they've got electric doors on their garage, things like that.

'Well, I'd put electric doors on the garage if they were needed, and I wouldn't if they weren't. I wouldn't go around telling the neighbours, I'm not much into status things.

'I suppose those that have made money in their own generation want everybody to know. All right, you may accuse me of that – monogram on the shirt [a detail I had gently teased him about earlier when he claimed not to have much interest in clothes] – but I hope I'm not that way.'

The Wares have lived in Stoke-on-Trent for five years. They met in London and married when Jenny was nineteen and Richard twenty. 'Too young, all that sort of thing. Our daughter's nine now and if she comes home when she's eighteen and says she wants to get married, we're going to start being petrified parents.

'I think the most difficult time was the first couple of years. We tended to have really good slanging matches and Jenny went home to mum on more than one occasion. When we learnt to live together and stop being so childish it worked quite well.'

Jenny worked as a legal secretary and they made a conscious decision to have some time on their own before the children arrived. Katy came in the fifth year of what is now a fourteen-year marriage. 'We've an awful lot of friends who've broken up. I think you've got to work at it. If you think the vicar or an agony column is going to sort out your problems, you're in trouble.'

He often refers to Jenny in his conversation and quotes her opinion. At one stage he shows her photograph with an obvious display of pride. 'If she really wants to get something out of me,' he says, 'she only has to flutter her eyelashes.'

The Wares have to entertain business people two or three times a week. Richard shares the cooking, 'quite complicated dishes', not because he doesn't think his wife cooks well enough but because, he explains, he finds it relaxing.

'I think the most difficult thing for Jenny has been meeting people . . . many would be quite important or quite senior. Say a charity do which Lord Forte attends. It can be quite daunting but now she likes it.'

I ask what, in his opinion, makes Jenny a good wife. 'She stand up for herself without being bitchy. She makes it clear what the rules are without saying, for instance, "You must be at home at a certain time." If I've

worked late a bit too often, she points out that I've gone over the line.
We enjoy our own company. If I'm home late for any reason and it's a
night when I've said we were going out for dinner, she won't complain
that because of business we've lost out but she makes damned sure we're
out the next night. So she gets her way but in a nice way.

'She puts up with all the travelling. There's nothing like being abroad
and wondering, "Oh if the flight's two hours late will she fall out with
me?"' Does that happen with some men, I ask? 'Oh yes,' he replies. 'I
had one salesman who cut an appointment to get back early. The customer
mumbled to me about it. He said the salesman had said he had to get
back because he had an urgent meeting on the following morning. I
covered for him and then called the man up and said, "Well, what's this
about an urgent meeting?" It turned out he had to back in the evening
to babysit so his wife could go to a WI meeting.

'I told him, "Make up your mind next time that either you don't go
travelling or you get your home life sorted out".'

I ask if there is anything he misses on the long trips abroad. 'It's almost
the reverse,' he answers. 'What you have to do when you come back is
get back to the real world. Occasionally when I'm back I'll say something
to my wife like, "This collar isn't starched." And she says, "Well you
ain't in a bloody hotel,"' he grins.

I ask if he does much in the house. He says he doesn't do as much as
he would like. 'I'm not very good on DIY. The standing joke with my
daughter if she sees me near a shelf, she'll say, "Don't put that up, daddy,
it'll fall down."' I explain that by 'help' I mean housework.

'I enjoy the garden,' he says. 'I like to do it myself. I'll shop for my own
things if I'm doing the cooking but Jenny does all the rest of the shopping.'

Does he count Jenny as his best friend? 'That's sort of a new way of
putting things,' he says. 'It's been in the press that that's the way you
should treat your better half but if it's the modern way of calling it then,
yes.' I ask what Jenny thinks are his strengths and weaknesses.

'She appreciates the fact we've done very well for ourselves together
because of certain abilities that I seem to have. She stops me thinking I'm
too clever. If I say I've got dinner with some Lord next week, she says,
"Oh that's nice for you." She bring me down to earth. I suppose she sees
me as hardworking . . . reliable.' It is not, he adds with a smile, necessarily
how he sees himself.

Tales of travelling salesmen's exploits are common. Once abroad with business done they are alleged to prowl, collecting sexual conquests along with the orders. I ask Richard Ware how he deals with such temptations – if indeed they are temptations. He says the answer is easy: quite apart from how he might personally feel, he is usually 'too knackered' to bother. 'Besides, I think it makes life too complicated. And it's unprofessional too. You see some men who've drunk too much the night before or whatever and it tells . . .'

Is there anything he envies about Jenny's life, I ask? 'She'll probably hit the roof if I say it but I envy the fact she has time and she can decide what she wants to do with it throughout the day. She would argue back that she doesn't *want* time to think about what to do. It's almost going to sound male chauvinist pig but she enjoys her woman's role reasonably well except for the fact that she'd like to have a job.

'Jenny says,' he adds later, 'that she sees a lot of me in my mother . . .' Richard Ware's parents were against the marriage and blamed Jenny for it afterwards, he says. He has tended to have a distant relationship with them both but more so with his mother. He is the only child; his father worked as a catering manager and the family moved frequently. They spent four years in the USA, moving there when Richard was eleven. He attended a number of different schools during his childhood. If it was traumatic, he says, he can't remember it now.

Richard Ware's father died quite recently. He had had a serious stroke. 'I had never seen a close relative die. I didn't know how I was going to react. I was very upset, obviously, but I didn't react in an emotional way. There were no tears.' I ask if that surprised him.

'I don't know. I like to think I don't worry about anything. I expected in a personal crisis I wouldn't perhaps have the same attitude. But I found I did. I don't know whether that's right or wrong.

'I feel happy that he died rather than being paralysed for the rest of his life, I know that's not what I would want so I felt relieved that it just happened – finish. I don't believe in life after death or anything like that. I was just happy that if you've got to go, that's the way to do it.'

I ask if the death has had a profound effect. 'No,' he says. 'My attitude to life is you're only here for seventy-odd years so enjoy it. And when it comes to an end, that's your lot mate!'

His parents, he explains, were ambitious for him. 'They kept pushing but all that did was tend to make me wonder why and I deliberately decided to go the wrong way. They wanted me to go to university and I left at seventeen with four 'O' levels, that sort of thing . . .

'I think they had their opinion about what should happen to me. If I didn't do it their way, there was no halfway house. I was totally wrong. Then once somebody else came into my life, it wasn't my fault, it was the person's fault who had interfered with my parents' plans for me.'

He says he now tries to encourage rather than push his children, he wants them to make their own minds up what they want from life. I ask if he has spent much time with them both, particularly as their childhood has coincided with a series of rapid promotions in his career? In addition, he also plays squash twice a week and has long been a rugby player.

Richard Ware occasionally takes his son along to rugby but 'he prefers football really and that's his choice'. They all quite often go swimming on a Sunday but Richard says that he does feel he doesn't give enough time to the children.

'Jenny is very good. She will remind me, "Go on, think about the kids." It's not that I don't think about the kids but you just get yourself into this unreal world . . .' Does he feel he knows them? 'I think we're now getting to the point where it'll be difficult, Katy being nearly ten, unless I can spend more time in the next two or three years.

'In fact, I think I've *got* to spend more time purely on the basis that they're now getting to the age where they no longer take your word for granted. They're becoming individuals and that's when you've got to learn to try to know them . . .'

We move on to the subject of friends. He says Jenny criticises him because he often calls business colleagues whom he brings home for dinner 'friends'. 'She says, "Well, you haven't got anything in common with them," which is probably correct, but I get on with people very well.

'Actual friends, I don't know how many people have anyway but I've probably half a dozen people that I could ring up at two o'clock in the morning and say, "Let's have a talk." But I wouldn't say I've got a best friend.'

If ask if he feels happy. He is unequivocal. 'Yes,' he says. Has he had any disappointments in his life? 'No,' he replies. 'Jenny says that that's probably the thing which will hit me the hardest. Up till now everything has gone, I wouldn't say as planned, because that sounds as if you've worked it out to the last detail, but there hasn't really been anything that has been totally traumatic. I'm not ambitious as such, I've just always needed a challenge and gone for the next one along the line.'

I ask how he felt when he'd heard he'd come second rather than first in the Salesman of the Year award. He smiles broadly. 'Beat the buggers next time.'

Graham Winstanley *Yorkshire*

The detached house on a Barrett estate in the small village of Barlby, twenty-three miles from Leeds, has three bedrooms, a skeleton of a garden and a W-registration Cortina parked in the drive. Eighteen months ago, three days before Christmas, the Winstanleys and their three children, Vicky, ten, and two sons both in their teens, moved in. The mortgage is £160 a month and it is the first house the Winstanleys have owned.

Inside, pride in the home is almost as visible as the large television set in the corner of the sitting-room. The colour scheme is beige and brocade and cream. A china Bell's whisky ornament, carriage clock and wedding pictures decorate the room. Graham Winstanley makes a mug of tea. At thirty-four, small and slight, he looks not a lot older than his son Richard, who is eighteen.

Grahan Winstanley's outfit is carefully toned; light blue shoes; light blue slacks, a maroon collarless shirt and gold chain. Considering he likes a pint – around four a day, he says – he must have sieves in his heels, his body carries hardly any flesh.

He has been a miner since the age of fifteen. His father was a miner, and his grandmother. His son and brother also work down the pit.

'I never heard anything else talked about at home. I don't know, it's just something I always wanted to do. I like jobs where you can get stuck in and finish. If I hadn't done that I'd have been a scaffolder . . . somewhere I can get stuck in and get some brass and then off home.

'Even when I was a lad I wanted to reach the status of being a collier. They wouldn't let you down the pits until you were seventeen and I couldn't wait. Firstly that was where the money was, but most important that was where the men were.'

Graham seems cautious by nature, but as the caution is slowly erased by familiarity he becomes more outgoing. He was born and brought up in the Leeds area. In nineteen years as a miner he has been part of an industry whose image has changed from muscle to MINOS, the Mine Operating System computer which now can control an entire colliery. In his teens, Graham used to lead the ponies down the pit, now he drives a ninety-four-tonne roadheading machine whose tentacles do what man once did (and still do in the older pits), tunnelling ahead. 'Where once we might have had twenty-seven on the face, soon there'll be three.' He hates the idea.

Anyone can be a miner nowadays, Graham says, and it shows. 'You have to take so much green labour on, you see. When you get green labour that means somebody who hasn't come out of a mining family or owt like that. They had nowt to do with it before, they are just a waste of time. They ain't got it in them at all. Probably one out of ten might make a miner. You can tell them straight away, as soon as you see a bloke down the pit at sixteen, whether he's going to make it.

'You can tell by whether he's rough and ready, he'll get mucky, he has a go, he never has a minute and he wants to be happy, he's thinking all the time – how can I get done? It's like seeing somebody kicking a ball. If it's all over the place you say he's rubbish.'

The comradeship is going; money is the acid which has destroyed some of the old solidarity. A supporter of Arthur Scargill, 'the best leader we've ever had,' Graham Winstanley does not belong to a political party but he is a strong union man. 'I don't think you should ever lose your roots . . . your feeling for other people anyway. I think that's what's wrong mostly with working people like me, say, fancy houses, fancy car. They tend not to back a union the way that they should. A lot say, "I'm all right Jack," and that's no good.'

The miners in Graham's area voted two to one against a pay and pit closures strike in November '82; at the time we talked, just before the strike, they were losing between £20 and £100 and more a week on the ban on overtime.

'If I had to go on strike now for two years I would,' he says. 'I'd throw all this in and see that I'd make do and that's it – even if we had to live in a tent. What's happened is, we make good brass here for doing probably less work than the blokes in Scotland shovelling by hand. They're in two-foot-six/three-foot seams and it's a hard job, is that. They come home and fall asleep before they've had their dinner. It's unbelievable. People now just want to keep on earning good money, they're not thinking about the coalfields any more . . .'

Eighteen months ago, Graham Winstanley graduated to the rank of survivor in the mining industry. He began working on the NCB's 'striking symbol of the rebirth of coal', the Selby Coalfield. The work is still black, even more unrelenting and just as punishing, but now it is 'modern'.

Selby was discovered in the 1970s; 2000m tonnes in five coal seams covering 110 square miles, the size of the Isle of Wight.

By the time it is completed in 1988, five pits will have eight hundred workers each. These men will be able to produce seventy per cent of the total production of the South Wales and Scottish coal fields with only ten per cent of the labour force. Graham Winstanley's first mine, Water Haigh, closed when he'd worked there six years; his second, Peckfield colliery closed thirteen years later and after a two-year 'loan' to Welldale, he is now at Selby. He doesn't expect to be a miner at sixty-five, or possibly even fifty-five.

He won't mind, he says, so long as he can retire with a 'decent carry-on, enough for a pint and a small car and a holiday a year. Nowt special, just a decent carry-on'. But the passing of a way of life that matters to him, he says, can have no compensation.

Selby covers the Vale of York, seventeen villages – one of which is Barlby, and some of which date back to the Domesday book. Most of the four thousand miners eventually employed will live in the area but the mining communities have gone; Barrett estates and white-collar commuters have taken their place.

Graham has never lived in a mining community and doesn't appreciate overly friendly neighbours. 'It wouldn't do for me, that, I like people to knock on the door.'

Now he earns over £200 a week but the lack of a bonus can as much as halve that. It also means shifts; mornings, afternoons and nights. Whatever the shift, he usually manages to make the pub at around two o'clock, latest. This week he is on nights. He got to bed at eight and would normally have slept until dinner time, visited down the pub more often than not for four or five pints, slept again and left for work at around ten p.m. He hates shifts. 'I disagree three hundred per cent with nights. You can't eat sometimes, it's funny. I mean when you come home, it's not so bad like the first day because you can eat a breakfast when you come home, but as the week goes on – it must be a time clock or something in your body – you feel like a dinner in the morning, you could do with some dumplings or something. It's the same as when you get up in the night, she'll make me say pie and peas or something and you feel like bacon and eggs, it's terrible. At nights, to me, you should be in bed cuddled up and that's it.'

The Miner is Graham's local pub, 'a bit of a man's pub really'. It has red brocade flock wallpaper and a real fire, copper-covered tables and simulated leather pews in the lounge. It also has darts, a pool table and a jukebox, and a handful of miners also out for a lunchtime drink who pull his leg about the company he is keeping. 'Does the wife know then, Graham?' says a miner who from his dress could be a Poly lecturer. 'They're not bad lads,' Graham says. 'They'll ask all about you tonight. I'll have some fun.'

At fifteen, Graham Winstanley went to see the boss about a job. 'Now lad,' the boss said, 'what do you want?' 'I've come about a job'. 'Aye, get in that office then and I'll be out to see you.' Graham sat there for three hours; the longer he waited, the more frightened he became, a baby trying to be a man.

'Finally the gaffer came out and said, "Come on lad," he took me up these stairs and there were all this machinery and I were fucking frightened to death. "What's your name?" he said. "Winstanley," I says. "Hmm, that's a very Conservative name," he says. I'll always remember that.'

At first Graham worked on the surface, sifting coal from dirt and stone, a job that was generally given to people who weren't 'a full shilling'. The noise was so intense people had to communicate in sign language. 'One bloke I remember used to cry all the time. A big strapping fellow he was, stocky. He were a Pole and he used to cry about Jews. He used to frighten me to death, he was strong as a blinking ox, he used to knock me flying.'

At sixteen he went down the pit. 'It used to be freezing cold down there, and I mean cold. They used to send hot bricks down to warm up your hands because you couldn't move. Sometimes you used to pee yourself you were so cold, you couldn't control yourself. I'm only skinny but I used to look like the Incredible Hulk, coats, balaclava – all sorts on.'

Mining has always been a love-hate relationship, he says. Now it's more hate, it's so repetitious. No one acts the goat so much. 'In the old days, it were just you with the shovel. You could go and see your mate, if he'd been on the beer all day, we'd help fill his car for him, set his props. We used to do all sorts of dirty tricks. There were no toilets down there obviously . . . it were a lot funnier, a lot more humour. If you can't laugh at work it's just a waste of time going to work to me . . .'

Graham Winstanley had to go through the same initiation rites as all the apprentices – forty and fifty young boys at a time down a pit. Grease

spread thick on penis and testicles; an enforced dip in the five-foot-deep
pool where the water was pumped from the workings to the pit bottom;
on the main haulage roads there used to be two electric wires running
along the roadways, the men would make a circuit with a knife and the
two loose wires would then be used to give a small electric shock; a bag
of stonedust would be propped on one of the air doors so that when a
boy went through it covered him from head to foot in white dust – a
state in which they might have to work their full seven hour shift. And
then there was always the knowledge of death or injury:

'I've seen one killed and lots hurt bad. When it happens to someone,
you just think, Well it won't happen to me. You've got to use your head
all the time. That's why they get a bit rough with you when you're
learning. They try and knock it into you if they have to, because at some
time it might be life and death to someone if you get it wrong. It's a bit
eerie sometimes. I remember one bloke died at the end of the gate and
his coat were left there. Any other time and it would have been nicked
but because he had died, the coat were left there for months and nobody
touched it. I wouldn't bother so much about being buried alive if I'd
thought they would get me out. One time they left them all down there
and I were as sick as a parrot about that.'

Graham now is chargehand in a team of four. It's not spoken about,
he says, but men know who is the best worker in the team. It's a matter
of pride to be the best – especially if you're nine stone. He's pushed
himself that bit harder all his working life.

'It matters to me a lot. Always has. Sometimes in the old days, your
hands would be covered with blisters but you'd carry on. If you didn't
fill your car up, you got kicked off or the older blokes would have a go.
Sometimes now you get physically tired and mentally tired and it must
be something like when you're running, like a pain barrier. Many a time
I've thought, I wish a lump would come down and hit me, just so that I
could've been taken out of that pit. I mean there's sweat running down
your face and you can't see ahead and the dust and the pain. It's
unbelievable. Anyway ten minutes after, you're as right as rain, you get
your second breath and you're off again . . .

'Most big blokes don't like work. I mean if you're shovelling for seven
hours, it takes some doing. You've got to know where to start and that
takes a long time to learn. I know where to start straight away. It's my
nose. By the time a big fella's filled two yards off, I could probably fill

six – not because he isn't fitter or stronger, he probably will be. But it's my nose . . .'

In Selby in the future, machines will take over much of the men's skill, some pride in the work has to go – is going – but the hazards remain. 'There's more machinery and there's more dust. Every five years, they give you a check-up. I've been fourteen year on the face and every five year I get the same old letter: "We're pleased to inform you that there's no change." A fella who works in the pit, there must be a change . . .'

Women down the pit, he says, he'd welcome. 'It'd be nice, yeah. There's a lot of light work, our Vicky could do some. But I don't think many of the men would welcome it. It's a different world down there. Even if you hate someone down there, you know if they get injured, you get them out, but if women were down there . . . it would cause a lot of arguments. There'd be blokes chatting them up so they wouldn't be working.' What he is saying is that brotherhood, the bonus, both would go.

Graham Winstanley remembers a different time, in the years that Macmillan was telling us we'd never had it so good. His father Jack worked in the mines and on the railways. Dolly, his mother, looked after three children, Jack didn't like her to have a job.

The boys would wear bumpers – reinforced pumps – to school but take them off when they got home to make them last longer. Christmas presents came from the jumble sale; a tin aeroplane one year, a cowboy suit the next.

'My mum were as soft as a brush. She used to cry a lot, she was always crying. She used to take my dad's suit to a pawnshop – it were a brown pinstripe – and she'd say to me, "Don't tell your dad." She'd take it on a Monday and take it out on a Friday. Same as club cheques for Christmas. She used to say, "Don't tell your dad," because he would've gone spare, He didn't believe in credit.'

Graham's dad is short and stocky. He never drank but Graham says he had a terrible temper. He was a member of the Communist Party and Graham remembers helping him to sell copies of the *Morning Star*. He was a scrapper, always fighting. 'He'd fight over anything, he were always losing jobs because of it. I saw him hitting a big fella, a big Pole – it was unbelievable. I thought he'd kill my dad but he didn't. My dad's changed now, completely. He helps with the washing-up, he doesn't fight. I can't remember him ever talking to me until I got wed at sixteen. He just started talking then on a fairly adult level.

'When I got wed I could smoke in the house too. Up to then, I didn't dare. About six year ago I started to get much closer to him. I asked his advice about something. I've never talked to him about the early years. I've never said, "You were an idiot when you were younger," like. We talk about politics. He loves politics. He's up my house all the time now.

'My mum used to talk to us a lot. Not about politics. She told us stories, you know what mums do and like.' The two, Jack and Dolly, would stay in every night. Graham would go to bed early and draw. On Saturday Jack went dancing alone. 'He were a dancing man. Looking back, he might have had a fancy woman, I don't know.

'My dad never hit us. He only had to shout and that were enough for me. If he'd say to me, "Graham, I want you to go to the shop," and I'd say, "Oh but I'm reading this," or whatever, "Hey, shop," and that were it. I'd be off.

'Me mum and dad got on. I don't know how, like . . . if I'd have been my mother . . . Dad would come in and sit in the chair, dinner were fetched on his knee, and his tea. He'd have a drop and he'd say, "Dolly, there ain't enough sugar in," and she'd traipse back to the kitchen and put sugar in and fetch it back. It's unbelievable. "All right Dolly," he'd say, and that were it. He never washed up, he never did anything in the house.'

Graham's wife, Anne, works in a fish shop. 'She works hard,' he says. 'You have to help out when they're working, don't you? If she weren't working, I wouldn't do owt. She always complains that I don't do it right, though, you know if I go round with the vacuum.

'I wash up, tidy up, use the vacuum. I never iron and I never wash clothes, I would never do that. I cook but only in the frying pan. She prepares it like first, I have to have everything ready for me first. She peels the potatoes and that. We always do the shopping together.

'I'd rather she didn't work. There's nowt nicer than coming home and your dinner's ready, it's grand, isn't it. Plus they're a lot fitter. They don't get headaches so often, they're more interested in bed.'

Graham says his wife likes to have a job. 'She were getting a bit stale. She didn't really watch television and she isn't really interested in politics, she's no basic interests. She'll read what I call them silly books, you know, love stories where everything ends up good . . . Most women seem to like them. I'd rather have a good book. I read a lot. But it's like a dream world they live in, life isn't like that.'

I ask him why he thinks the dream world is needed. He smiles. 'Well, because men treat them so bad. I don't know. They're mostly taken for granted and things like that. Once you marry I don't think you appreciate them as much as you should.

'In sex I think there's a bit more feeling with women. A bit of warmth and respect. With most blokes you stay with a woman half an hour, ten minutes and that's it. They won't even remember their name next day. But a woman would be hurt and that's the difference.

'I can never understand women. You must get a certain amount of pleasure out of sex. I mean men are always chasing aren't they? It must get on your nerves. Basically it's on my mind all day.

'I have a good sex life but to me it's like an urge, it's a drive. It must be going back to Adam but you've just got to get rid of this thing. How these single fellas who go without it for three or four days manage, I don't know, it's no good for me, that.

'Sometimes my wife does it for me, you know, but she never lets me know. You see women who are divorced or widowed and they can go without it for years. I would say most women are a bit like that.

'But I think most women do have satisfaction from men. If there's some feeling with it. But I think there are more men than women highly sexed. It's like a conquest to men. It's the natural thing to do. We're here to reproduce and woman are more passive, like. Even in the animal world . . . look at cats, I mean they nearly get killed . . .

'Men talk about it all the time in the pit but a lot of it's fantasy. Half of what they say wouldn't be physically possible. And it's not done to talk about the wife or the girl friend.

'To me sex is like – what can you say – I once read something where it said, "Sex should be just like an old oak tree, it's got that many branches." It's like playing a violin, you can play it badly or you can play it well . . . I'd do anything a partner wants apart from causing pain or owt like that. I never feel sexually repressed or inhibited. It were always expressed openly in our house.

'You know say, when the Tiller girls were on at the London Palladium, my father would whistle and all, "She's got a grand pair of legs, Dolly," he'd say. And she'd say, "Oh Jack, give up." I do it in my house now. If I'm reading a paper like Page Three I'll say, "That lass is all right, son," and they say, "Oh, dad." My daughter asks questions and I'll answer openly.'

I ask him how he would feel if a group of women passed remarks in the street about his body. 'I think that would be an ego-booster. I wish some women would yell at me,' he replies, smiling. Then more seriously he adds, 'I don't like rape as a male fantasy myself. Physically one woman couldn't rape me but several women . . . I wouldn't like it, no I don't think so . . . Unless, say, there were three of them and they say, in a nice manner, "We're going to undress you . . ." Now that would be a different thing. But just to get hold of you, that would be terrible. If a fella raped a woman and came in here and we knew, he's likely to get beaten up. We've no time for owt like that, it's no good.'

Graham met Anne in 1963; Gerry and the Pacemakers were singing 'You'll Never Walk Alone', 'She Loves You' had come and gone in the Top Ten. Graham was fifteen, Anne six months older. She was shy and attractive – it took him a long time to persuade her to make love. I ask why he persisted. 'I don't know, if there's something there you can't have, you tend to go for it, like. I don't know. I just liked a woman like that where nobody's been before. She was attractive, she still is. You've got to have everything in a marriage – you've got to have attraction and something you can't have. I suppose if a woman went to bed every day, twice a day, you wouldn't want it that much . . .'

Anne became pregnant, Graham was happy to marry. Her parents reacted to the baby well; when he asked his dad about marriage, Jack said, "No, you're not getting wed." Angry, I was. It were the first time I could have hit my dad. I needed their permission because I wasn't earning enough to support her and the kid. I said I'd stay home from work and smash every window in the house if he didn't agree. But he came round in the end.' Graham was sixteen in October and they married in February. He earned £4 a week and the rent on a flat came to 27s. 'I said, we'll be all right, we'll buy a spoon a week.

'We didn't realise what was involved when we got married . . . it was a struggle, we came through but with great difficulty. Plenty of others have split up for less . . . She used to leave me like regular. We never had nowt. My mother used to fetch us tins of soup. I used to come from the pit and have a tin of soup, I used to be starving.

'Anne used to say, "Is soup all right?" and I'd say, "Oh yeah, fine." I used to take three tomatoes and about six slices of dry bread to work and that were it. But she always used to give me – I don't know where she got it from – one and six for a pint or two a day. I used to get halves and go in the pub at sixteen and spend an hour there with the men. I felt if I could go in the pub, I was a bit grown up . . . Anne has a good heart, she knew somehow.'

Graham's admiration is reinforced by the knowledge that he almost lost the relationship which he now says is central to his life.

At eighteen and for the next seven years or so, he was thieving, staying out late. 'It were the excitement, the money. You needed money to go places like clubs and that. It upset the wife immensely but she came through it and stuck by me.' Why did she? 'I've no idea, because she loved me, I like to think. I don't know . . .

'I was afraid she would go. You know a bloke needs somewhere that's home. You know a fella is often like a knave in a castle, you can go with as many women as you like but you still want to go back home . . . Sometimes if I was with someone else, I'd feel remorse . . .'

If Anne had had an affair would he have taken her back? 'It would depend on the circumstances. I'd have flattened her, that would have been the first job, no doubt. For two years I did a lot of that, scrapping and fighting with others and hitting her, stupid stuff.

'It started because she used to be very annoyed about me coming home late and I could understand that. But I used to be very vain, I still am. She began to scratch my face and that upset me. She could have thumped me, kicked me, owt but scratch my face and that were me finished. If she were my wife or no, I'd knock her down. I used to hit settees, walls, anything . . . it were frustration because we had no money. I used to blow what I pinched in a night and then I wouldn't go to work the next day. I regret it all now a lot . . .

'I don't regret what I did for myself because it were pleasure for me, it were great. But I regret what I did to her. She is a good 'un. It must leave a bit of a scar somewhere, you know, she must remember these things. She doesn't talk about it . . .'

Graham stopped because his brother shopped him as a deterrent and a man of sixty told him he'd give him a hiding if he didn't lay off Anne. The fighting he does less of now, but to him it still seems a fair way of communication.

'Fighting – there's nothing better. You have a few words with a fella and then you go outside and settle it. You fight it out and come back inside and buy him a pint and that's it. Its over.

'You do better to take on a chap bigger than you. He'll thump you but you'll black his eye first. After, you get the sympathy. "Well at least you hit him hard." He gets, "What do you want to pick on him for?" And he won't hit you again because whatever happens, you've hurt him and he'll remember. I've never been frightened at the time; the adrenalin gets you going.

'I only believe in clean fighting, one-to-one. None of this three on to one and kicking and knives. I'm a scrapper like my dad but I'm not like I used to be . . . I mean if I came in the pub with my wife and somebody looked at her, that would be it. I was terrible jealous. I still am. I'll go over to the bloke and say, "Do you want to come and sit next to her?"

'I mean, you know how blokes are, I've done it myself, undressing women with their eyes and all that. I've been walking through a shopping centre with her and somebody just looks and I'll go straight up to them and say, "Who do you think you're looking at?"

'And it's so stupid. The wife runs off, she's so embarrassed and ashamed. It *is* stupid, I feel really terrible after . . .'

Graham says there is nothing he envies about a woman's life. 'But I suppose you wouldn't like to be a man? My wife says, "I'm coming back as a man next time."' He laughs – and he laughs more often now; his shyness has gone.

'I think a woman's luckier. She can get anything she wants if she attacks it in the right way. You can make money, to be crude, by basically just using what you're sat on. You have power over men. A woman can take any man out of a pub that she wants to; a man couldn't take any woman out. So she has the power.'

I ask how he would feel if a woman with money took him everywhere, paid for everything, ran his life, could he live like that? No, he couldn't, he decides after thought. 'That would be a kept man, wouldn't it? I wouldn't like that.'

Perhaps some women see marriage like that, I suggest, and he pauses for a very long time. 'Yeah, well that's true,' he finally says. 'I don't know, perhaps women have more of a fascination in a type of bloke or something . . .'

We talk about children. 'I weren't in the room when Richard was born, I was outside,' he says. 'I started crying, me. It was the first time for ages,' he adds without embarrassment. 'I wasn't crying Sob, sob, just the tears trickling down. I was there when Vicky was born and I thought it were great. I wouldn't like to go through all that women go through at childbirth though . . .'

What he wants for the children, he says, is what they want for themselves. Vicky is the bright one, she keeps him at the library trying to answer her questions. 'She's always straight to the point.'

'I hope she'll be a good one, I shall teach her all I know and what I've been like, tell her about her roots and where she comes from and what's what.' Will she be happy to settle down? 'I should think so, yeah,' he replies. 'I don't know, that'll be her decision and if she don't want to get wed, she don't get wed, it's whatever she wants to do. You sort that out as it comes, don't you? But with a girl it's a bit different. With the lads I can say, "Hey, pack it in I'll give you a clout." Now with her I couldn't clout her, you know that. I couldn't give her a belt like the lads like. I'm always frightened of hurting her. I mean with the lads I used to get them on the floor, and fight with them when they were younger. So it's a different level of law if you like.'

Does he take her to play football or anything?

'Her? No, no. She isn't really a sportswoman – to what the lads were like, but she isn't really into sports.' What does she do? 'Reading, writing. She's always . . . She'll just sit on the settee reading and writing on her own. It's unbelievable. She's quite clever.'

Does her mum tell her not to get married or anything, I ask.

'No, no, never. I don't think that's ever come up, actually. She'll say, "Don't finish up like me with someone like your dad. Better be better than him," you know that sort of thing. And they both have a good laugh.'

In the afternoon, back at home, Graham makes more tea and shows photos of a recent wedding where Vicky was a bridesmaid. If he had his time again, he says, he would still have courted Anne but 'I would've used my loaf, like. It were my fault. There were none of those things like the Pill. We've come through a lot and what we've got now is good. I don't know what Anne thinks,' he adds as if uncertain he wants to ask.

'If I had a lot of money, I'd like to travel, see the Seven Wonders of the World. Educate myself by travelling about. I've always wanted to see the Taj Mahal. We go on holiday to the seaside every year but that's it. I've always wanted to go abroad but could never afford it.'

'We'll go,' he adds, smiling again, 'As soon as we can get these lot married off. I've got a good carry-on,' he says. Mining has mostly given him what he wanted; a pride in a craft, a chance to be one of the men; decent money. 'When I was little, I used to see blokes walking by blacked up and I used to think, One day, I'll be there. Well that's what I've done.'

Neville Wright *Sheffield*

The road from Sheffield to Rotherham resembles the mouth of an old crone; full of gaps and blackened stumps. Buildings are boarded up, closed down, autographed with graffiti. Neville Wright says he can remember when Steel Peach and Tozer, still in business, once employed thousands upon thousands of men and their factory stretched for four and a half miles. But he was thirteen then and it's different now.

On one of the walls of a deserted building, a 'No Parking' sign has been amended. 'Parking' has been crossed out and 'Cuts' written below in neatly identical lettering. It looks official: No Cuts. In the late sixties when Neville Wright began an apprenticeship as an electrician, the unemployment rate in Sheffield was barely one per cent. Now it is thirteen times that officially; probably more.

Steel was always a highly specialised industry in the area – cutlery, silverware, a market in which steel is sold by the pound not the ton. It generated the massive factories but it also spawned the small businesses, and craftsmen with a love in their work. Employment for them and their fellow steelworkers was – and is – a matter of pride, an essential part of 'being a man', a breadwinner. It never was just about having a pound in your pocket.

Pride perhaps explains why traditionally the men and women of Sheffield have never accepted the myths about unemployment. They have always fought back against the idea that those who are jobless are therefore work-shy, scroungers, the martyrs of self-inflicted poverty. Neville Wright knows the history well. In the thirties, he will tell you, 60,000 men, women and children protested in the streets at the cuts in public assistance. Earlier still, in June 1922, the Battle of Walkley took place almost on Neville's doorstep.

Neville Wright and his wife, Diane, moved into Tennyson Road, Walkley, six years ago. It is now a Housing Action Area. At the foot of their terraced street, a bulldozer is at work, flattened rubble marks the area where families previously lived and died. The houses that remain, from the outside, seem unchanged since the turn of the century. The cosmetic surgery made possible by grants is only visible once you step inside.

The Wrights have a decent bathroom, kitchen and a dormer bedroom in the attic. It is still cramped living. Two up and down, a door which opens from the street into a sitting room smaller than a boxing ring. Walls are like tissue paper, a back garden is the size of a giant's window box. If the man or woman next door comes out to tend the tulips, you're as close as standing in a bus queue.

The claustrophobic dimensions of day-to-day living make 'neighbourhood' a concept for some as constricting as wire mesh; for others it still carries a few of the connotations of the thirties. It means companionship and support; more qualified now than then. Then, people trusted in the fact that each was as badly off as the other. Now, affluence, mostly imagined, is the mould which disfigures some of the traditional neighbourhoods – even Walkley. Someone knows someone else who is on the Social Security but you should see the size of their telly, the new car, the holiday snaps from Benidorm . . . etc. etc.

It is hard to visualise a Battle of Walkley ever taking place now. Then, sixty years ago with 40,000 unemployed in Sheffield, Harold Cundy, a labourer, his wife Annie and their two children, both suffering from measles, were evicted for rent arrears caused by lack of work from '8 Court, 2 House, Providence Road, Walkley' – an address which says as much as any description of how people lived.

Members of the local Unemployed Workers Branch and their supporters tried to reinstate the family. 'We are not going to allow the authorities to turn a man into the street who is unemployed,' said one of the leaders. Police on horseback, 'the Cossacks', appeared. The result was blood on the cobblestones. One unemployed man died (killed in the crush or felled by a policeman's truncheon), many were arrested. The funeral was attended by thousands.

Nowadays, the gestures of defiance are small. Neville Wright is a volunteer in the Centre *Against* Unemployment; the choice of words is crucial. It is not the defeatist-sounding Unemployment Centre. Neville has been out of work for two years. He, his wife and four children live on £60 a week – his debts add up to around £2,500. 'When you have to decide on what you do with your money,' he says, 'the children's needs have first priority, the debts come second. Children can get through anything if well fed and well loved – loved is the main thing.'

In 1973, the *Financial Times* described Sheffield as 'a tightly knit, rather insular community. In addition to its . . . self-confident masculine quality, it also has a deep conservatism . . .' Four years later, Norman Shrapnel in the *Guardian* described it as 'an heroic town'; such manly descriptions.

Neville would probably agree with 'masculine', 'heroic', but definitely not 'conservative' – at least, not as far as he's concerned. Unemployed he might be but he has never been more active. Soon after losing his job, he became involved in the Housing Action Area Committee; he joined the Labour Party, he listened to the arguments of Militant and now counts Trotsky as his hero.

In the course of an average week, he helps out as a welfare rights adviser at the Centre Against Unemployment, he sells *Militant* on Friday and attends a weekly meeting, he is, when we meet, helping to organise a Broad Left Conference, he is investigating the possibilities of a municipal funeral service (£200 a funeral as opposed to £500 on the free market), he spends two evenings a week at the Polytechnic on a course in Applied Social Studies, he is trying for a mature student's place at Sheffield University to read Social and Economic History; his academic qualifications are nil, his appetite for knowledge only recently awakened.

I had contacted the Centre Against Unemployment and asked for a man of thirty-four or thirty-five. Neville happened to be standing close to the 'phone. You don't have to tell Neville about the statistics on poverty. He knows them all and can, if asked, recite them like a karma.

Over seven million live in poverty in Britain (the Wrights are six of them), a 72 per cent increase since Margaret Thatcher came to power in 1979. The richest 10 per cent own 58 per cent of all marketable wealth, the poorest 50 per cent own only 6 per cent. A Child Poverty Action Group and Family Services Unit survey shows that 80 per cent of people on state benefit borrow to pay for housing and fuel bills. Neville can vouch for that.

He used to spend £10 a week on cigarettes. He cut down to a £1 a week on tobacco, but a few days before we meet he sits on his Falcon pipe and breaks it. A new one will cost £9. When you're poor, it's not only the large events in life of which tragedy is made; it's the small events too.

Neville is in his sitting-room reading a fat book on Trotsky. The room is homely. A rainbow of colours comes from the three pairs of children's pyjamas draped across the radiator. The three-piece suite is green leatherette, the decor is brown flock wallpaper; on display are a number of photographs of the children, Nevill aged seven, Michael, six, Matthew, five, and Joanne-Sherri, three.

Next to the television is a small bookshelf which holds books mainly concerned with politics and labour history. Neville writes his essays from midnight to four and then has a lie-in in the morning. He is small and stocky with red-blond hair, a moustache and a strong sense of humour.

He signs on the dole every second Thursday; from time to time he has to meet the Assessment Officer who decides if he is *really* trying to find work – although in a city with a limited number of vacancies, this shouldn't require much effort.

Neville talks about 'gainful' employment. The dictionary definition of 'gainful' is profitable – it's only a phrase, but in Sheffield its precise meaning applies. Soon after he became unemployed, he says he saw a job advertised, living in 'all found', £12 a week. Just a few days ago, a job had been advertised for a forklift driver in Sheffield Market, £36 a week. 'They know they can get away with it.'

In the seventies, Neville had a variety of jobs. He changed frequently because he was always in pursuit of good money and/or a proper training scheme. He began as an apprentice electrician, moved on to a factory which produced electric motors, moved on to a carpet-cum-furniture warehouse where he stayed for two years. Next came an apprenticeship as a metalsmith which in reality turned out to be a job as a warehouseman, then he was a welder for eighteen months and in 1974, he joined Acheson Electrodes, a company which makes electrodes for use in electric air furnaces. He trained as an inspector for eight months and remained in the job for four years. He was forced to leave because the work was aggravating an arthritic condition.

The electrodes are made of graphite, basically pencil lead, so it was the original dirty job. The money was good, he says, £105 for a three-shift system; £130 on a night-wage. 'I got shingles working down there. You had loose overalls but the shit would get down in the elastic of your pants and work its way into the belt lining of your trousers and get ingrained into your midriff and cause shingles. I had skin problems on my ankles too. I didn't hate it but you'd work for Thursday at four when you got your wage packet.'

He feels jaundiced towards apprenticeships. In the electric motor repair shop, the pressure was intense and he was expected to be subservient. 'In the end I just rebelled against it and didn't give two shits.'

'They had initiation rites. One was to smear Bostik on your pubic hairs. One day I spent eight hours chained to the firm's van with one arm through the window with the window wound up, other arm chained to roofrack,' he laughs. 'I had to wait for them to let me out. I was never weepy about it. I'd see the funny side. Sometimes in an apprenticeship you're O.K., you find an old-timer who really nurses you along, otherwise you just suffer pain and degradation.'

In 1978, Neville began minicabbing, self-employed. He worked long hours so the car got battered, so he needed more money to pay the garage bills and the cycle began. The long hours took a toll. In six months, he received seven endorsements and was banned from driving – that was 1982.

The Wrights, shortly before he lost his job, had been given a seventy-five per cent grant for modernisation to the house, a builder had begun work. Now, they are paying the builder off at the rate of £7.50 a week – and they also have debts with two finance houses. The financial situation frightens him to death, Neville says.

In the past two years, he has applied for the job of a Welfare Rights Worker, a trainee educational welfare officer and a temporary campaign assistant to fight against the abolition of South Yorkshire County Council. One day, he would quite like to be an academic or a social worker.

'I've decided on a complete change of direction. If I don't work between now and retiring, I'll hope to be in some form of education all my life. I'll no longer chase jobs I don't want.

'The jobs I apply for now are like a kid's dream about becoming a footballer; do something you enjoy and get paid well for doing it. That's my policy now in my working life. I'll never go back to clocking in again.'

Neville has a vision for himself of the future; he has a full life which keeps him out of the house five days and a number of evenings a week; if work ever gave him a sense of worth and an identity, his commitment to politics does so even more strongly – but what about Diane?

She has the children more of the time; the budget to balance. Neville says she hasn't the same degree of interest in politics as he does but she *is* avidly 'anti-Tory' and she dislikes the middle class. He smiles: 'That's why she pissed off today, she thought that's what you'd be.'

Diane and Neville's families live in the same street. In January 1975, the two began a courtship. In August, they married. In the intervening months, they managed to save £2,000 between them. Neville had good money and Diane too earned a high wage in buffing, glazing knives and forks.

Nevill, the first son, was conceived very shortly before the day of the wedding. The two had decided to go to Blackpool on a dirty weekend, Neville senior says with a broad smile. Once they got there, they discovered Diane's dad had raided her handbag and removed her supply of the Pill: 'but we weren't going to miss out on a good chance.'

Diane, now twenty-seven, has had four children in five years – one reason was the desire for a daughter. Once Joanne-Sherri made her début, Neville had a vasectomy. 'The Pill should be used as a tactic rather than a long-term objective,' he explains. 'I think fellas who decide the family is complete are being selfish by forcing their wives to continue . . . it's drug abuse then. I'd have been quite happy with boys or girls but if we were going to have just one sex, then I would have preferred boys. It's for selfish reasons of being closer in things you might enjoy, Sheffield Wednesday, football . . . but since Joanne has come along my views have changed somewhat. She's growing up a proper little tomboy anyway but I *can* be as close to her as the boys.'

Neville says he doesn't help that much in the house. Once a fortnight he has the children on a Saturday morning so Diane can do the shopping. He babysits on a Saturday night, when she goes out with her mother to bingo, plus one other night in the week for a drink, if Diane gives him four or five days' notice. I ask if a revolutionary shouldn't begin the revolution in the home and act more in the spirit of feminism.

'I take advantage,' Neville says and smiles. 'Diane isn't that politically aware, she doesn't worry about sexism. Diane plays her role and she enjoys playing her role and she's the perfect mother. Her role is being the mother, being my wife.

'She's not servicing me but I see her as playing a revolutionary role too. She is allowing my political activity to go on, and for that I am thankful. If she wanted to demand more time of me she would be quite entitled and I would have to give the situation some thought. I would have to start sharing that time somewhat.'

I ask if it bothers him that there's a gap between his revolutionary thinking and practical life – or is feminism simply lower down on his agenda?

'If women want to say something then I want to hear,' he replies. 'There's nothing I would like better than to hear it from my wife. I might consider myself sexist if I was to force Diane on the same political plane as me – that would be downright bullying. You might come in from outside and think, Well, this fellow's a shit, he's quite content to see his wife doing all the jobs around the house . . . I do it because I think Diane *wants* to do the jobs and provide for the kids. She likes to make it as enjoyable as possible for the family, she gets a lot of satisfaction as a mother.'

What does he want of life? 'I want a different society, one that doesn't discriminate against people who have nothing to sell but their labour. I think it can be achieved by people waking up to the fact that they have nothing to lose but their chains.'

Does he think, I ask, that women are different from men – more homebodies than activists? 'No, I don't think they just want to be in the home, because that's a tie.

'If a woman wants a family, then from day one she has to be explicit about what she wants, and what rules that family are going to follow, or she will be forced into the role of mother.

'If Diane pressured me, I'd have no alternative *but* to respond to that pressure. I might lose out in one area of activity in which I'm involved but I'd hope that the reason why I was being deprived meant that Diane was becoming more politically aware.'

Neville's view is that the onus is on women to demand change – but first a woman has to become aware enough to know she has a *right* to ask. Had he tried to encourage Diane's interest in politics?

He laughs, tickled by a memory. 'Yes I have, we did two weekend courses at Northern College. She enjoyed one or two sessions but it didn't create a big enough spark to draw her towards that kind of thing as a pastime or a lifestyle.

'She doesn't read much,' he explains, not in criticism, more as an observation. 'I talk to her about political situations, how I perceive them. I try to reduce it into simple terms. It's the same thing I do when I'm out on the streets in my role as an activist. I think I do influence Diane slightly. But she's a very tough person in her own right.'

I ask if he thinks one partner is permanently more dominant in a relationship or whether it alternates. 'I think it alternates,' he says. 'If Diane wants to know something about politics, she comes to me wanting to know and I'm dominant. But in other things more akin to a family unit, all things are equal.'

She doesn't pressure him to find work, he says. 'She fully understands the situation, any effort on the jobs front is futile.' She also supports his efforts to improve his education. 'I do get some snide comments, the fact that I'm returning to education at my age. Perhaps because it's something she didn't envisage when we first started going out together.

'At times, she's quite critical, in as much as when the nice weather's around quite often I'm doing something when I could be out with the kids. I suppose I get a guilt complex about that to a certain extent but in education it's important that you don't fall behind. If you do you have to turn yourself into a zombie to re-establish yourself.

'I try not to fall behind but we do have occasional days out. My mum's got a caravan down on coast so we can get to the seaside for a few days.

'Weekends are sacred,' he adds and laughs again. 'If I started getting involved at weekends that would probably finish it. Me hand on me heart, she'd ask for a divorce.

'I think perhaps marriage does keep you together,' he adds later. 'That little insignificant piece of paper. I mean there have been several potential explosive situations in our married life where had we not been married that might just have resulted in one of us pissing off.

'I don't think women get security from marriage. I think Diane gets security from me. Now I'm being totally honest, if these explosive situations did occur I would be frightened to death to leave. I don't know whether it's the same for women but it's the same for a lot of fellas.

'I'd be frightened because I'd be putting myself into a situation where you have to build a new world on your own rather than build a new world together. It's different if it's all happening around a third party because a fella thinks I'm all right here, but on my own, I'd be genuinely scared.'

Why, I ask him, does he think men philander if they get security from marriage? Why risk that security? 'I think when a fella looks for sex with another partner, what he's really looking for is some sort of glorified posh wank, I think a fella can enjoy sex, ejaculate with any woman and that's it.

'I think for women a sexual coming together means that woman has to educate a fella into exactly what stimulates her because our creators made it more difficult for a woman to be stimulated.

'I don't think a woman can find as much satisfaction in a one-night fling as a fella can. A woman can't find immediate sexual satisfaction. I don't know, I've never asked a woman.'

A lot of men, I suggest, believe that women aren't that interested in sex, that if women didn't have sex for the rest of their lives they wouldn't be bothered.

Neville laughs. 'Diane would,' he says instantly. 'It's important. Sex is a two-way thing. You've got to be caring and attentive enough. I think in a new relationship all men are probably the world's worst lovers. All your timing is out unless you think about stewing cabbages.

'We've had some difficult times sexually. When I was working taxis, I'd work all night, come home in the morning and Diane wouldn't feel like it. She'd come upstairs at teatime feeling all randy and I wouldn't feel like it so consequently I'd probably do myself a favour in the morning. It was a situation where sex didn't occur as much as we both would like. We were living two different clocks.

'Whether she went in for masturbation I don't know. Diane has never talked about masturbation, she's always denied it and I've always openly admitted it.

'Sex sometimes is just a physical relief for the two of you. Sometimes, it's an emotional coming together. Initially you might be laid together or sat together just chatting, not working towards the objective of orgasm and then it just happens.'

I ask about his feelings on rape. Does he believe a man gets to a point where he can't control himself – or is it a crime of violence?

'If a man wants sex without respect for what a woman thinks then all he is looking for is self-gratification. I think self-gratification is why masturbation exists. But Christ knows how I would react if Diane was raped. You know . . . fucking hell . . . she must have done something . . . or did she?'

I ask how he feels when he is with a group of men and they are, for instance, being explicit about what they might do to a Page Three woman, given the chance. 'It's voyeurism,' he says. 'They would like a situation where Page Three would jump out and say, "I'd really like half an hour with you." They can't have that so they have a woman captive on Page Three instead.

'A lot of what men say they do sexually is just romance. It's a trap that all men fall into. To me, it's just acting in the crowd.

'I do assimilate well with women,' he says. 'When some fellows are trying to portray a sort of macho image, it sort of sickens me. In the sixties, hippy thing, I felt that there were no problems if you suggested going to bed or whatever because everything sexual was open and explicit.

Whereas now because of the feminist movement, men are more aware of female sensitivities and tend to get frightened off. It doesn't make any difference to machos because they're not bothered whose bum they'll nip, but for the rest . . .

'In socialist aware circles it's difficult for some men to know how to start a relationship. It is a constant worry, like we've got to allow that fellas are the hunters without being sexist. But if a man makes an advance is that a sexist gesture? Or is it a genuine sort of an attempt to try and bring people together on an emotional plane which at the end of the day might still have sexual objectives? I think a lot more would be achieved if women had more meetings that were open to men – we'd know more that way.'

Neville says he and Diane knew from the fifth or sixth week of the relationship that they wanted to marry. 'I liked the fact that she weren't pretentious, she were quiet, she didn't travel in a circle of friends out to impress each other, we hit it off sexually quite well from early on . . .

'The fact that she conceded sexually so early on made me want to know more about her past. She were quite open about it. One or two things about her past made me wonder a bit . . . At one time she had had a free attitude when it was just sex for sex's sake and that took some overcoming on my part . . .

'I supposed I didn't want to be in a situation where me friends might look down on me, say, "Oh yeah, but I screwed your missus." I'd never want that situation to happen. I could find probably closest friend in the world and if it turned out that he were one of my wife's past, I'd have to shoo him off very quickly.

'The relationship was unbelievable, especially in the first few months when you tend to be more sexually active than you ever are in the relationship again. I think I've always been in love with the idea of being in love. You get the feeling of hurt or feeling sick in the pit of your stomach because if you're not with somebody you want to be with then that's it. Though I steer clear of defining what "it" is.

'We didn't sleep together openly with parents knowing about it except for one occasion two days before wedding. I got kicked out of her house. I were pissed as a fart, it was my stag night and I thought I'll not go off tonight, but I got kicked out . . .' He laughs.

His interest in sex began at around nine or ten, he thinks. 'You fall into your little play group which excludes the opposite sex for a period of time.' At thirteen, Neville moved on to social evenings and postman's knock. 'I'm surprised at teenage pregnancy nowadays because then, speaking as a fella, you used to think it something just to get a hand down somebody's pants.'

At sixteen he 'lost' his virginity. A girl of fifteen consented to intercourse with six or seven, Neville included. They took turns, going into a bedroom one at a time. I asked if the girl was educationally subnormal. 'I wouldn't say that. I was in the third stream at school, out of eleven streams. She was in a different school but probably fourth or fifth stream. We thought she was a slag.'

Relationships tended to last six months to a year on average until Neville joined the hippy scene at the age of twenty. He left Sheffield one Friday to hitch-hike down to the Isle of Wight Festival and returned fourteen months later – he had been celibate throughout that time, more interested in acid than sex.

He had long hair, wore loon pants and beads. He found a job as a washer-up in Ryde and had about 100 LSD trips in just over a year, he reckons. He smoked marijuana but never used 'hard' drugs. 'We laced a pot of tea with acid and gave it to six pensioners . . . we used to have some laughs . . . they started acting strange but unless you are actually on a trip you don't relate to the experience.

'I had bad experiences every time coming down. I got this fear of spiders. If I saw a speck of dirt, it would turn into a spider. It would have a heartbeat and it grew bigger all the time . . .'

Neville Wright's father died two years ago at the age of seventy. He had been a professional footballer in his youth, playing for Birmingham, Crystal Palace and Sheffield Wednesday Reserves before the war. Later, he became a toolmaker. Neville's mother did 'women's work, underpaid areas, laundry, factory . . .'

Neville was born with a short and contracted femur. His father volunteered to give a bone graft to his son, which ended his football career. At seven, Neville went through a wall on a sledge and smashed his leg again in seven places. One leg is now ten inches shorter than the other. He walks with a limp but until he lifts his trouser leg it is impossible to guess that his own foot rests on an artificial ankle and foot so that both legs appear to be the same length.

'I got whacked in football once and when they took me to the hospital, the doctor saw what he thought were something like a broken chair-leg sticking out,' Neville says, still enjoying the joke. '"Fucking hell, what have we got here!" he says. It was my artificial ankle . . .' Humour and determination have obviously been his two shields against the prejudice shown towards his disability.

He played in the school football team. 'I tended to be apple of everybody's eye because I was in the team, bad leg or no bad leg. I think if anybody had got to carry a disability then it's better that they carry it from birth. I had a lot of piss-taking I suppose when I were a kid but I used to cure that by knocking shit out of them and proving that I were as capable. If you beat up somebody,' he adds, laughing again, 'they will have respect for you.'

At eight, Neville's mother gave birth again. His brother, David, was born epileptic and with a hole in his heart. The drugs he was given retarded his development. Now, at twenty-five, he lives with Neville's mother. His mental age is about eleven. Drugs have caused his teeth to fall out and Neville says he is a virtual recluse. The burden fell mostly on his mother, and it exacted a price.

'My mum had this nervous problem even as a teenager and my dad was aware of that. When I was seventeen, my mum had a nervous breakdown and went into hospital for four or five months. I definitely felt guilty, I didn't want to go and visit because I didn't like what I saw. My dad had really got to pressure me to go. I would go once a fortnight. I couldn't handle it.

'It was something that gradually came on my mum. We came home one day and she wasn't there mentally, she wasn't communicating. She didn't talk much about her problems anyway. I don't suppose I asked much. She were about forty-five. I think it was due to twenty years of worry, what with me being born imperfect and then David repeating the process. I think twenty years took its toll.

'I've always said exactly what I felt to me mum in a family situation. I've never gone in for this respect thing for parents because it's just an accident I'm here. So I've always said my piece. Sometimes I've got a clip for it and sometimes I haven't.

'I was very wary not to get in them situations after she came out of hospital because I wanted to lighten the load as much as possible and still do.

'My mum and dad were married thirty-three years when he died and I were quite worried how it might affect her but she overcame that. She's always tended to be the family's dustbin for problems. If she had a fault it was that she cared too much about other people and perhaps not enough for herself.

'My dad was very definitely head of the household. My mum was very subservient when my dad was around, not otherwise. She was a good mother, a caring person.

'If dad got to arguing, she'd never involve herself until it got really heated then she would try to ease the situation. I can remember when I was six or seven, dad would chase me round the house determined to give me a clip, mother would probably step in between and her pleading would always work.

'Still, I've always felt I've never been as close to me mum as me dad although I love her. My mum couldn't share my interests. I wouldn't have imposed my interests on her anyway because the only three things I could talk about were boozing, football and screwing.

'I got on very, very well with my dad. We were close but I wouldn't take my problems to me Dad because I thought I ought to be able to handle them myself. Us kids, friends, used to share problems amongst ourselves – and give each other a load of crap,' he adds, smiling.

'I don't open to people easily. I have to you because this is an academic exercise but not normally.'

Neville seems to talk more easily and in greater detail about his father than his mother. He says one football programme gave his dad's height as six foot four, 'but I only ever remember him as about five foot ten,' he laughs affectionately. 'His makeup were very contradictory. He was a tough man who commanded a lot of respect in his circle, which were Working Men's Club, he commanded a lot of respect for his macho image but at home he could get quite weepy about things. He never helped in the house, he had the excuse, he grew up in the thirties and forties when it wasn't expected.

'When my mum went into hospital me and my dad looked after David, he had pills which had to be administered four or five times a day. If it wasn't adhered to he'd throw a fit on the floor. My dad did the cooking, he proved to be a very able housewife, the old fella . . . David couldn't avoid being a nuisance – he's still got a lot of the rebel in him and who can blame him?'

Neville says with his own children he has no trouble in showing affection. He was at each of the births and the force of their numbers means he had to give a hand 'with nappies and that' when they were young. 'I had a few days off when Nevill and Michael were born. I was taxi-driving when Matthew and Joanne came along and my time was more my own anyways. We were lucky in that Diane never suffered from post-natal depression or anything like that.' I comment that four children in five years must have been quite a physical strain for Diane.

'She's paid for it by losing her figure. She's got to take some responsibility for that because she never used to do her exercises. I used to bully her a lot.'

I ask if it matters to him what Diane looks like. 'I suppose it does to a certain extent. I'd have to be lying if I said it didn't. I'd like her to lose weight partly because she'd be more attractive, I think, more important, for health reasons. We've both got weight problems. Sheffield's got a tradition in medium engineering for women too. It's heavy work so you tend to educate this big appetite over a period of years and it's cheap food too. I find it hard to draw meself away from a big plate of chips.'

He has a broad mix of friends, he says, but none as close as Diane, whom he *can* talk to if he needs to.

One friend, Neville adds, enjoying a joke, serves up middle-class food, 'trendy food, rice with bits, I wouldn't say it tends to be tasteless but it's not like steak and kidney.'

The people he knew in school he still sees but he doesn't have much in common. They are into mortgages and success and a new car bigger than the last. 'The wives are into posing and they go around boozing. At end of day I don't know how they can live with themselves. I look back and think what a load of mugs we were, people just thrust together.'

In the middle of the afternoon, Neville gets ready to go into the Centre Against Unemployment. It would be a mistake, he warns, to think that unemployment had somehow done him a favour. It might have made him more aware of his potential in education but it hasn't done his family any favours at all . . . no holiday, no treats, bargaining with the Social Security all the time for necessities such as an overcoat.

'Unemployment can turn some men into something which is undescribable.' he says. 'I think the men who feel emasculated though are those in their sixties, the older ones. I think the younger ones don't set much store by working class ethics like "a job is important". They can't, can they? It would drive them mad. I consider that I *am* working, I *am* the breadwinner. I see being a revolutionary as a full-time occupation. I'm lucky that my working-class forefathers made enough ground for that to be possible.'

I ask if he worries at all that the changes in his life might make him outgrow his relationship with Diane. 'I don't think I'm going to grow away,' he says after thought, 'partly because I've got a lot of respect for Diane. We're nailed together as a family unit. If somebody did come along who was more academically akin to me then I'd be frightened to leave anyway because I've got four kiddies. They would be sacrificed. After the kids grow up, if I still felt the same, I'd have a rethink.

'I wouldn't mind being seen to weep,' he explains later. 'I've always been like that. I've been tough, I've been brash and I've always felt I can face the world and situations. But to some extent, I've always felt emotionally slightly effeminate.'

On the way to the railway station, we go on a tour of Sheffield, a city which he obviously loves – as much for its history of working people as for its bricks and now deeply scarred mortar. He says his goodbyes, his knapsack and anorak a flash of green in the traffic. 'Keep up the fight,' he says.